I0793214

IMAGES
of America

Rochester's Downtown Architecture 1950–1975

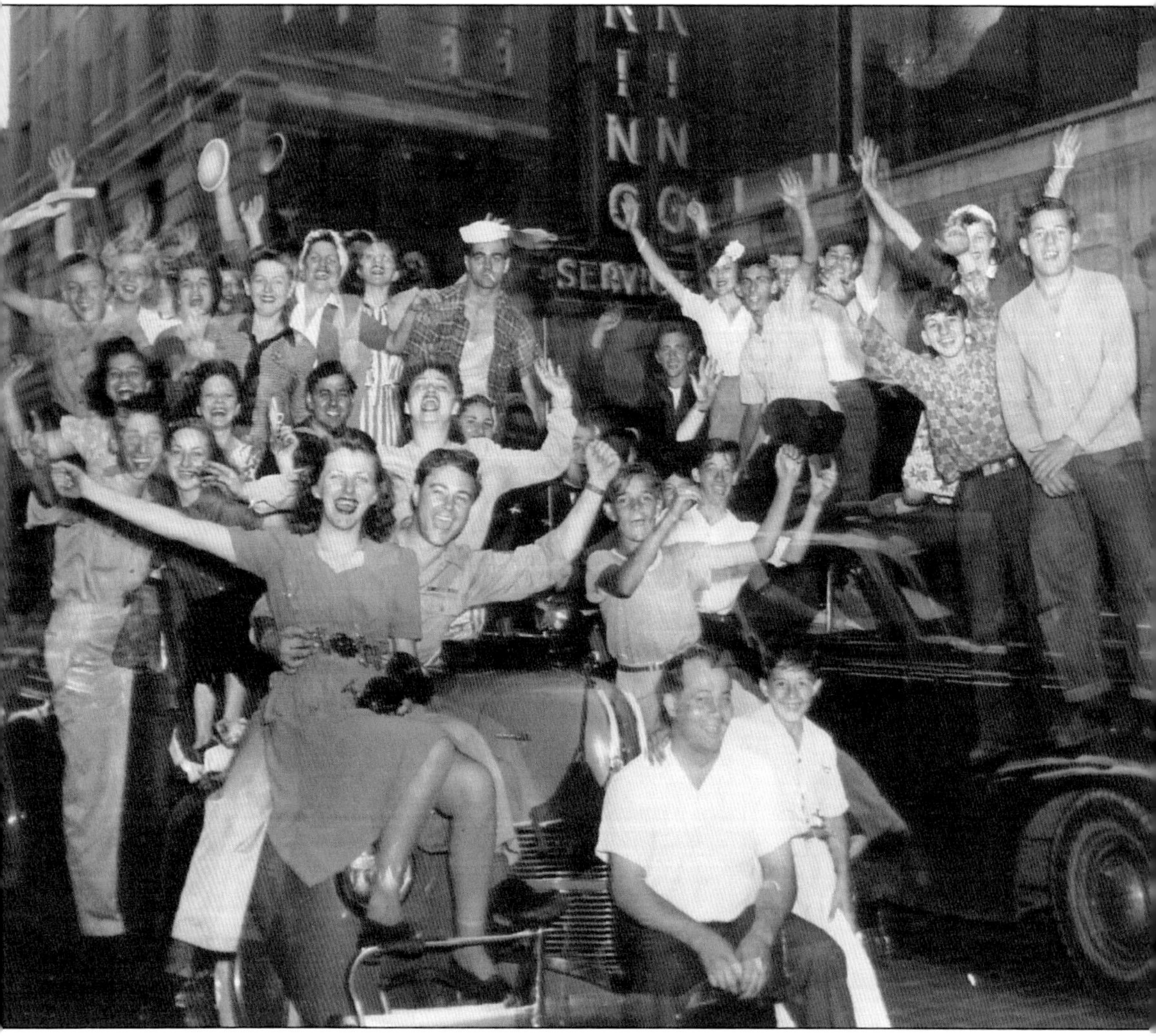

More than 100,000 Rochesterians celebrated the end of World War II on V-J Day in 1945. For those coming home from the front, the familiar city they returned to was on the edge of a period of unprecedented prosperity and growth. It would also go through a physical and social transformation. The city's population would reach its peak and then begin a gradual contraction, just as the surrounding communities would experience an explosion of population and development, along with the building of highways that provided easy access to these "outer ring" communities. (Rundel Library's Local History Department.)

ON THE COVER: This aerial view of the Monroe County Civic Center was taken by city photographer Samuel L. Grassadonia in 1972 and illustrates the massive scale of the project. (Rochester Municipal Archives.)

IMAGES
of America

Rochester's Downtown Architecture 1950–1975

Daniel J. Palmer

ARCADIA
PUBLISHING

ISBN 978-0-7385-7250-5

Published by Arcadia Publishing
Charleston SC, Chicago IL, Portsmouth NH, San Francisco CA

Printed in the United States of America

Library of Congress Control Number: 2009936094

For all general information contact Arcadia Publishing at:
Telephone 843-853-2070
Fax 843-853-0044
E-mail sales@arcadiapublishing.com
For customer service and orders:
Toll-Free 1-888-313-2665

Visit us on the Internet at www.arcadiapublishing.com

To Laura, whose patience and faith freed me to realize a dream.

Contents

ACKNOWLEDGMENTS

There are many in our wonderful archives and research community to thank. First and foremost, I must thank the staff of the Landmark Society of Western New York. They took my enthusiasm for our city's architecture and gave it focus. Many thanks to those who allowed me to use their image collections for this book including: Ira Srole at Rochester City Photography Lab, Larry Naukam and the staff at Rundel Library's Local History Department, Michele Rowe and the staff at Rochester Municipal Archives, and Matt Dudek and the staff of the *Democrat and Chronicle*. Special thanks are owed to Richard O. Reisem for taking the time to meet with me and for his encouragement to pursue this project. Thank you to Arcadia Publishing for taking a chance on a new era of history with the Images of America series and to my editor, Rebekah Collinsworth, for her guidance and encouragement throughout the process of creating this book. Love and thanks to my wife and family for their support and understanding.

All images used in this book are courtesy Rochester Municipal Archives (RMA) and Rundel Library's Local History Department (RLLHD), unless otherwise noted.

INTRODUCTION

Rochester is sometimes referred to as "America's First Boomtown," due to its rapid population growth in the mid-1800s. Much of this growth centered around the river that runs through town and the natural power of its waterfalls that, once harnessed by industry, led the city to become known for its processing of wheat into flour and the manufacturing of various goods. The downtown area grew rapidly in these years. Crowded groups of low-rise stone, brick, and wooden structures sprang up along the river and the surrounding streets in an era before zoning and urban planning.

From the late 1800s to the early 1950s, not much had changed. The occasional bank building would replace older structures, and the city would build its central library in 1936 on the edge of the former Erie Canal Aqueduct and over a still-active raceway (a channel of water that powers a mill or hydroelectric plant), but not much else was built downtown.

Following the end of World War II, and with the country finally recovery from the Great Depression, Americans held optimism for the future and desired to improve their standard of living. The building of suburban residential communities offered many the chance to own a piece of the "American Dream." These homes were built on larger plots of land than were possible in the crowded city and offered modern conveniences not found in the city's Victorian-era housing stock. Federal highway policies and money built expressways that led workers from their offices in the city center to their homes in suburban communities like Henrietta, Greece, and Webster in less than 20 minutes. Financing for mortgages and automobiles became easy for many Rochesterians, and the city began to see its population shrink from its 1950s peak in the 300,000s to a projected 200,000 in 2010.

In many ways, downtown was given a suburban makeover as well. Crowded streets of two- and three-story buildings were cleared and replaced with projects of a scale and density never before seen. Streets were de-mapped, as whole sections of downtown and its edge neighborhoods disappeared. What replaced those small-scaled and decorative structures represented the state of the art in architecture and planning in the 1960s and 1970s. Massive complexes of modern buildings spread out and grouped along large plazas reflected the new philosophy in architecture of functional design that focused more on the geometry of the composition as a whole, and the use of prefabricated materials, than in delighting the passerby with ornament and classical references. The use of natural materials such as marble and limestone continued but was often replaced with "curtain walls" of glass, concrete, and steel. In a daring move, Rochester's retail leaders and city government collaborated on a plan to build an enclosed shopping mall at the heart of downtown. When it opened in 1962, Midtown Plaza was hailed as an innovative project that would save retail in downtown Rochester. Unfortunately, suburbanites were more likely to spend money at a nearby mall than to venture into the city, and the city's shrinking population could no longer support the once-vibrant shopping scene on Main Street. Therefore, retail in the center city would continue to suffer, finally collapsing when local retailers Sibley's,

Forman's, McCurdy's, and local grocery chain Wegmans all closed their downtown locations by the end of the 20th century.

Later examples from this period reflect a trend at approaching the design of a high-rise as a habitable sculpture, often expressing the building's structure in its exterior. The Lincoln First Tower, Xerox Square, and the Marine Midland Building are standout examples of this attempt to make modern architecture more lively and interesting to the layperson. High-rise housing and adjacent parklands were built to replace the aging blocks of homes and apartments at the edge of downtown and along the Genesee River. They were priced to give both senior citizens and young families a chance to enjoy affordable, but modern living spaces, as well as the recreational opportunities available at the neighboring parks.

The project that changed the look and feel of downtown more than any one building or project, however, was not a building at all. The Inner Loop is a depressed expressway that rings the downtown area. It was under construction throughout this era, its effect on the physical fabric of downtown much like a miniature Cross Bronx Expressway, demolishing neighborhoods, severing streets, and physically separating downtown from the surrounding city. The Inner Loop was always a controversial project; some refer to it as a "moat." The prospect of filling in portions of the Inner Loop and replacing the neighborhoods it displaced has been a topic of discussion for years and continues to this day.

As these structures reach their third, fourth, and fifth decades of existence, the question of preservation must be raised. Midtown Plaza is slated to be demolished in 2010, with a small portion to be retained as a residential tower and shopping area. Large projects like the Genesee Crossroads and the Monroe County Civic Center are aging and in need of renovation. The decision whether to reuse, renovate, or remove these buildings will shape the look and feel of Rochester's downtown for the next 50 years.

One

Community War Memorial

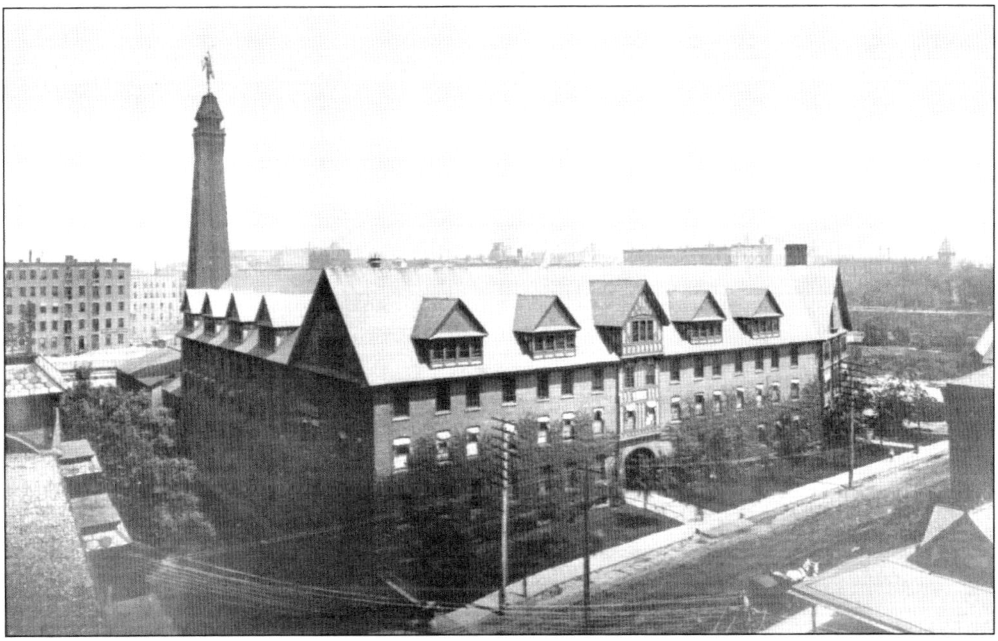

Built in 1882 from designs by local architect James G. Cutler, the Kimball Tobacco Factory was a fixture in downtown Rochester for over seven decades. An early example of adaptive reuse, the factory was, from 1924 until the early 1950s, rented as an annex of overcrowded city hall, a few blocks away, and served as the city's library until the Rundel Library was built across the river in 1936. (RMA.)

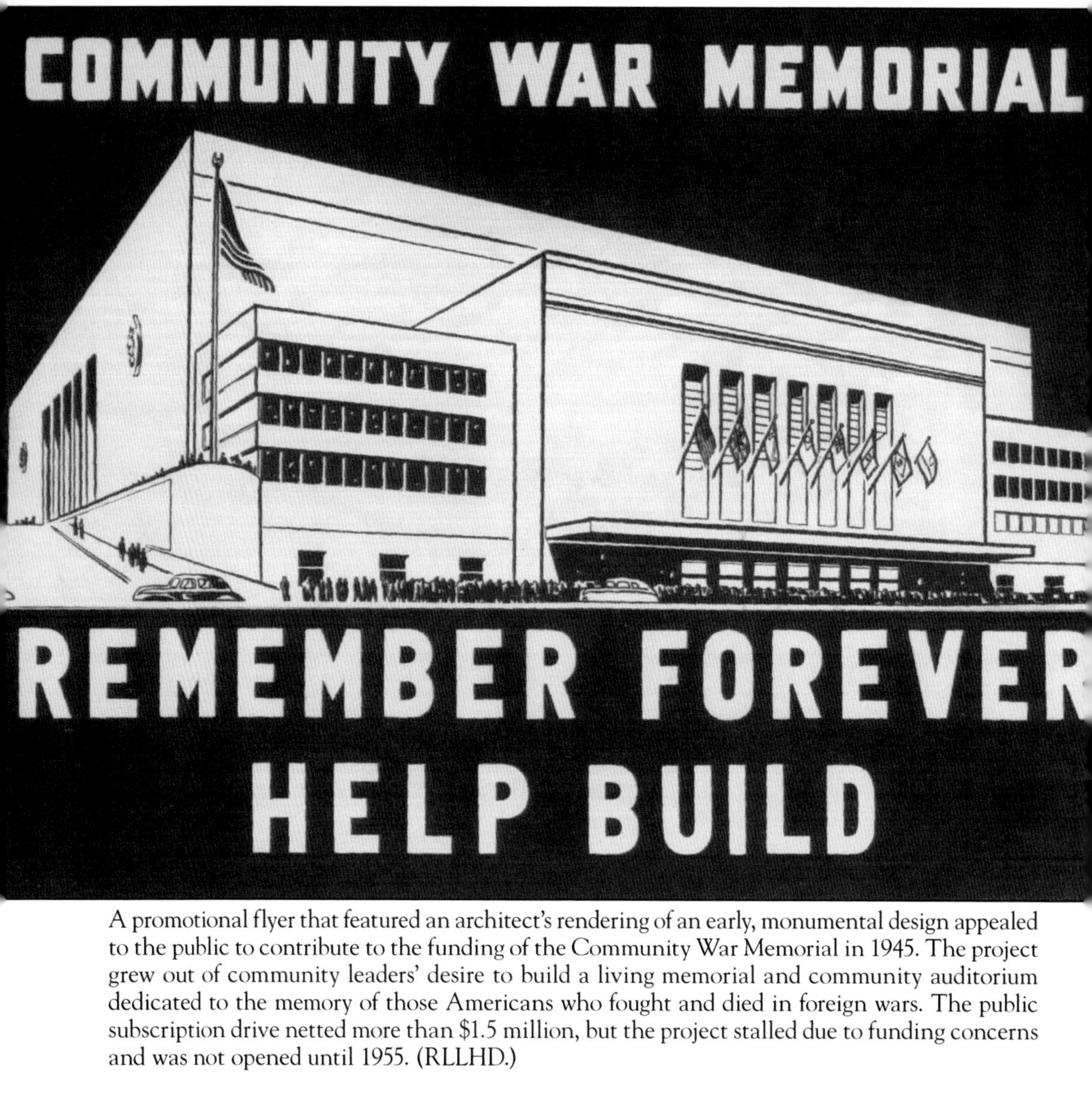

A promotional flyer that featured an architect's rendering of an early, monumental design appealed to the public to contribute to the funding of the Community War Memorial in 1945. The project grew out of community leaders' desire to build a living memorial and community auditorium dedicated to the memory of those Americans who fought and died in foreign wars. The public subscription drive netted more than $1.5 million, but the project stalled due to funding concerns and was not opened until 1955. (RLLHD.)

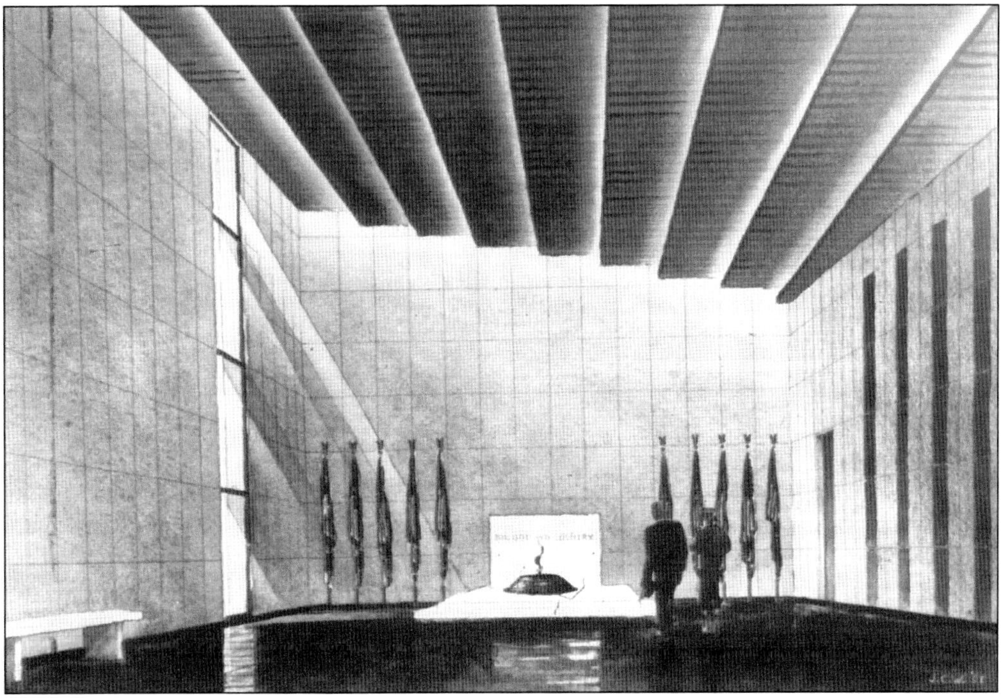

The architect of the Community War Memorial, Leonard A. Waasdorp, after touring the nation's memorials and being disappointed with their use as glorified lobbies and traffic lanes for pedestrians, was determined to create a truly dedicated and sacred space to honor the fallen soldiers of war. He designed a large room separate from the main building and insulated from outside noise. Travertine would line the walls, and terrazzo flooring would lead to an "eternal flame" surrounded by flags. (RMA.)

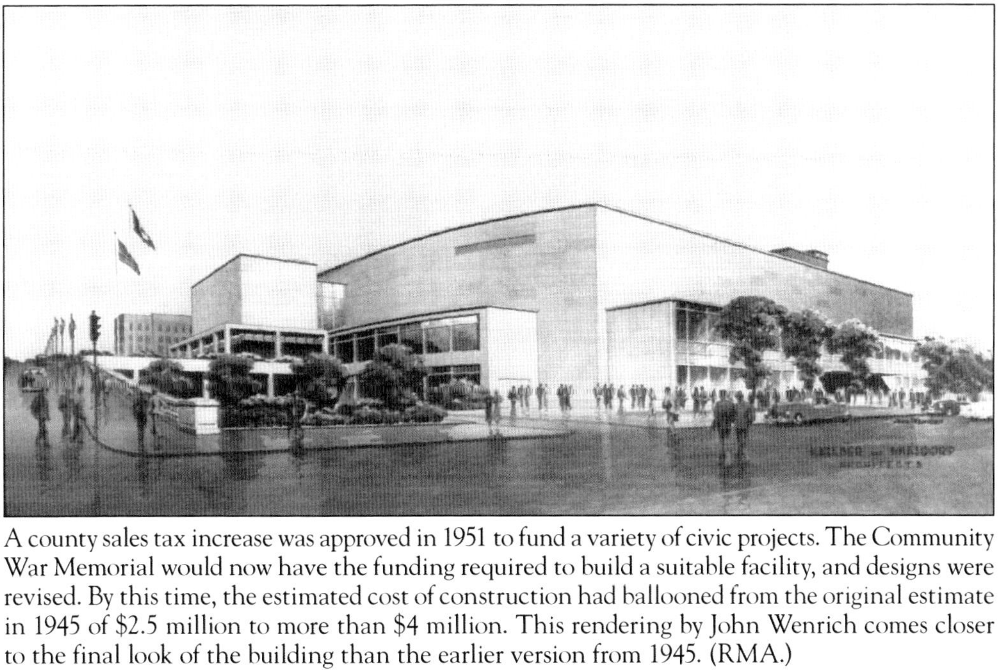

A county sales tax increase was approved in 1951 to fund a variety of civic projects. The Community War Memorial would now have the funding required to build a suitable facility, and designs were revised. By this time, the estimated cost of construction had ballooned from the original estimate in 1945 of $2.5 million to more than $4 million. This rendering by John Wenrich comes closer to the final look of the building than the earlier version from 1945. (RMA.)

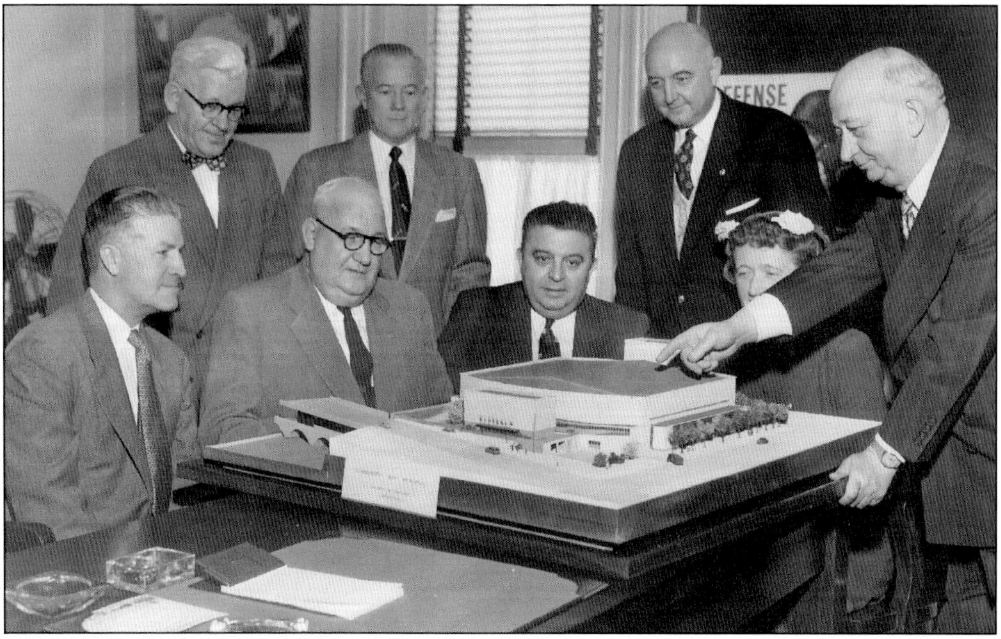

The final design for the Community War Memorial is presented to Mayor Samuel B. Dicker (far right) and other local leaders in model form. The structure at the front of the model is the "room of remembrance" chapel. The wing on the right side of the arena, behind the row of trees, is the main entrance of the building. The architect wished to keep the chapel from being used as a lobby and kept the two functions separate. (RLLHD.)

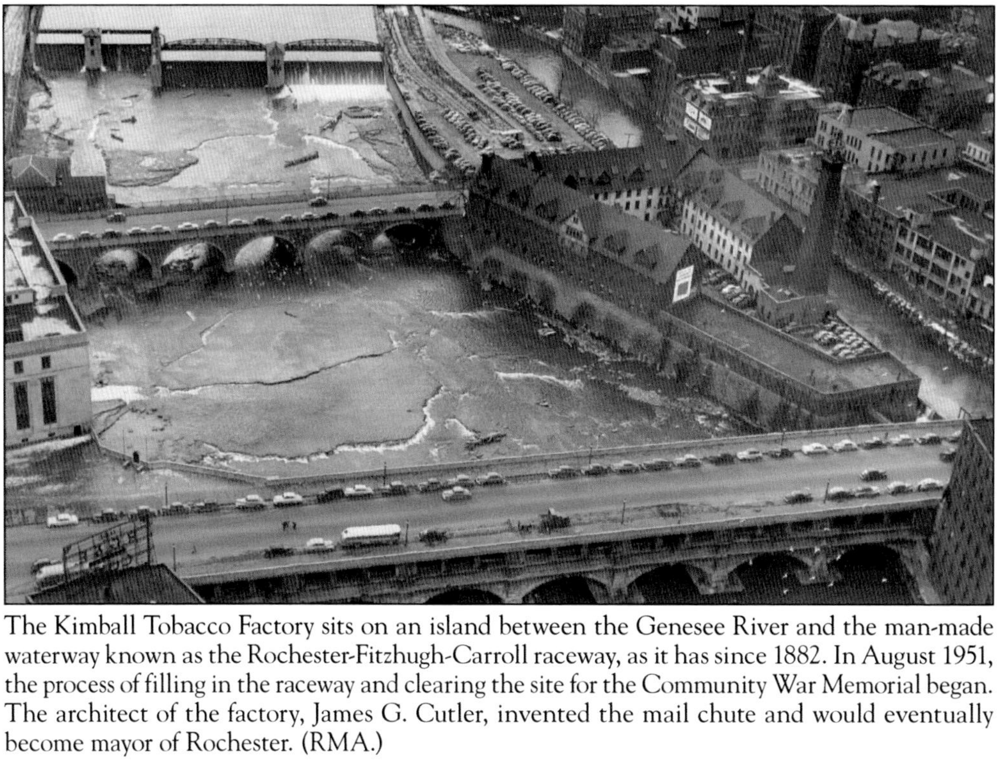

The Kimball Tobacco Factory sits on an island between the Genesee River and the man-made waterway known as the Rochester-Fitzhugh-Carroll raceway, as it has since 1882. In August 1951, the process of filling in the raceway and clearing the site for the Community War Memorial began. The architect of the factory, James G. Cutler, invented the mail chute and would eventually become mayor of Rochester. (RMA.)

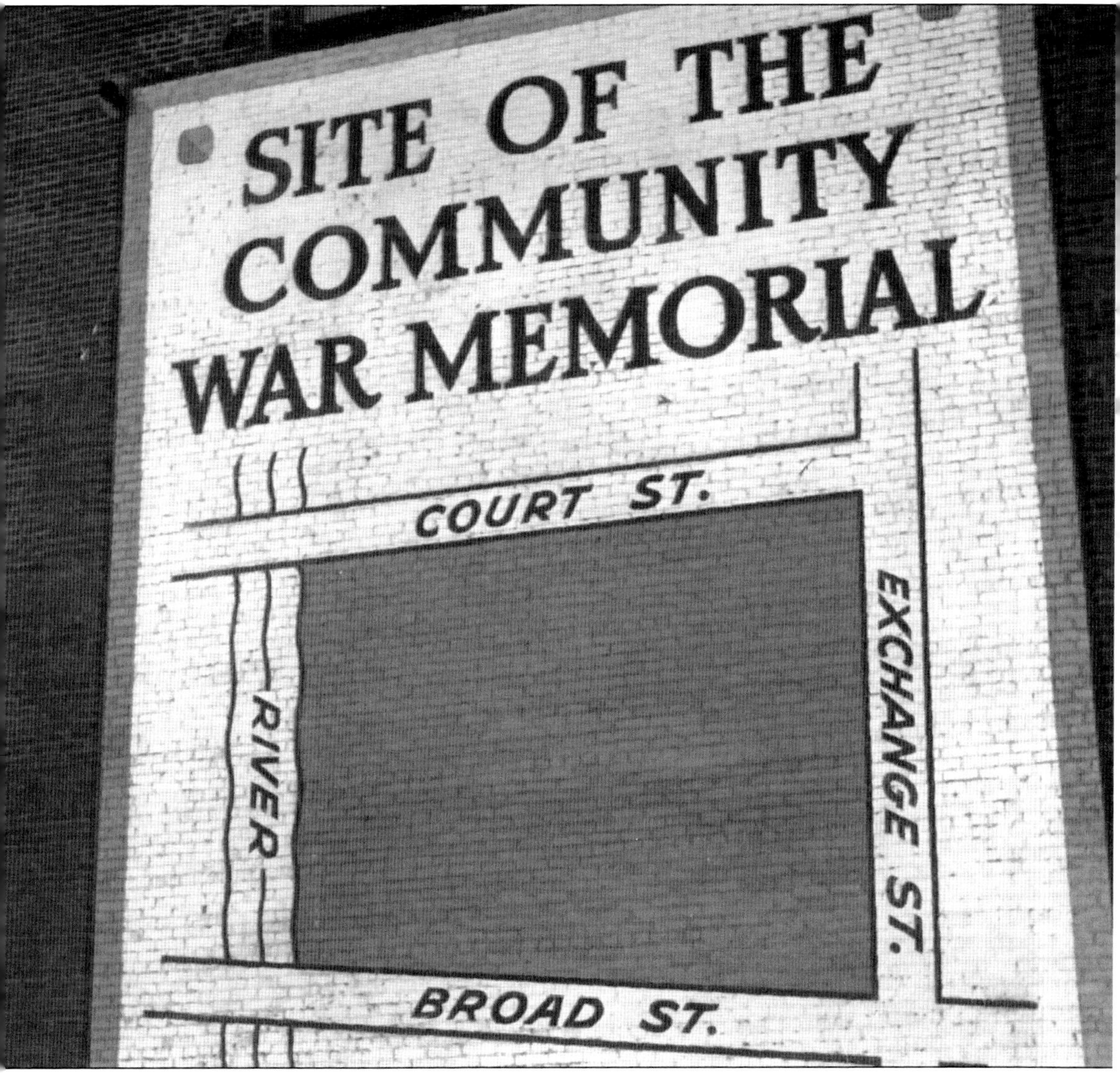

This sign painted on the side of the factory not only announces the construction of the Community War Memorial, but also illustrates how the island will become a super block. While it was the first time in downtown that streets and blocks would be combined into a multiple-acre plot, it would not be the last. Downtown would become home to at least six more super blocks as the density of the old city was replaced with sprawling complexes grouped around large plazas. (RMA.)

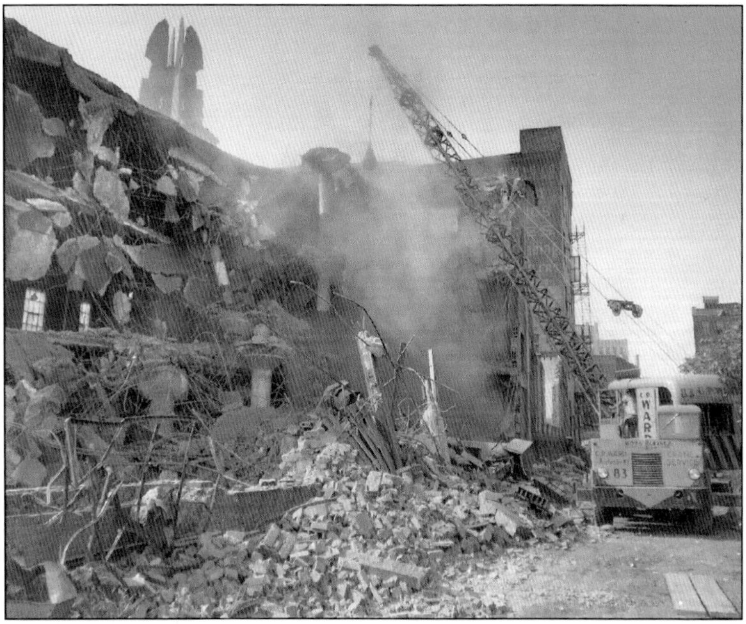

The demolition of the buildings facing Exchange Street is underway in early 1953. The mushroom-shaped columns and reinforced concrete of the floors show that not much had changed in building technology from the innovations of the late 1800s. Factories and parking garages would continue to employ this type of structural support well into the 1900s. (RLLHD.)

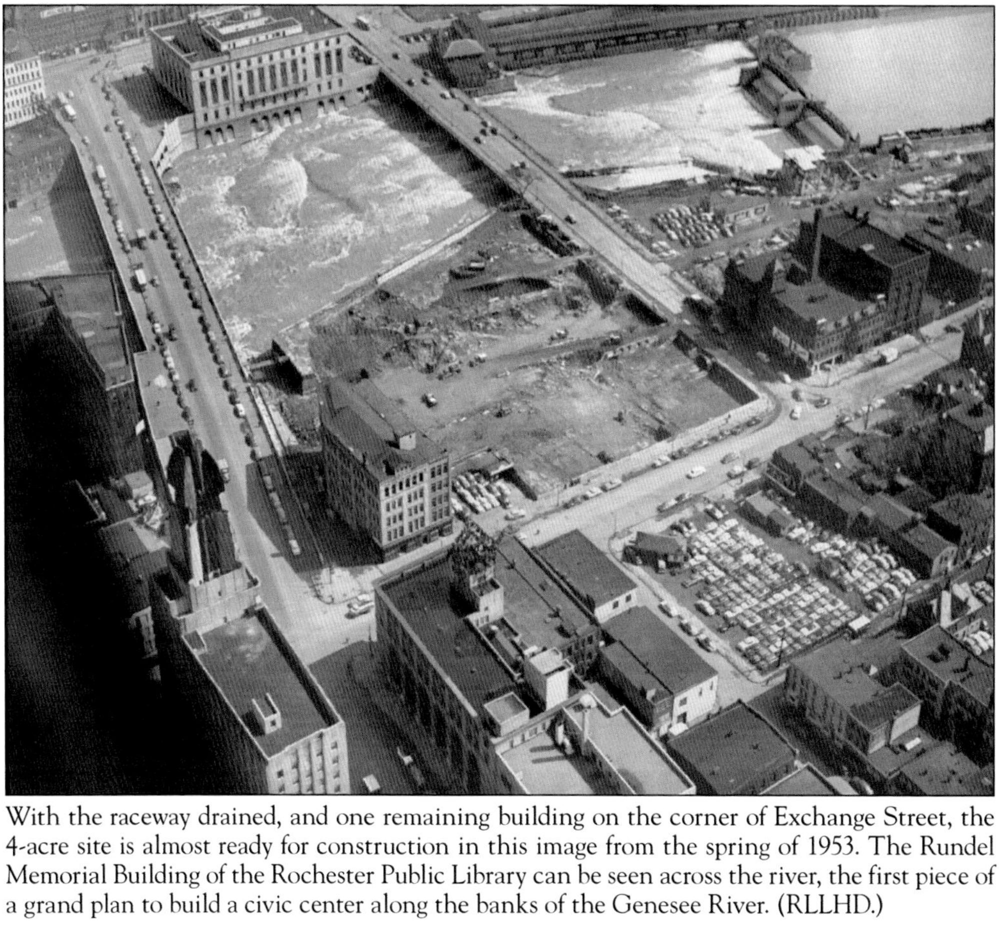

With the raceway drained, and one remaining building on the corner of Exchange Street, the 4-acre site is almost ready for construction in this image from the spring of 1953. The Rundel Memorial Building of the Rochester Public Library can be seen across the river, the first piece of a grand plan to build a civic center along the banks of the Genesee River. (RLLHD.)

Workers on the roof of the Barr and Creelman Building continue the process of site clearing for the Community War Memorial in April 1953. Soon the distinguished Romanesque structure would no longer grace the southeast corner of Broad and Exchange Streets, as it had since the 1800s. (RLLHD.)

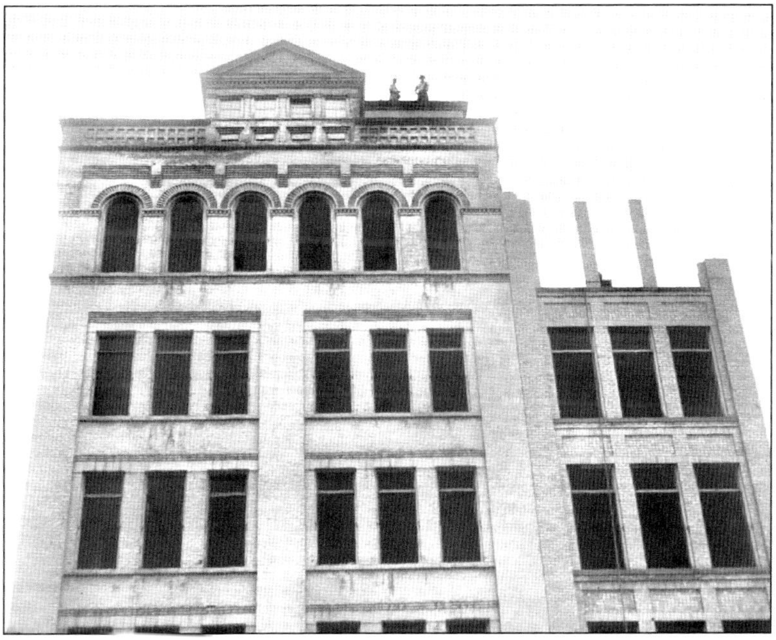

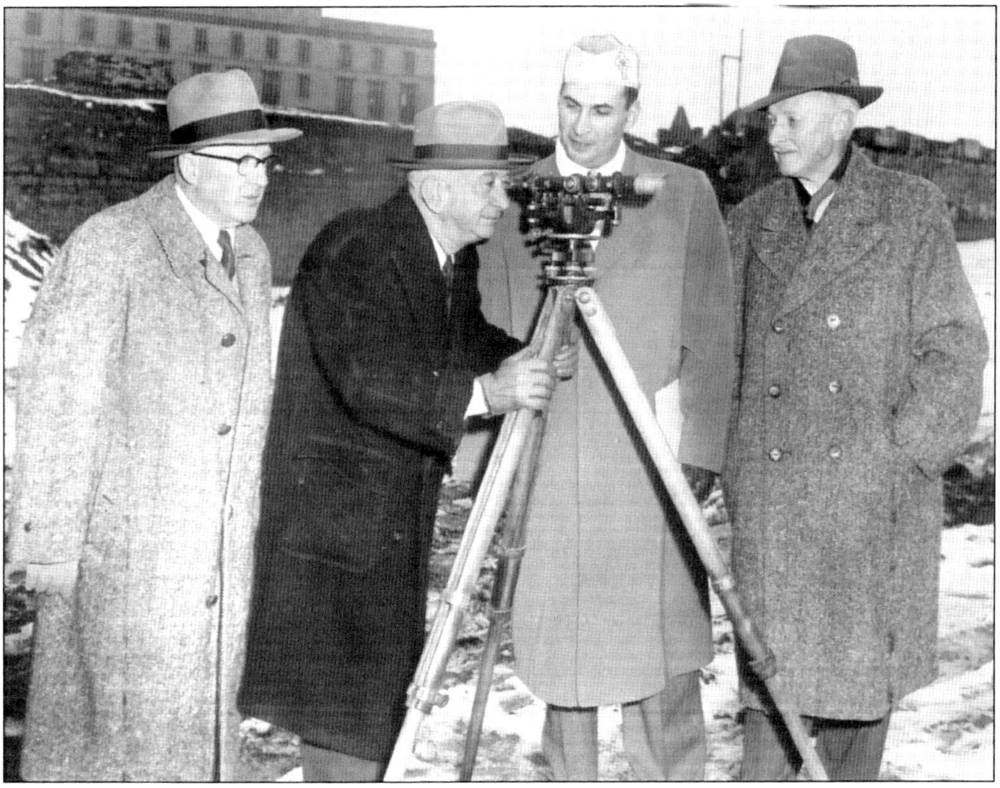

Mayor Dicker (second from left) checks the accuracy of the surveyors at the Community War Memorial site. The head architect for the project, Leonard A. Waasdorp, is seen standing on the far right. Before long, the Community War Memorial would begin to rise. The Rundel Memorial Building can be seen in the background. (RMA.)

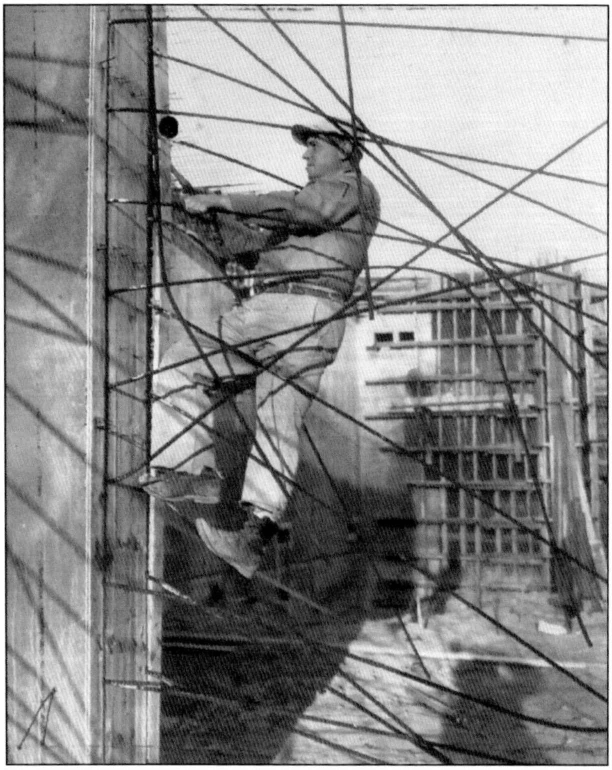

Steel reinforcing bars protrude from concrete columns at the base of the Community War Memorial, and they seem to have this worker trapped. The building would soon rise above street level, as the structural steel was delivered and erected in the fall of 1953. By the summer of 1954, the steel structure would be finished. (RMA.)

The steel structure of the "Room of Remembrance" memorial chapel is complete as the auditorium's steel begins to rise along the riverside in this image from January 1954. The Rundel Memorial Building, sitting atop a hydroelectric raceway at the edge of the Genesee River, can be seen in the background. (RMA.)

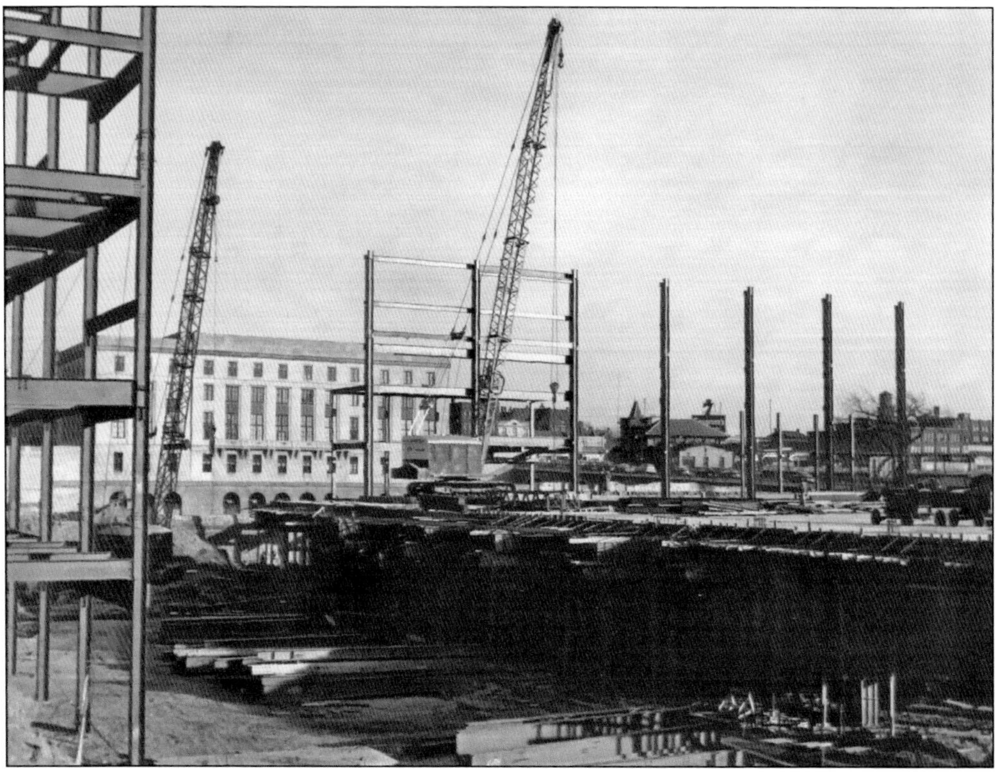

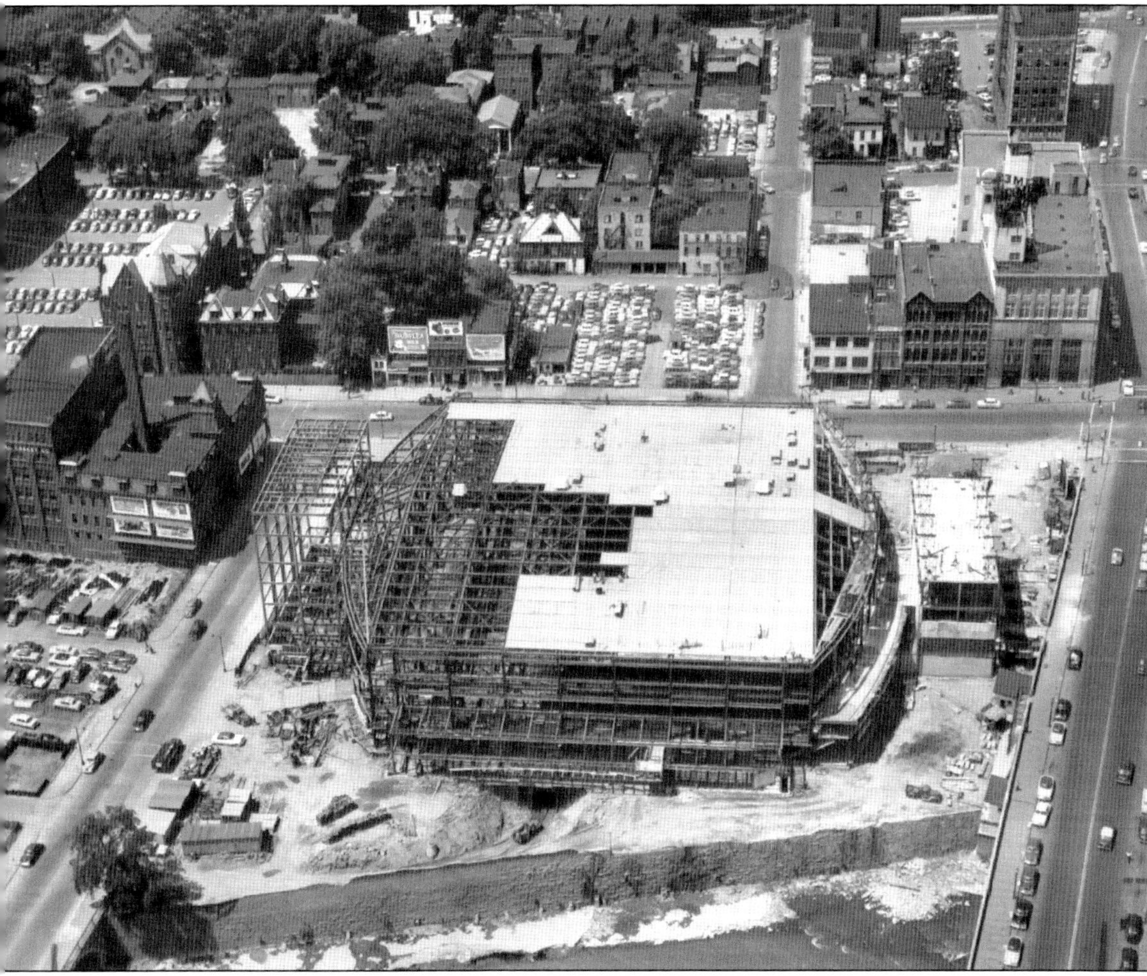

By June 1954, the steel has been erected, and the roof is more than half complete. The roof will cover a column of free space, spanned by ten 260-foot trusses. Just above the construction site is a section of the city's Third Ward, slated to become the home of the Monroe County Civic Center. (RMA.)

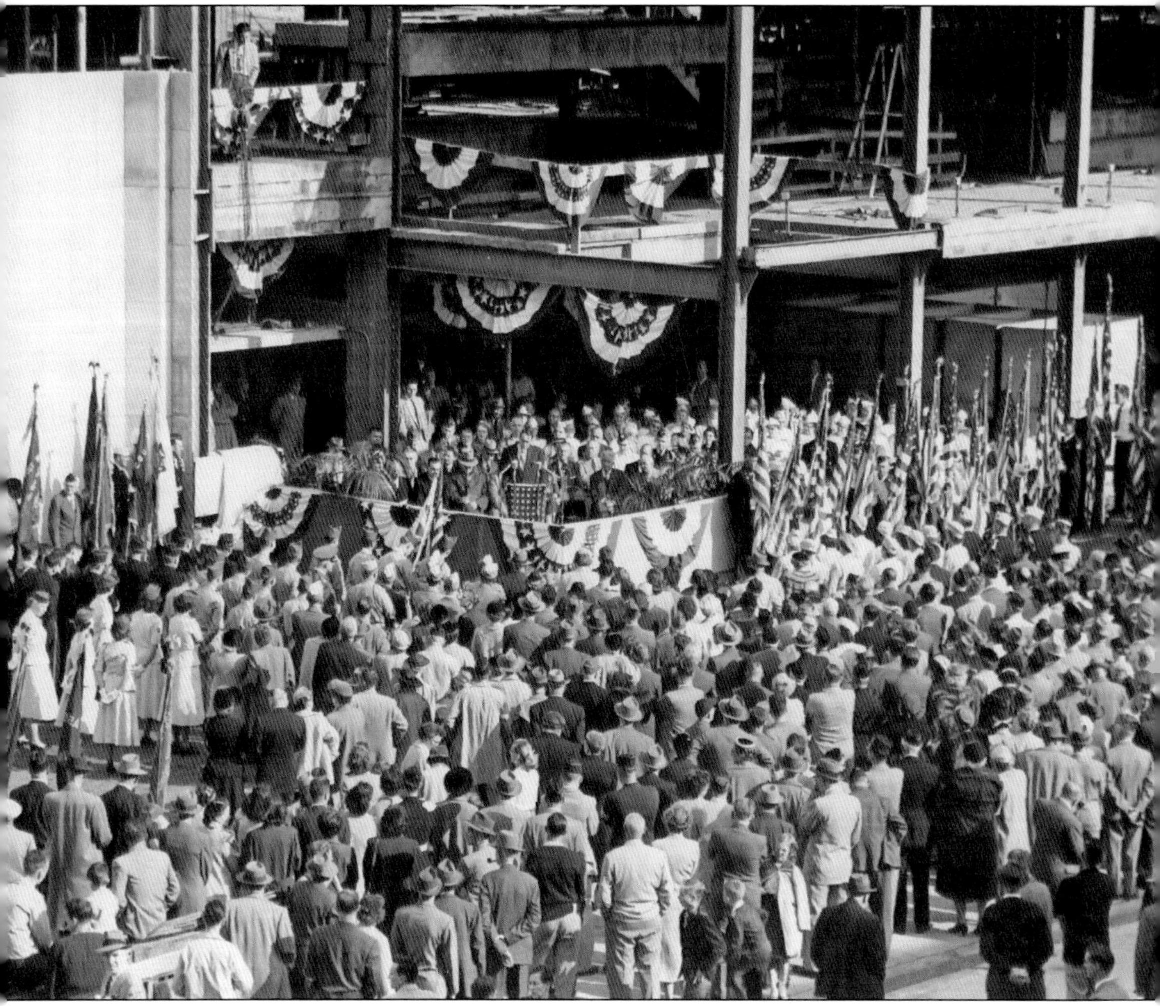

City councilman and future mayor Peter Barry speaks at the laying of the Community War Memorial's cornerstone in September 1954. Approximately 800 people attended the ceremony to hear speeches from local leaders and distinguished guests of honor. (RMA.)

Wanda Pietrzak and Clayton E. Handy, members of the war memorial commission, flank city historian Blake McKelvey as they add items to the copper "time capsule" that will be placed inside the cornerstone. Items included newspapers, photographs, the city council resolution providing for the building's construction and character, and, of course, issues of McKelvey's famous *Rochester History* booklets. (*Democrat and Chronicle*.)

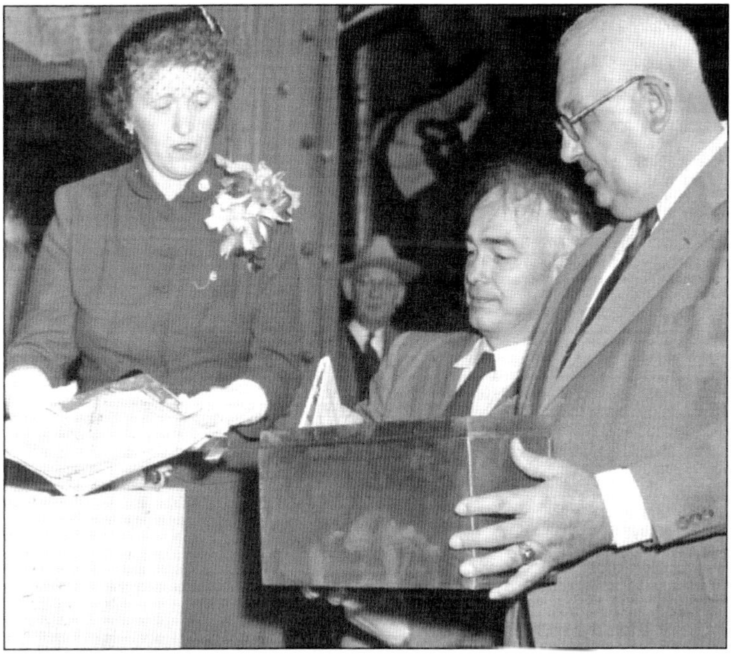

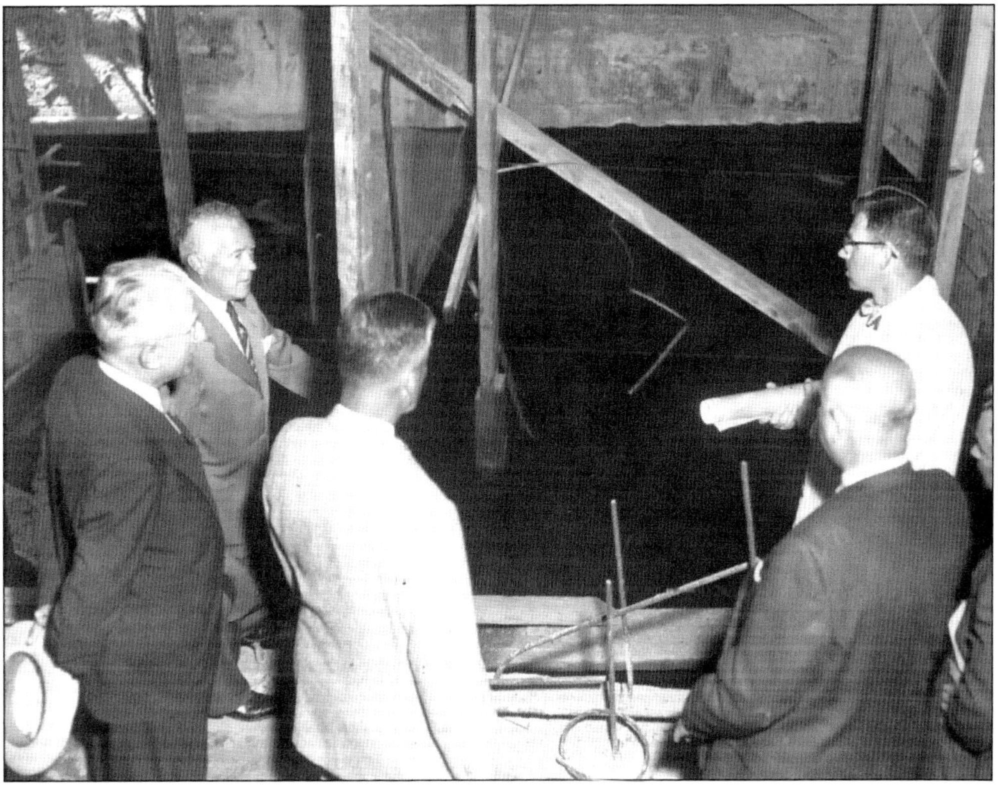

A ramp leading from the subway beneath Broad Street to the Community War Memorial was briefly considered but then deemed unnecessary. A few years later, the subway would be shut down as light rail gave way to the automobile. (RLLHD.)

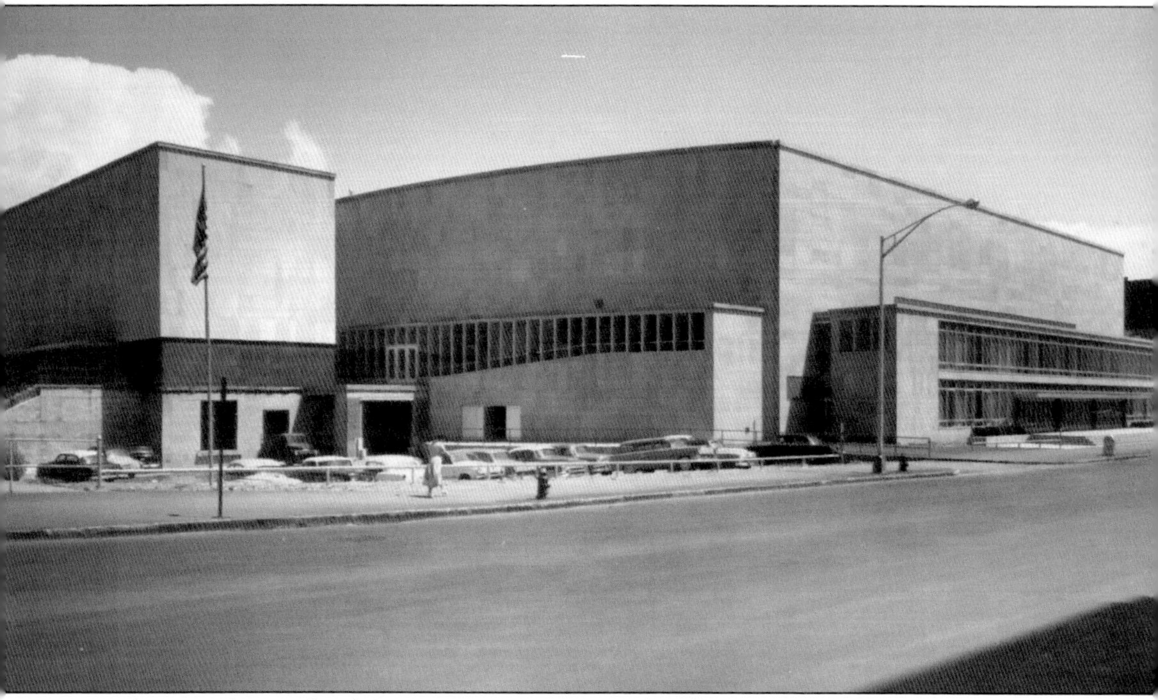

The recently completed Community War Memorial—all 2,800 tons of steel and 8,700 panels of limestone of it—shines on a sunny day in 1955. The architects chose Indiana limestone because it would match the nearby Genesee Valley Trust and the Rundel Library's limestone, and it was believed that the Monroe County Civic Center would also use it throughout the gigantic complex planned across Exchange Street from the arena. (RMA.)

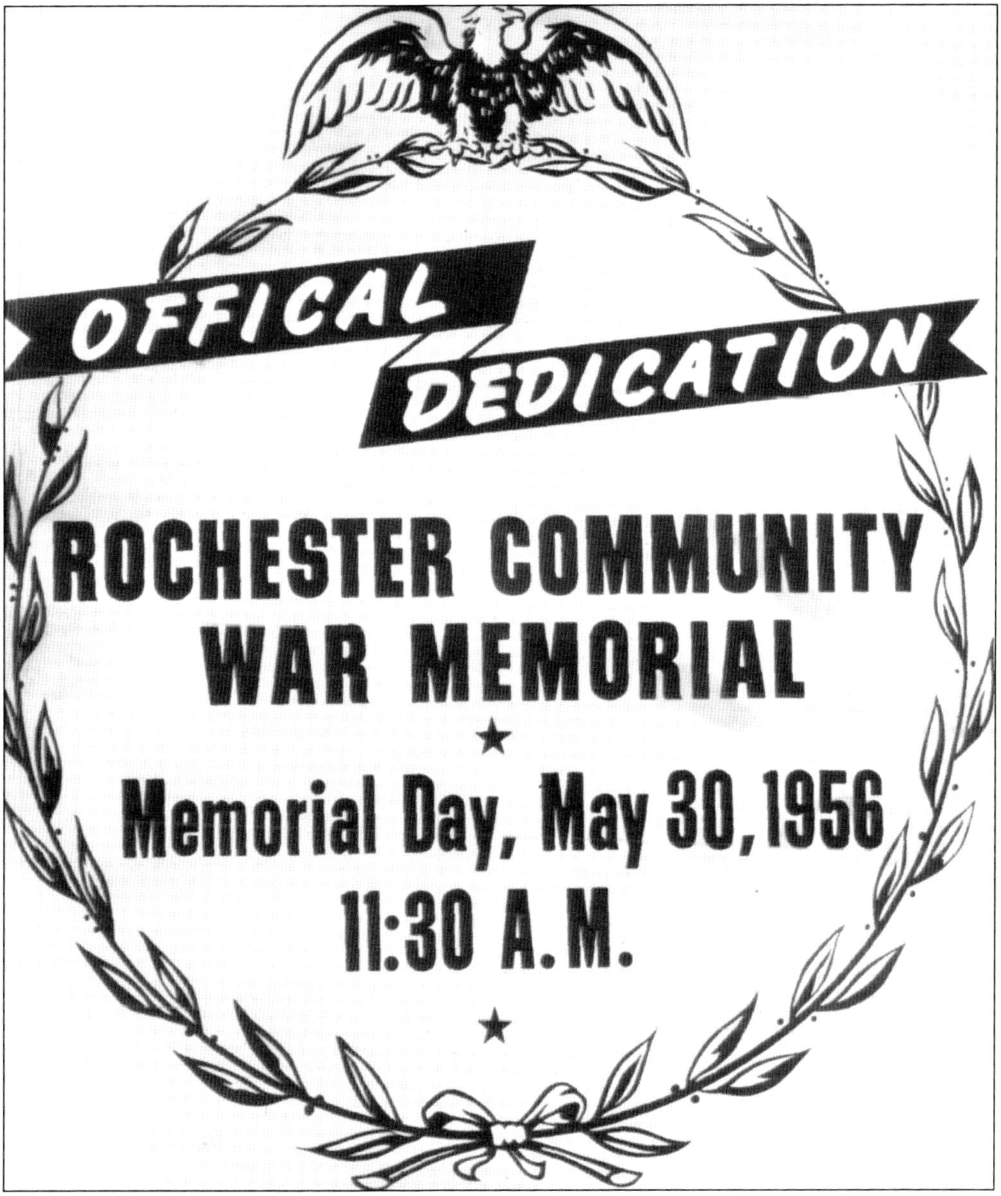

The Community War Memorial, after 11 years and $7.5 million, was dedicated on Memorial Day in 1956. The building officially opened in the fall of 1955 but was not completely finished until the following spring. Note the misspelling of "official." (RMA.)

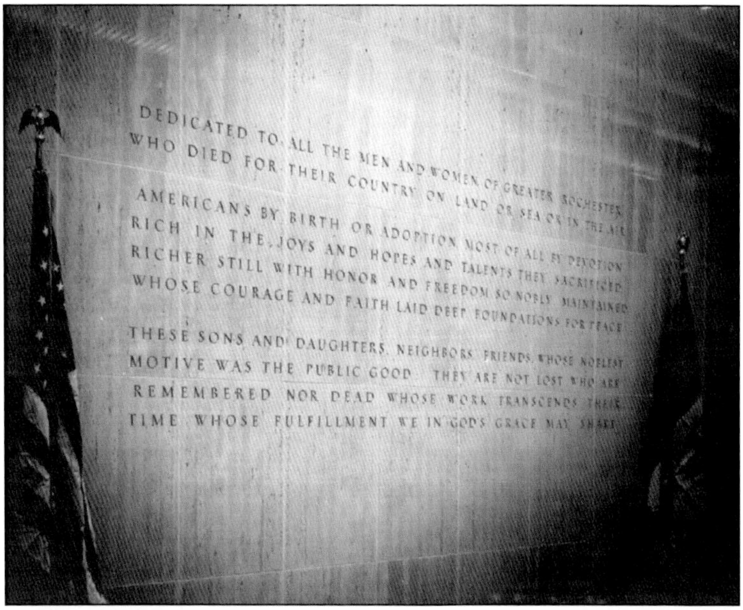

These words, carved into travertine, were written by city historian Blake McKelvey and John Slater, professor emeritus at the University of Rochester, to honor the fallen veterans from the Rochester community. (RLLHD.)

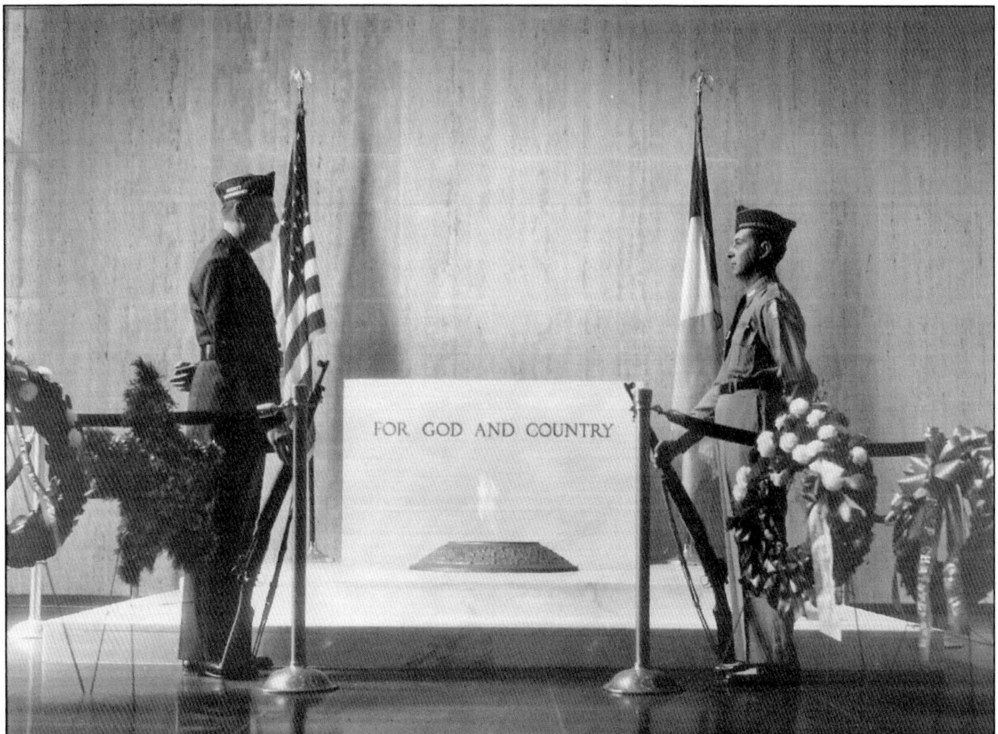

Two soldiers stand guard at the eternal flame, the focal point of the Community War Memorial's chapel. In the 1990s, the arena would be radically changed, and the chapel would be replaced with an enormous, glass-walled entrance lobby. The flame would be relegated to a spot in the corner of this cavernous and loud room, no longer the focal point of a tranquil "room of remembrance." (RMA.)

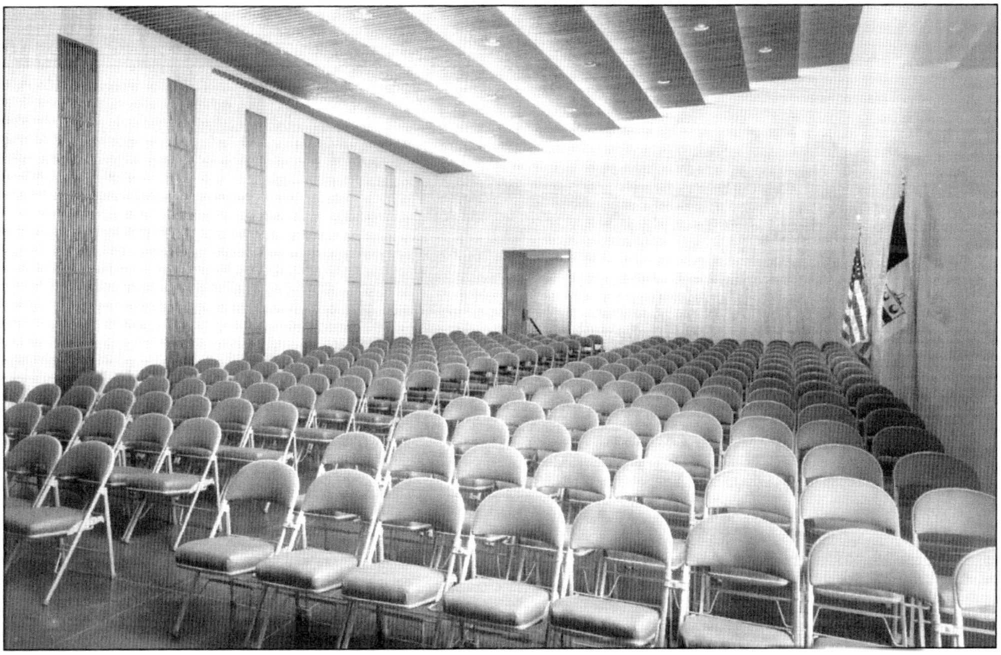

The ceiling is a series of walnut panels stepped back and backlit to give the effect of it floating above the chapel. The walls are covered in travertine, and terrazzo covers the floor. The chapel had room to seat about 70 people, as in this image from 1956. (RMA.)

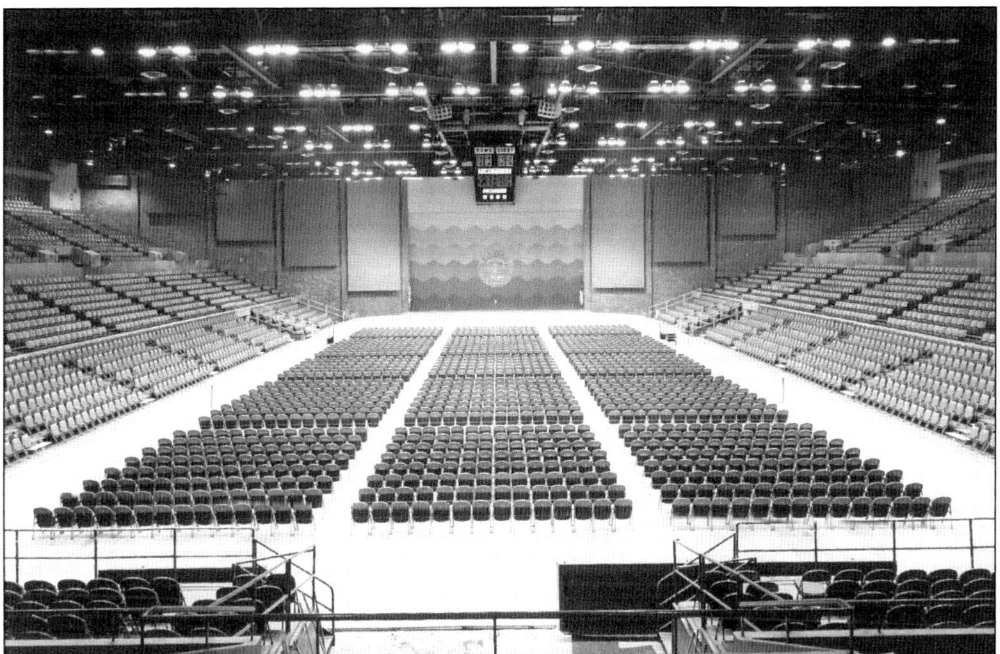

For most events, the arena would seat about 5,500 people. With floor seating added, the capacity became over 7,000. The stage area can be seen at the far end of the arena in this image from 1957. The 1990s renovation would remove the stage and build tiered seating in its place, expanding the seating capacity to more than 12,000 people. (RLLHD)

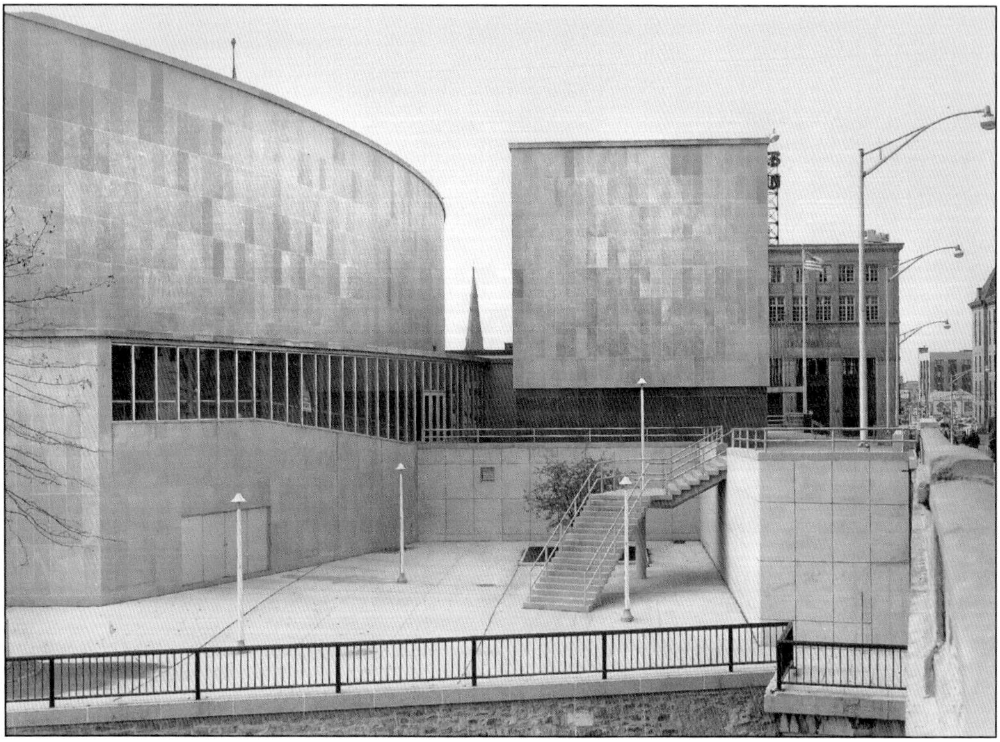

Steps from Broad Street lead to the riverside plaza, with its lovely tree plantings and unique views of downtown. The memorial chapel is seen just above the staircase. The official name of this plaza is Rochester War Memorial Park. Sculpture would be added on the opposite end of the park in the 1960s to complement the, by then, mature tree plantings along the river. (RLLHD.)

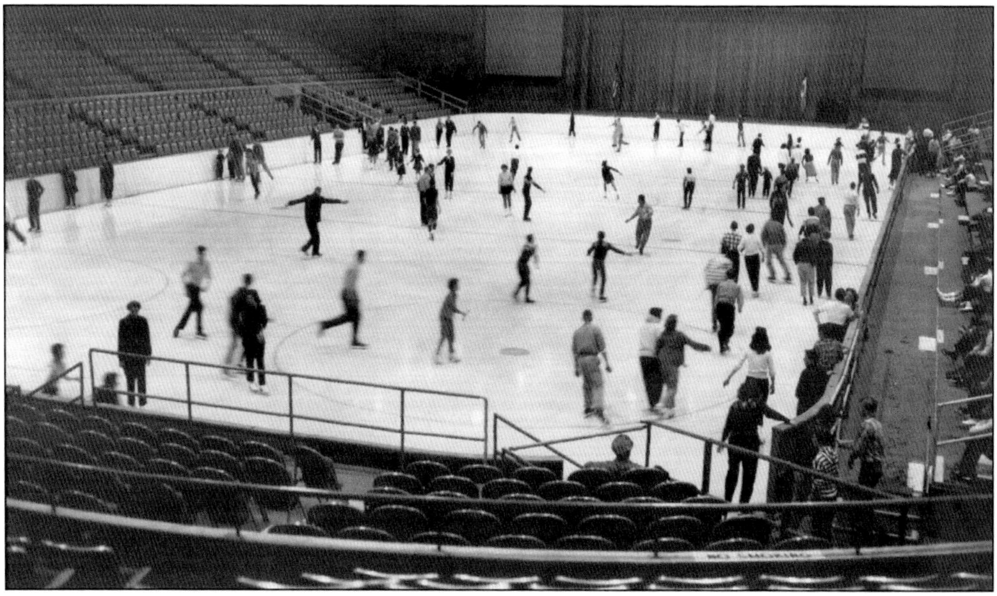

The public enjoys a festive time on the ice. Normally the realm of the rough-and-tumble stars of minor league hockey's Rochester Americans, the rink at the Community War Memorial takes on a more leisurely feel in this image from December 1956. (RLLHD)

From high above the arena floor an engineer controls the audio system, fine-tuning volume and tone. The latest in high-fidelity equipment was installed that not only filled the arena with clear and loud announcements, but also piped hushed music into the memorial chapel and provided audio communications between the people working at the Community War Memorial. (RLLHD.)

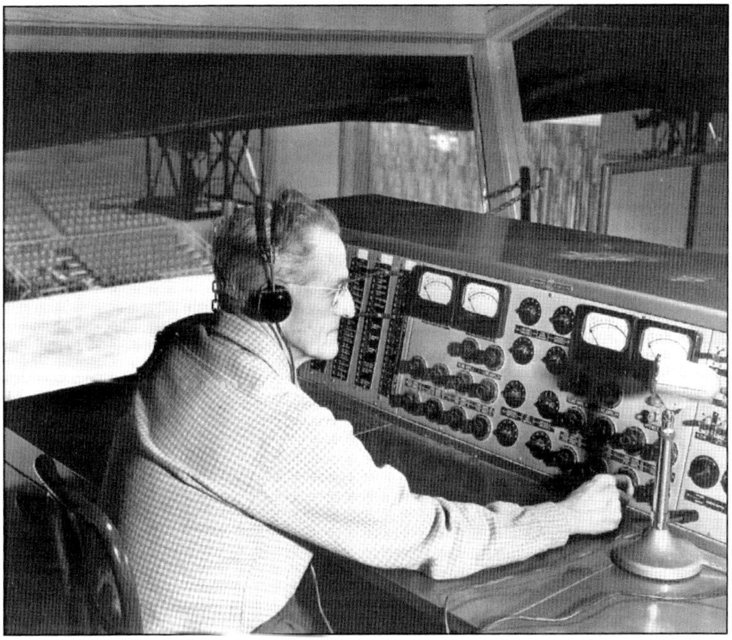

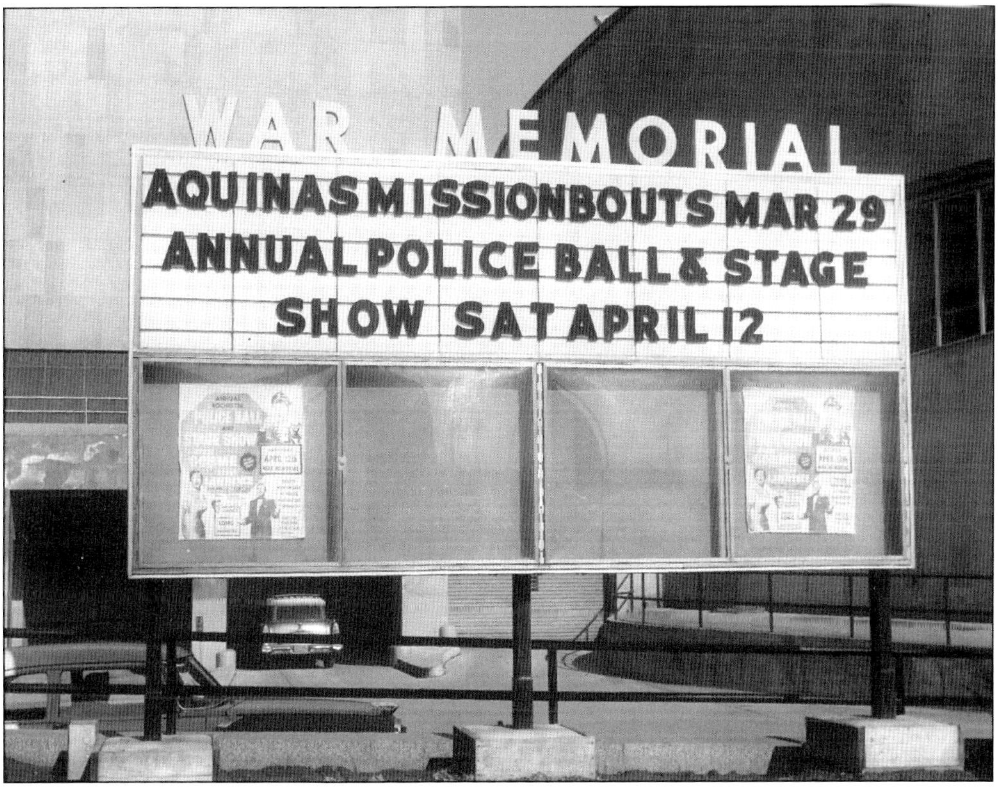

Upcoming local events are announced for the Community War Memorial on this stylized billboard that screens the loading docks located below the memorial chapel. In the 1990s, the Community War Memorial would be renovated and altered. This section of the building is now a glass-enclosed entranceway and lobby. (RMA.)

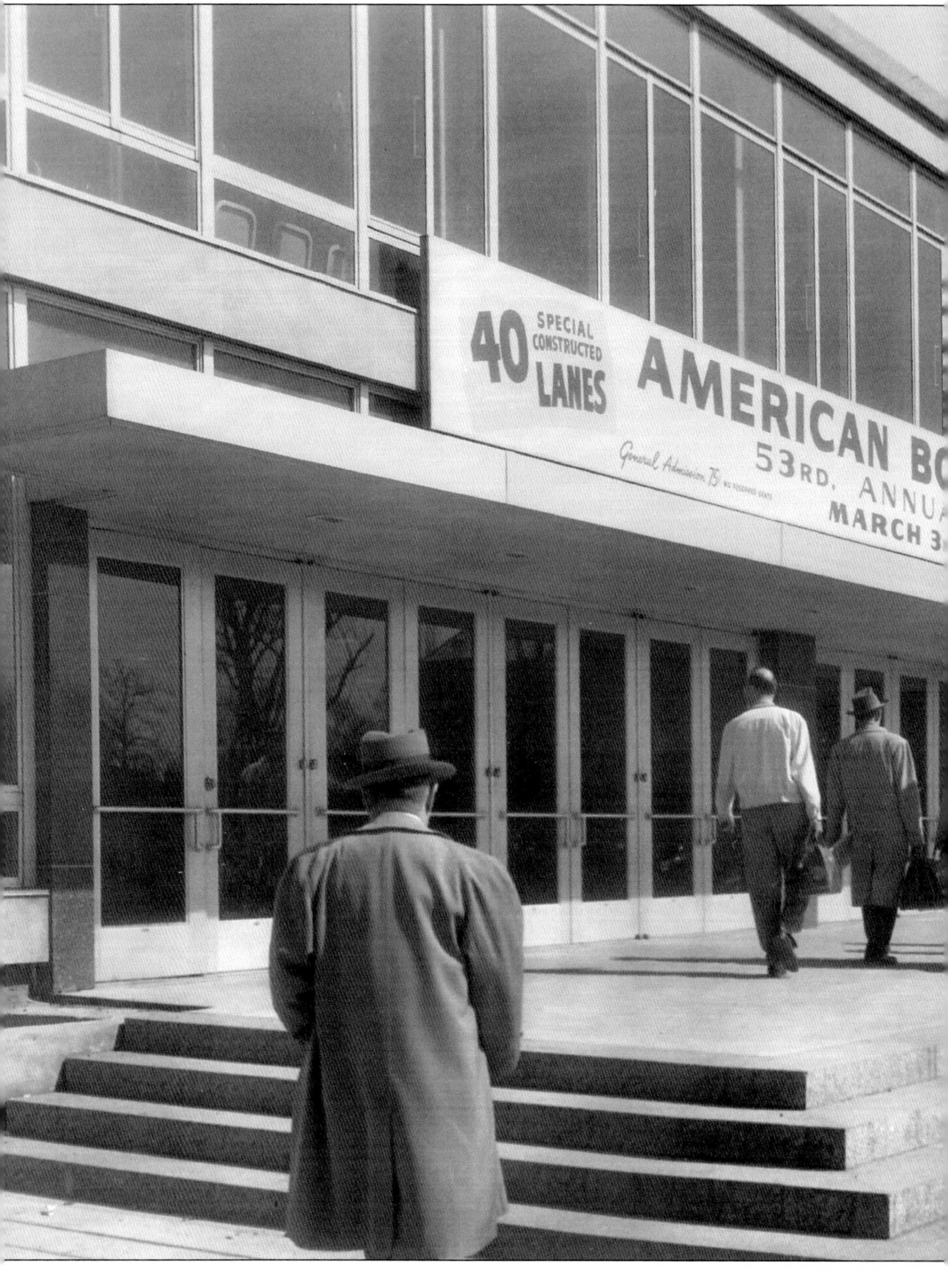
40 SPECIAL CONSTRUCTED LANES
AMERICAN BO
General Admission 75¢
53RD. ANNUA
MARCH 3

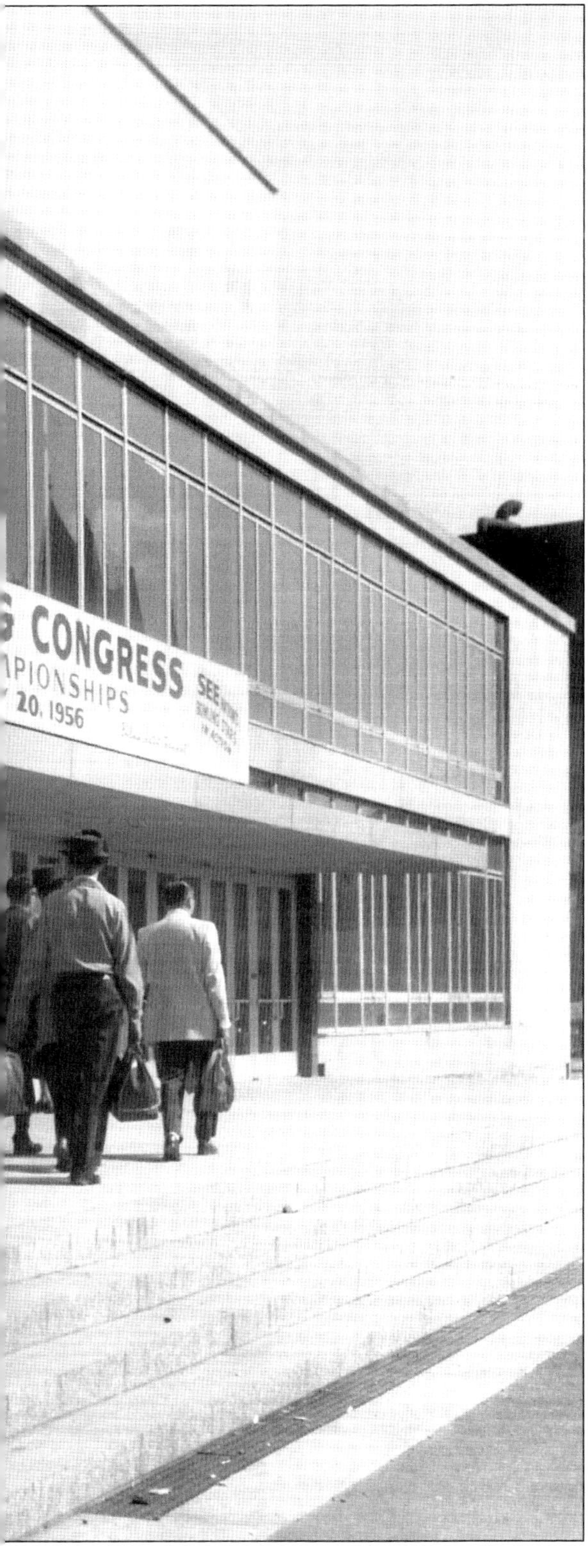

One of the important events held at the newly completed Community War Memorial was the 53rd Annual American Bowling Congress Tournament. These bowlers, bags in hand, approach the arena's main entrance on Exchange Street in March 1956. The Community War Memorial would continue to play host to events of every kind, from the 1956 NBA All-Star Game, to professional wrestling shows, to rock concerts. It is best known as the home of the Rochester Americans. The minor league hockey team has played its games at the arena since 1956, and over the years, it has become a community treasure and point of pride. (RMA.)

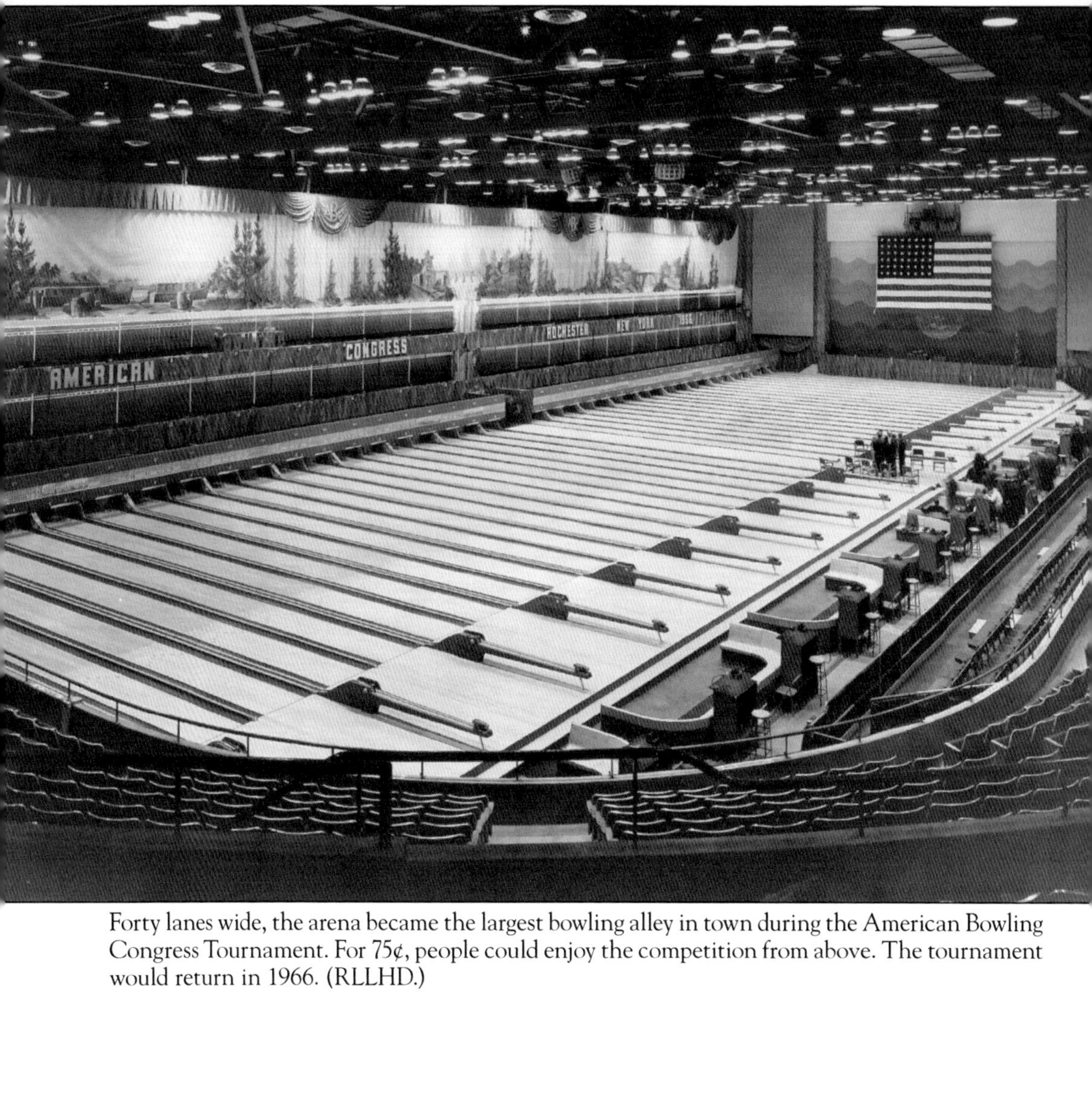

Forty lanes wide, the arena became the largest bowling alley in town during the American Bowling Congress Tournament. For 75¢, people could enjoy the competition from above. The tournament would return in 1966. (RLLHD.)

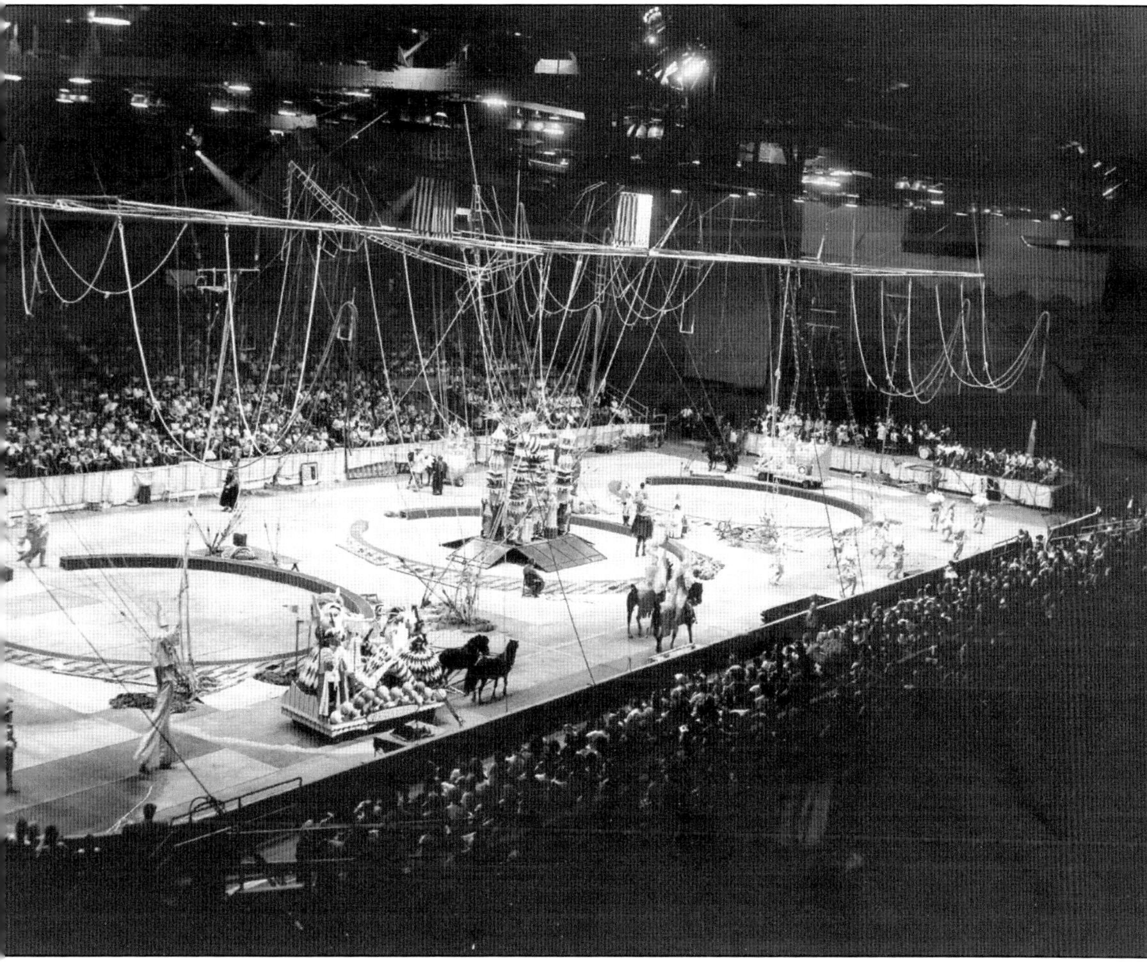

The Community War Memorial proved popular with traveling shows. The circus comes to town in this image from the 1950s. In 1998, after two years and $41 million, the arena reopened as the Blue Cross Arena at the Community War Memorial. Rossetti Architects were responsible for the building's new facade of brick and glass. The limestone box that is the structure of the former stage area on Court Street is the only part of the exterior that retains its original 1950s look. (RLLHD)

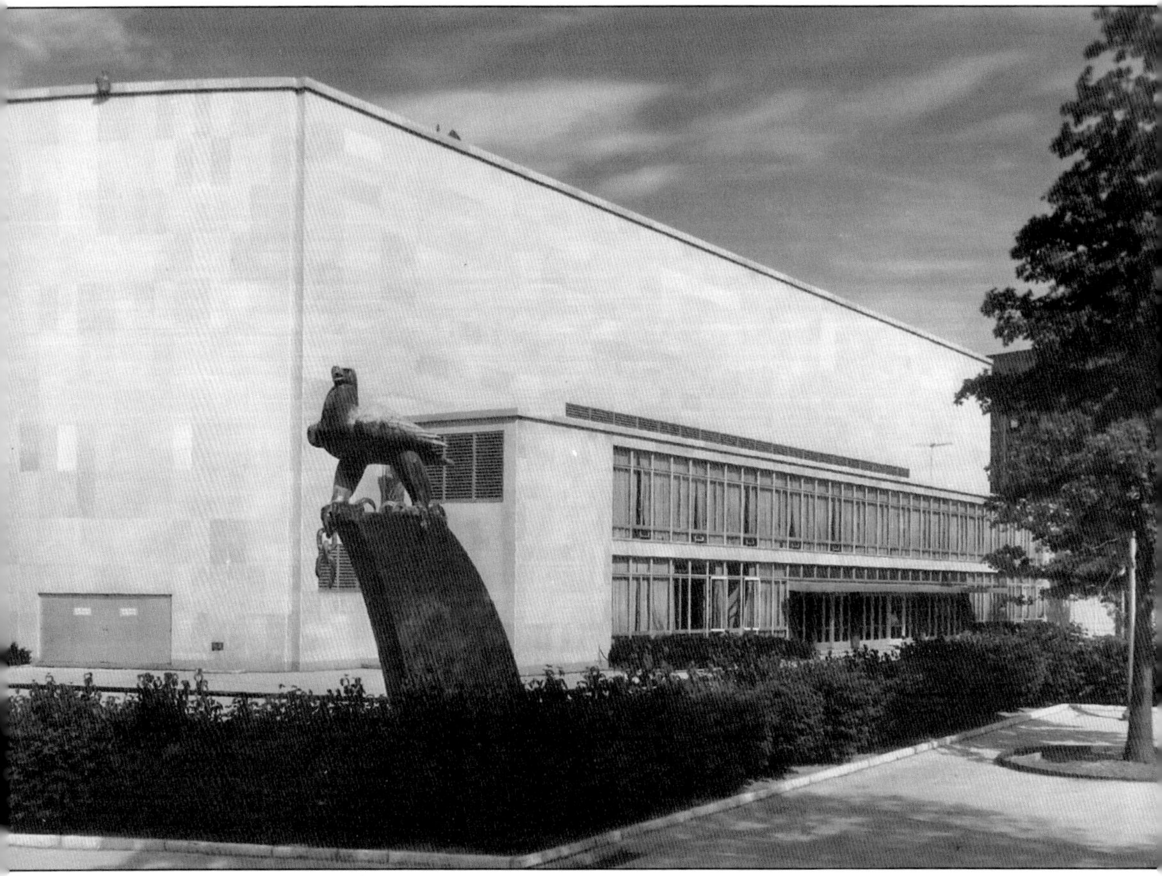

This regal memorial to the fallen of the Spanish-American War proudly stands on the Court Street entrance to the Community War Memorial's riverside plaza. Created in 1941 by New York artist Carl Jennervein, it was moved from Franklin Square to this setting in 1960. Notice the maturing trees, now four years removed from their plantings as saplings. The plaza and monument survived the 1990s renovation largely intact. (RMA.)

Two

Monroe County Civic Center

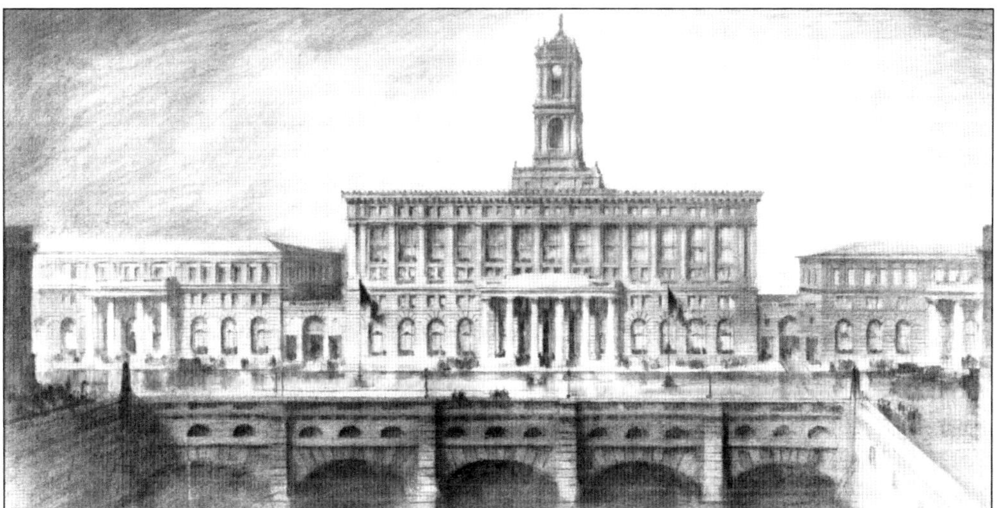

The idea to build a civic center had been bandied about since the early 1900s. Local philanthropist and founder of Kodak, George Eastman pushed for a complex of buildings to be constructed along and across the Genesee River between Court and Main Streets. This early proposal features a Beaux-Arts city hall with clock tower sitting astride the Genesee. The Broad Street Aqueduct is seen in front of the proposed complex. (RLLHD.)

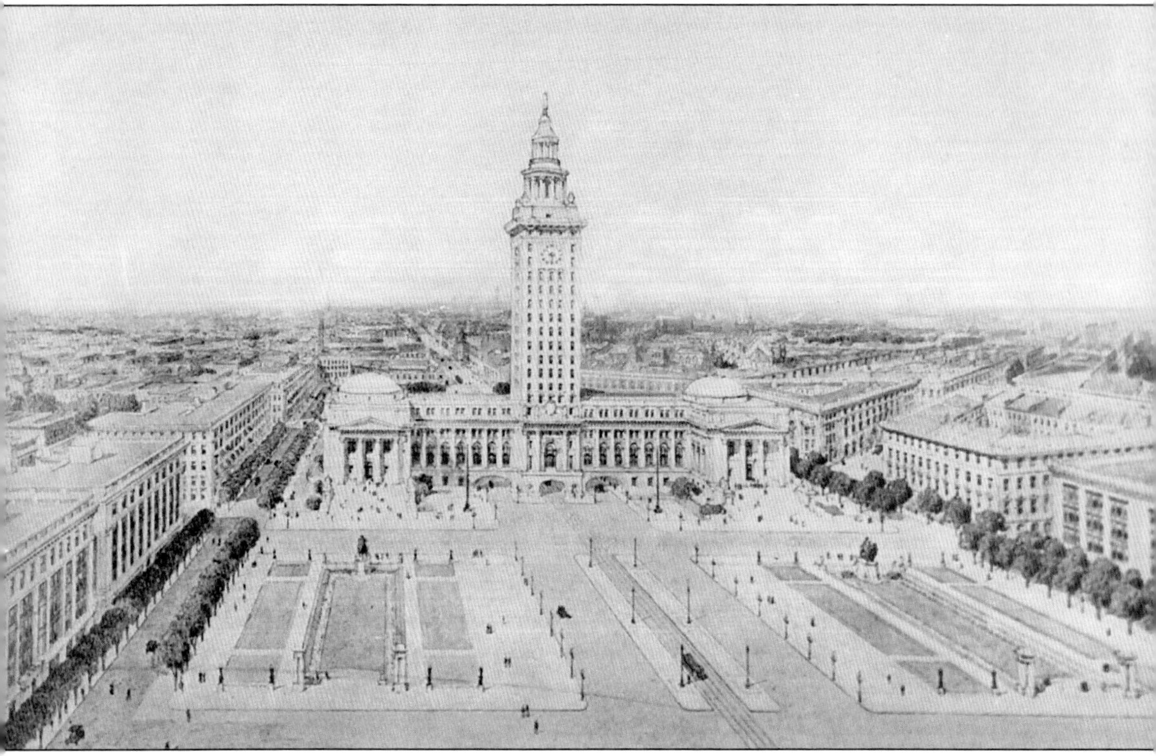

The team of Arnold W. Brunner and the famous landscape architect Fredrick Law Olmstead proposed to add some European flavor to the look and layout of downtown Rochester with this rendering from the early 20th century. Streets and whole blocks of buildings would be created and centered on twin memorial plazas fronting a high-rise city hall, with automobile and rail traffic passing under its monumental arches. (RMA.)

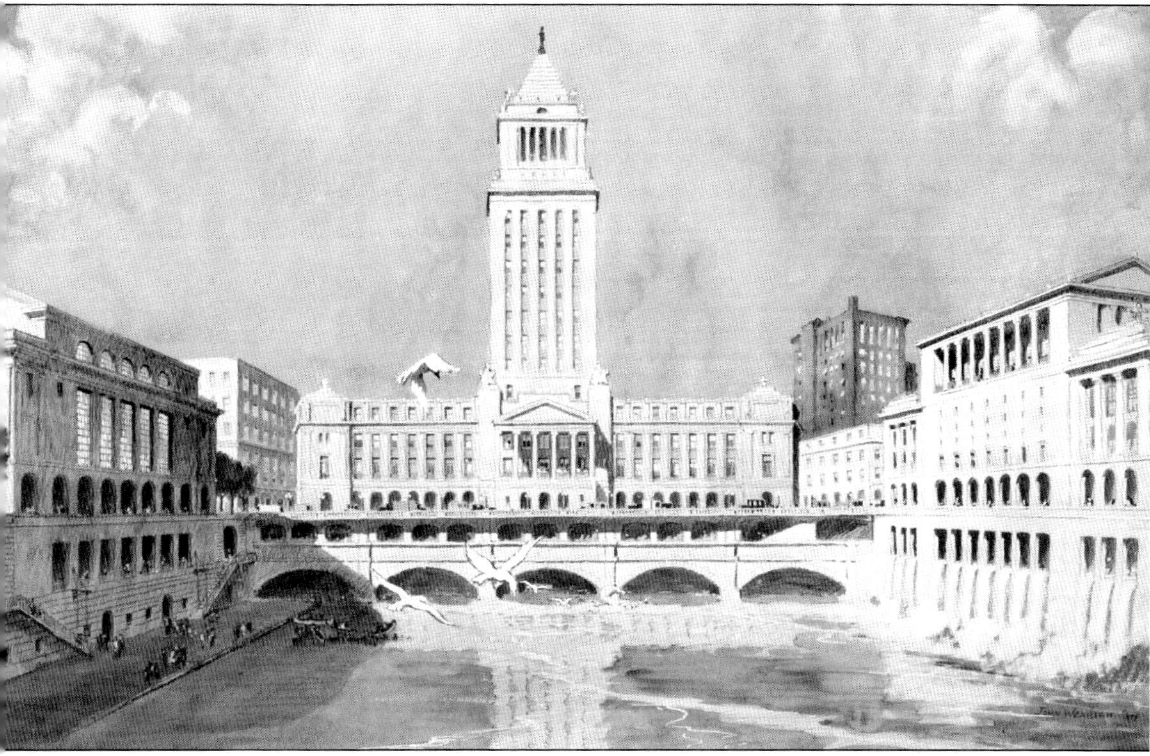

Here John Wenrich beautifully renders local architects Gordon and Kaelber's 1924 concept of a civic center for Rochester. Wenrich later worked for New York architect Raymond Hood and was responsible for the lush and wonderfully detailed drawings of the various design stages of the Rockefeller Center complex in the 1930s. He returned to Rochester following that period and continued to work here for a few decades more. (RMA.)

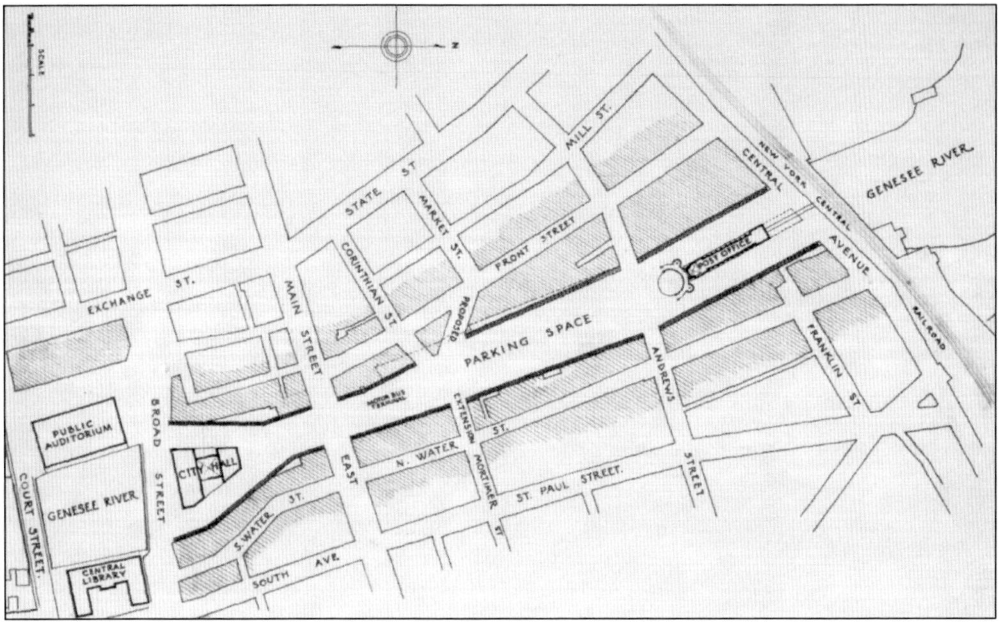

The Genesee River would be completely covered by a boulevard from Broad Street to Central Avenue at the edge of the 100-foot-tall Upper Falls in the plan by Gordon and Kaelber. In addition to the towering city hall straddling the river, there also was planned a new central post office with a public auditorium and the city's central library facing each other between Court and Broad Streets as well. (RMA.)

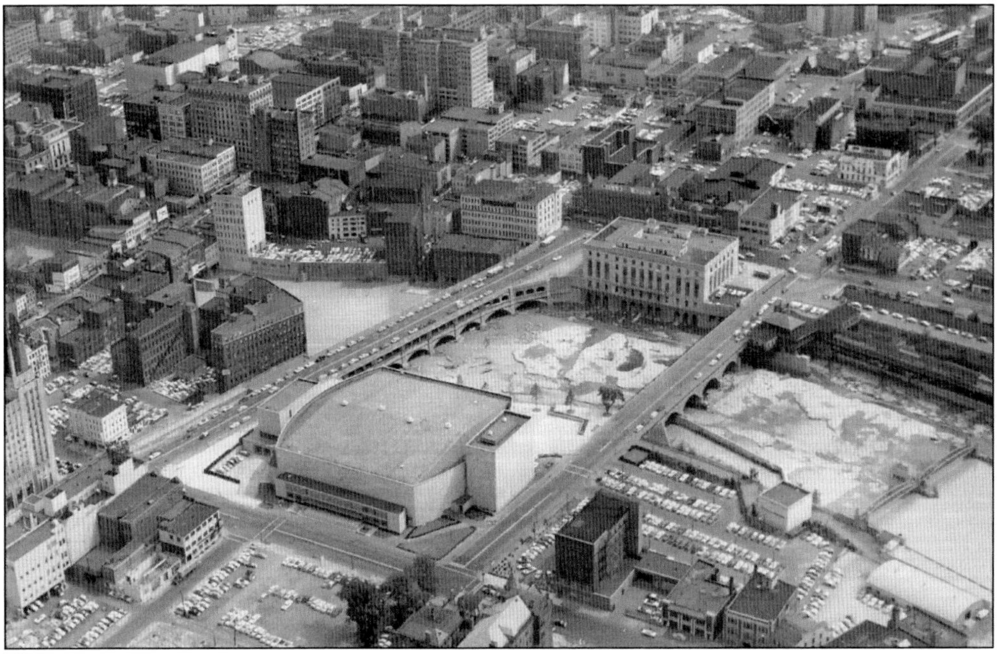

Although much of the Gordon and Kaelber plan was not realized, two of the components were built. William Kaelber designed the Rundel Memorial Building to house the city's central library on the eastern bank of the Genesee in 1936. Twenty years later, the public auditorium would be built across the river from designs of the firm that succeeded Gordon and Kaelber. (RMA.)

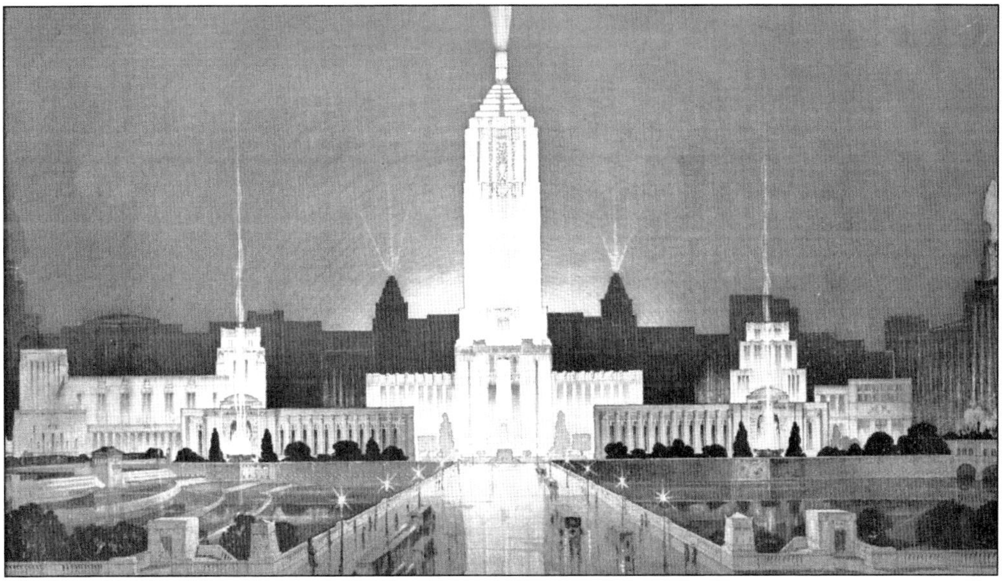

This unabashedly vertical, art deco concept from 1931 could be straight out of a Flash Gordon comic. Towers with powerful beacons reach skyward in the Rochester night, while enormous ceremonial flames burn in front of the wings of the pyramid-topped city hall. Unlike previous proposals, this would be built along the western banks of the Genesee River south of Broad Street. (RLLHD.)

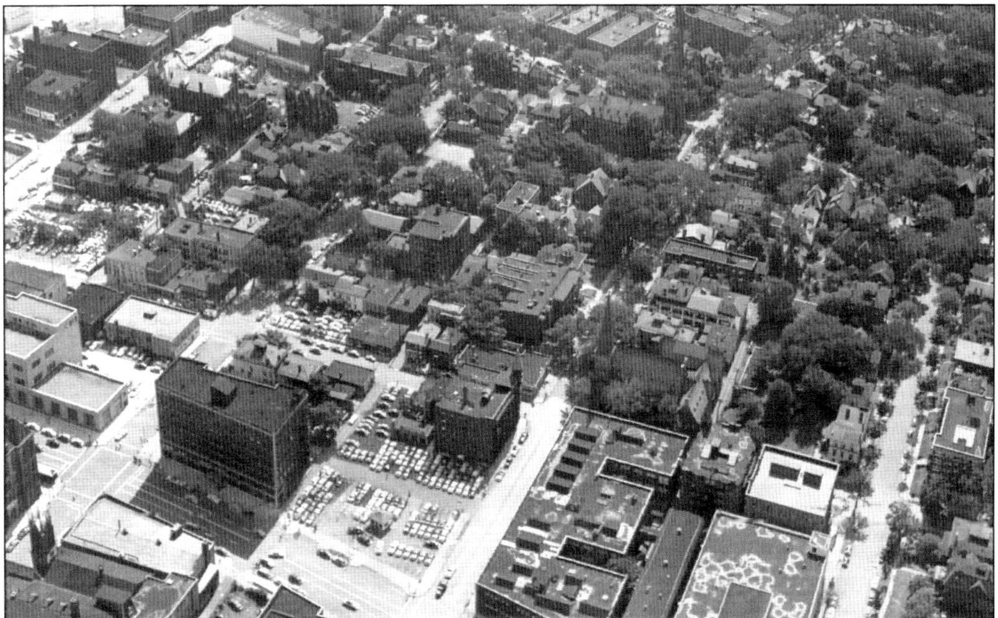

This section of the city's Third Ward was chosen as the site of the Monroe County Civic Center when local leaders restarted the planning process in the early 1950s. This area would include some of Rochester's oldest and most opulent homes, as well as parks, churches, small businesses, and apartment buildings. The Rochester Institute of Technology would call this neighborhood home until its ultra-modern suburban campus was built in the 1960s. (RLLHD.)

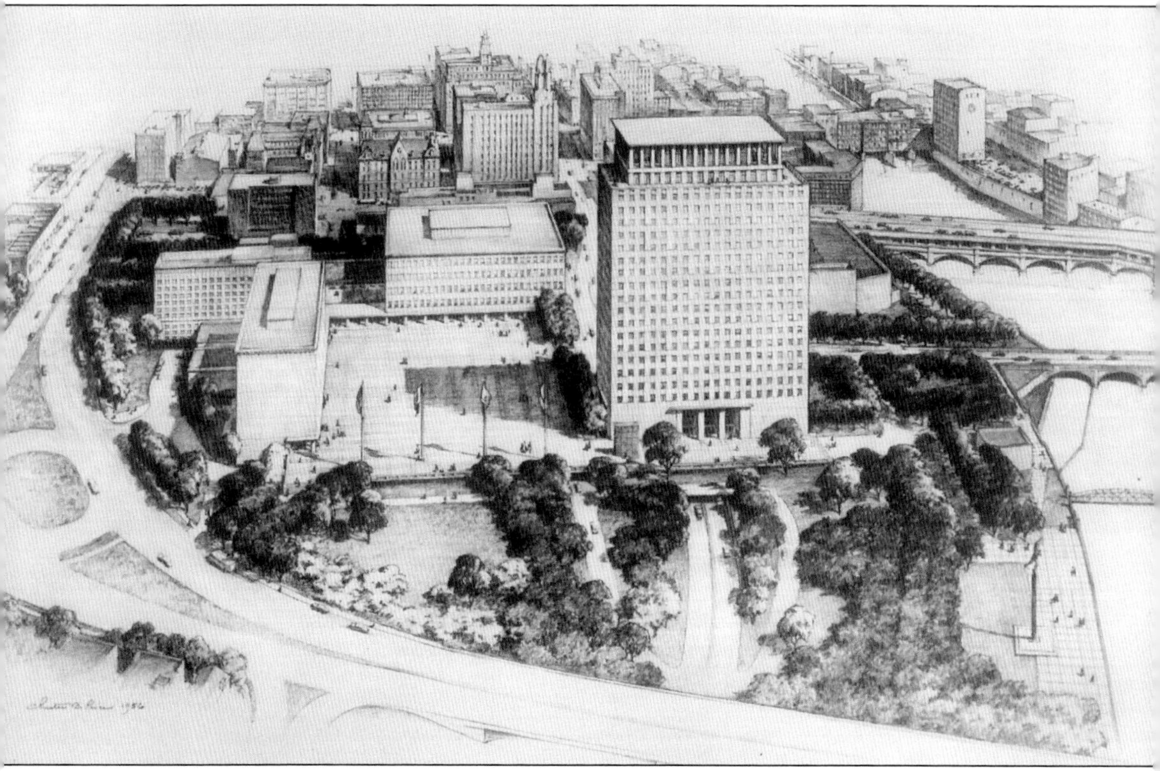

This 1956 rendering by Chester B. Price shows the Monroe County Civic Center as designed by a team of local and out-of-town architects. A towering city and county office building, with a two-story main entrance and an observation deck, straddles Exchange Street and is the focal point of the surrounding complex of low-rise buildings. An open-air plaza that was designed to have a capacity of 30,000 people for civic events tops a 1,300-car garage. Stairs to the right of the tower lead down to a river walk promenade that connects with the riverside plaza of the Community War Memorial and features the return of the sculpture of Mercury placed atop an obelisk, just south of the Court Street Dam in the lower right of this image. (RMA.)

A model of the Monroe County Civic Center is on display at the county courthouse in this image from the fall of 1956. Across the river, two unidentified buildings appear near the Court Street Dam. (RMA.)

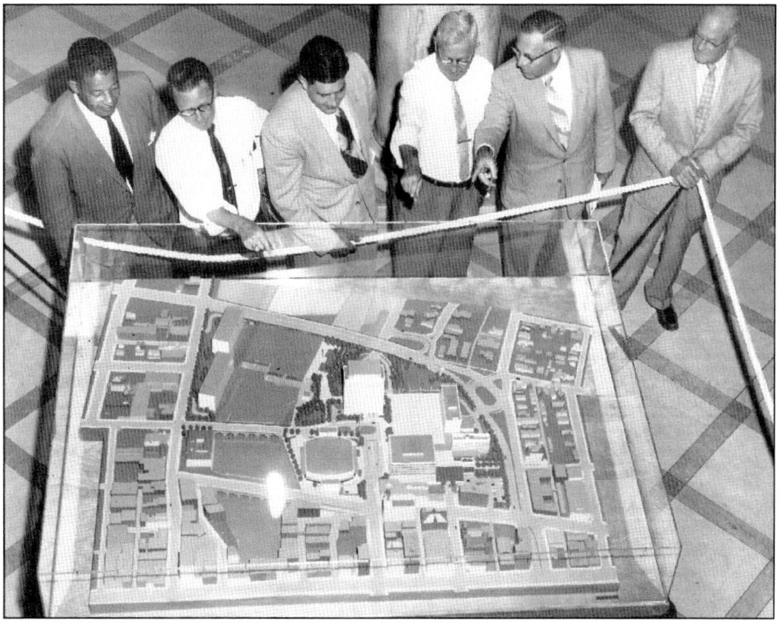

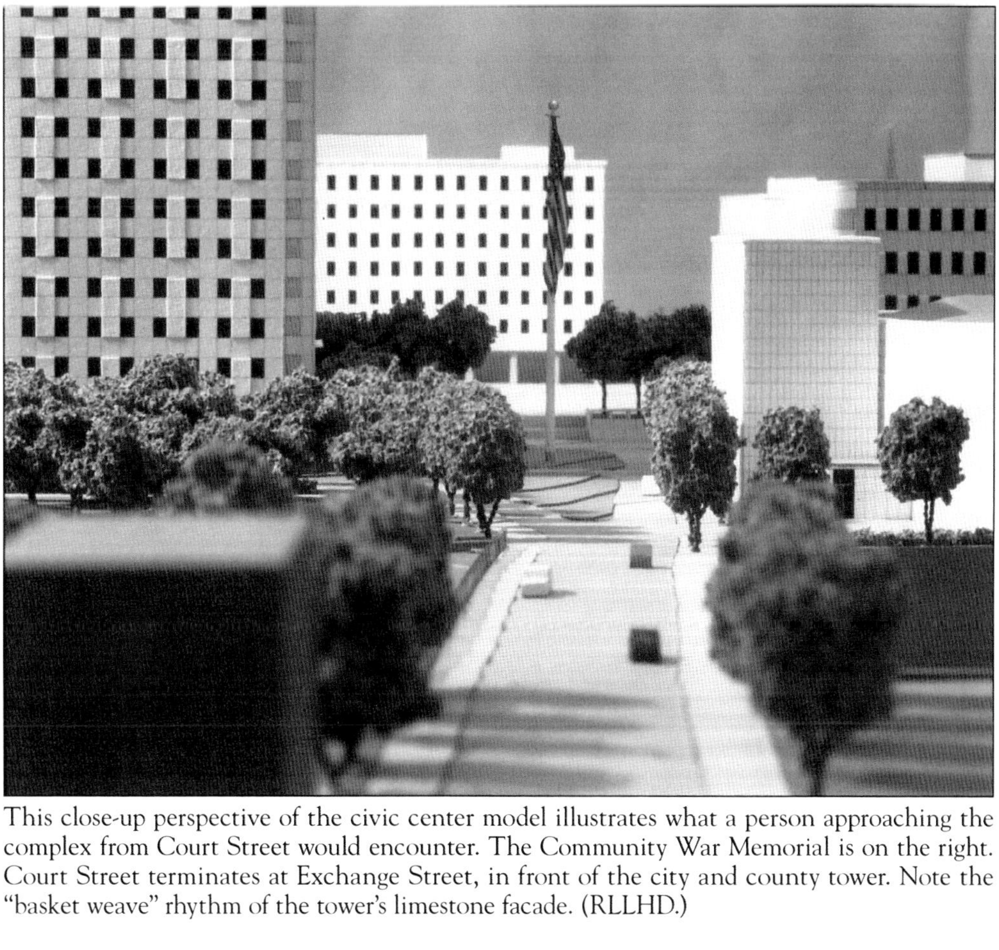

This close-up perspective of the civic center model illustrates what a person approaching the complex from Court Street would encounter. The Community War Memorial is on the right. Court Street terminates at Exchange Street, in front of the city and county tower. Note the "basket weave" rhythm of the tower's limestone facade. (RLLHD.)

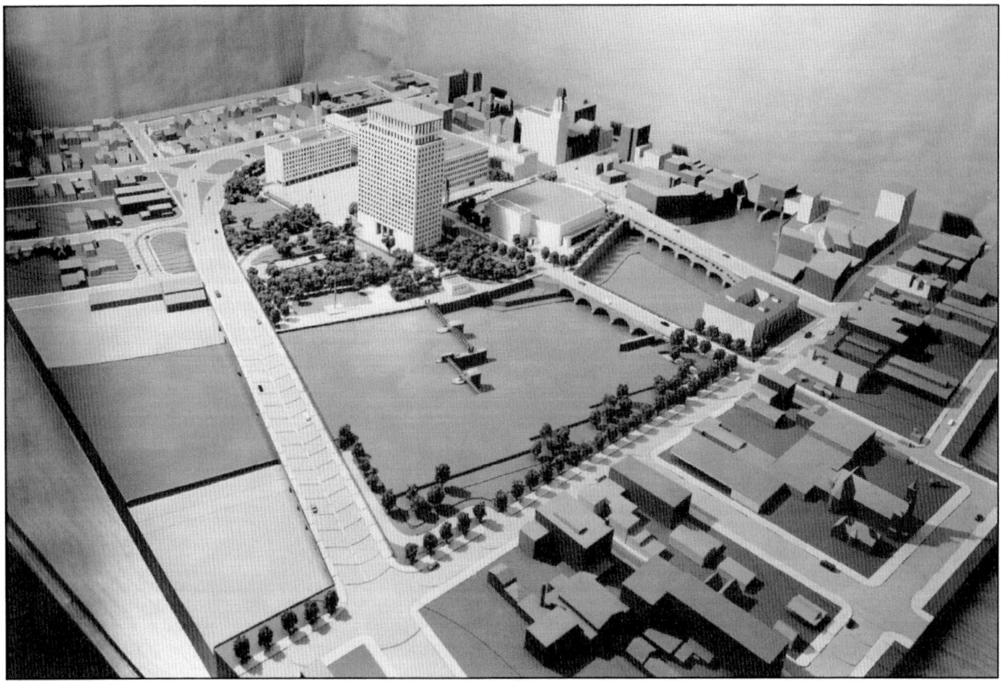

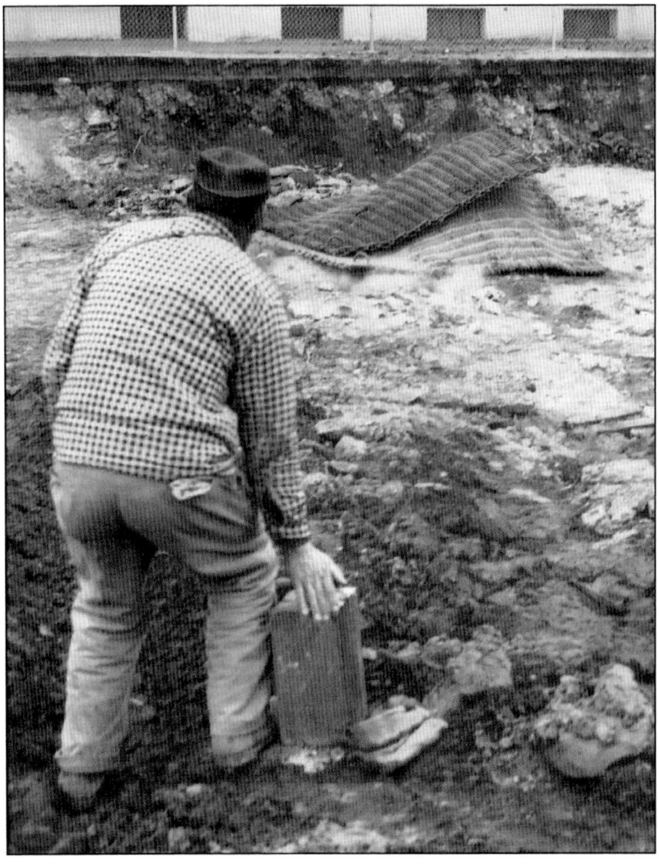

An aerial view of the model is seen here. South Avenue is in the foreground, and the Troup Howell Bridge carries the Inner Loop expressway across the Genesee River to the left of the civic center. (RMA.)

A demolition worker presses the plunger to blast the rock beneath the metal mesh during site preparation at the Monroe County Civic Center in 1957. The metal mesh would protect workers and bystanders from the shrapnel of the exploding stone. (RMA.)

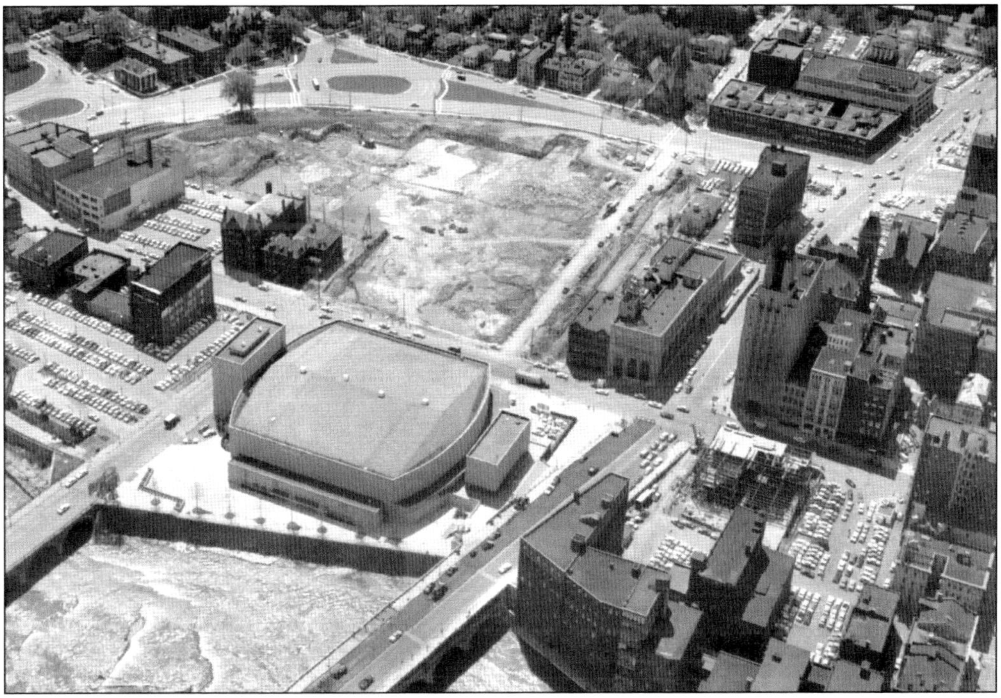

By early 1958, most of the site has been cleared, with only a few buildings remaining along Exchange Street. Over 150,000 tons of rock and soil were excavated and used as fill on projects throughout the county. The large building with the gabled roof above and just to left of the Community War Memorial is the soon-to-be-replaced city police headquarters. (RLLHD.)

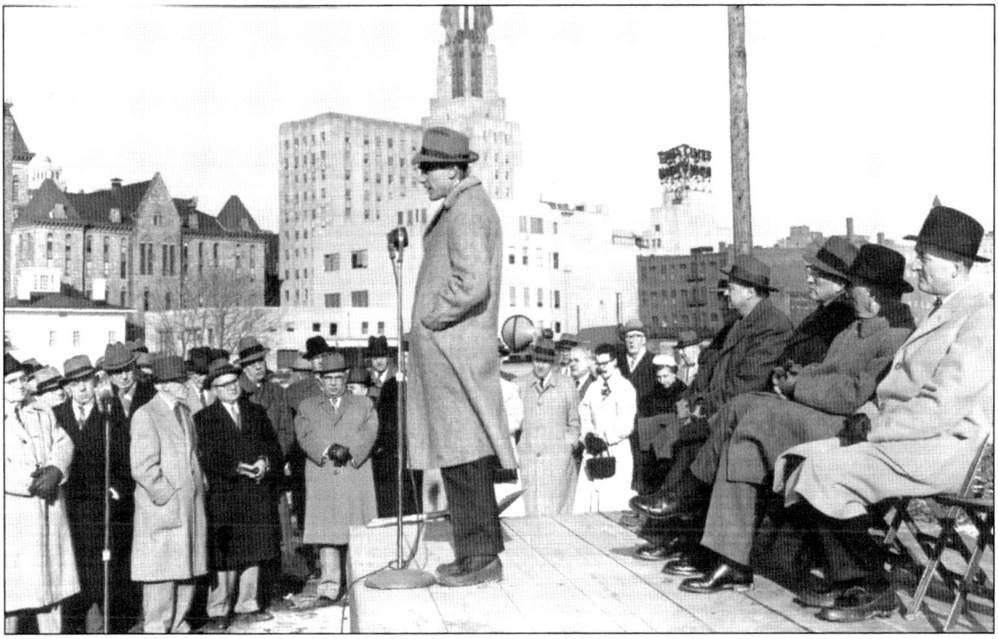

Mayor Peter Barry speaks at the ground-breaking ceremony for the Monroe County Civic Center in this image from January 1958. It was estimated that the civic center would cost $50 million and would take five years to complete. (RLLHD.)

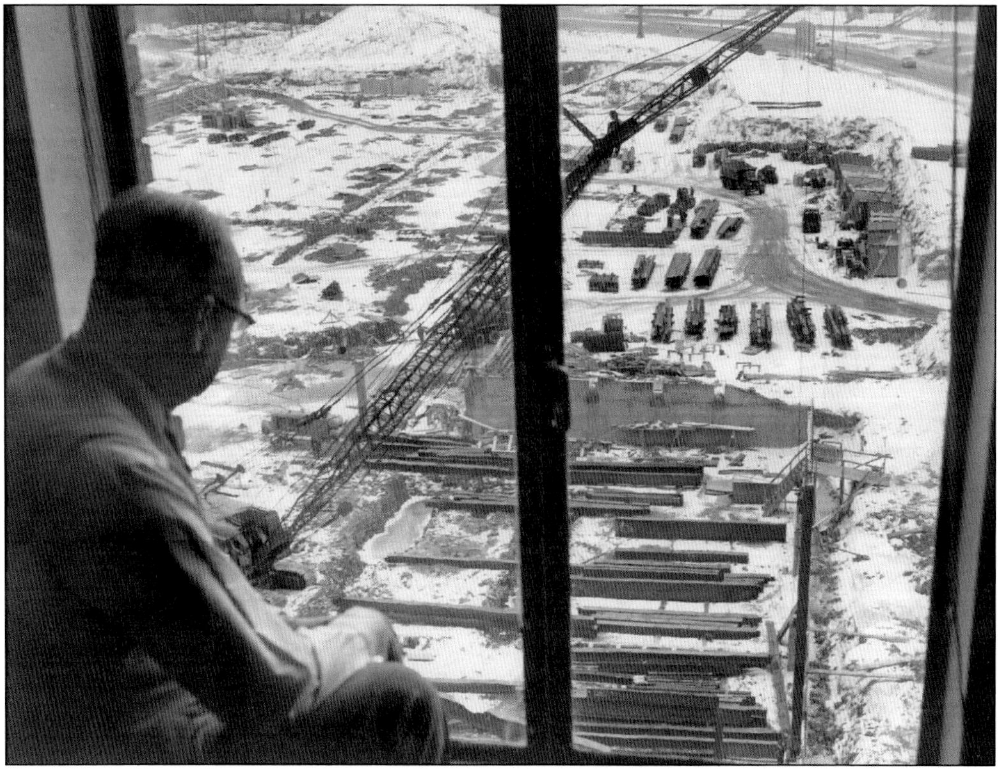

Amid delays and unforeseen difficulties, the first building did not start to rise until the spring of 1959. Project engineer Harold McElwain watches the first steel column for the police's testing lab being erected. (*Democrat and Chronicle*.)

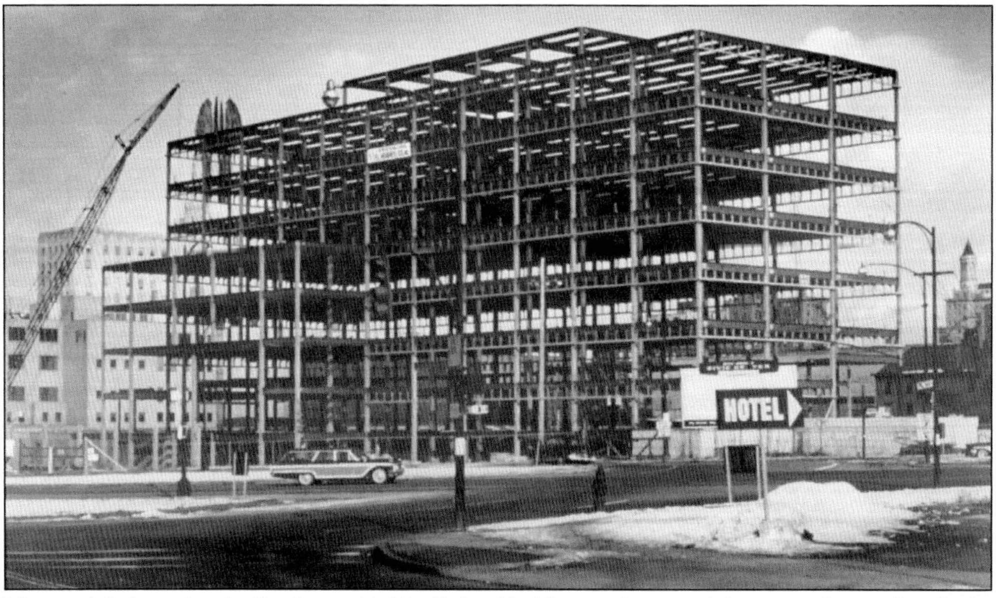

The steel skeleton for the Rochester Public Safety Building and testing lab is complete and ready for the application of its Indiana limestone facade. All of the buildings that were constructed in the initial phase of the complex would have this distinguished and handsome stone cladding. (RMA.)

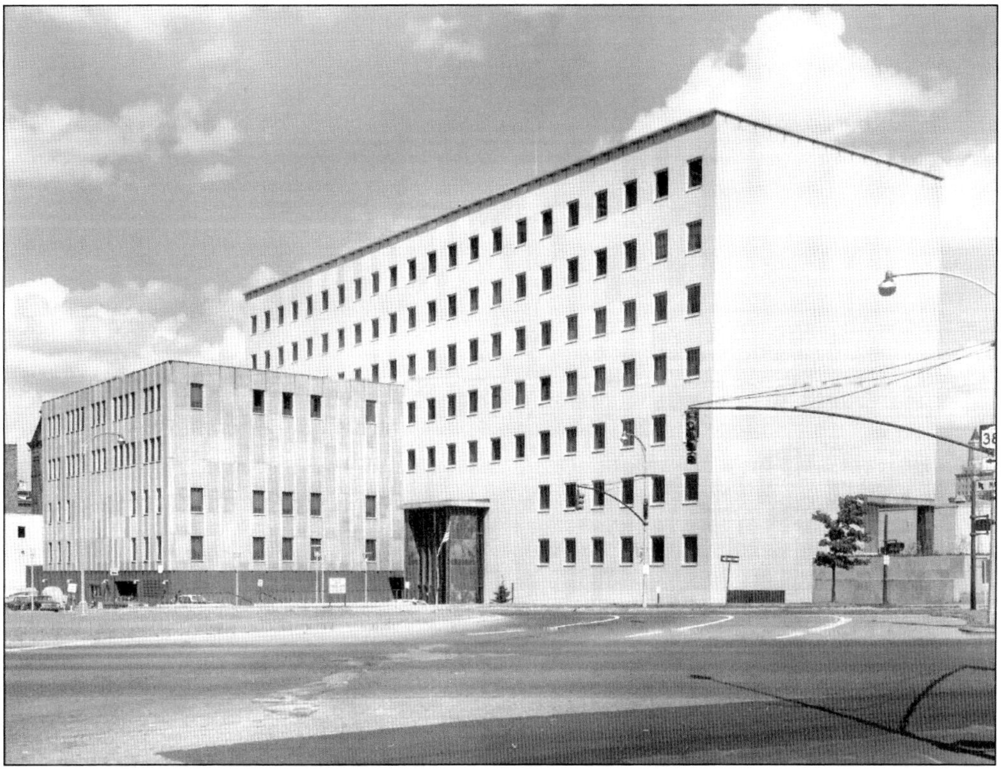

Limestone, marble, and granite are in place in this similar view of the newly finished public safety building and testing laboratory. The building is now ready to assist officers in their efforts to combat crime in the city. Its two-story-high entrance is similar to the main portal of the proposed city/county office tower. (RLLHD.)

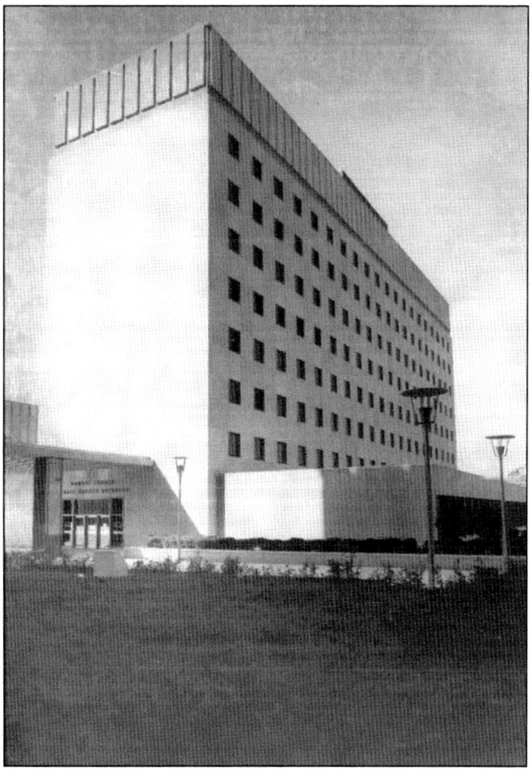

The controversial "high rise jail," officially known as the Monroe County Public Safety Building, not only houses criminals but the county sheriff's department as well. An addition, more than double the original jail's size, was built in the early 2000s. The architects of the new wing designed it to compliment the older building, with similar features like square windows and a distinct, if minimalist, cornice. (RLLHD.)

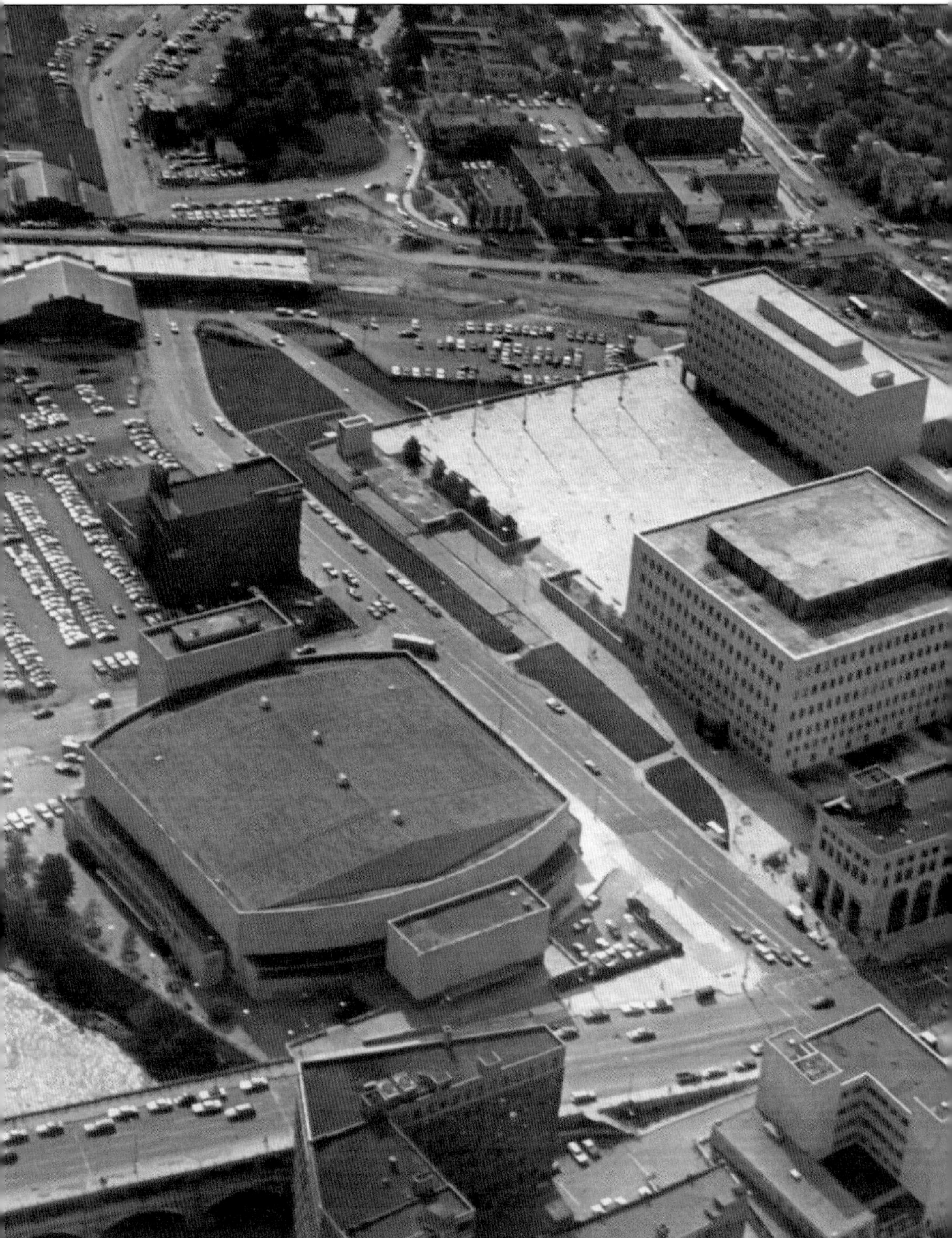

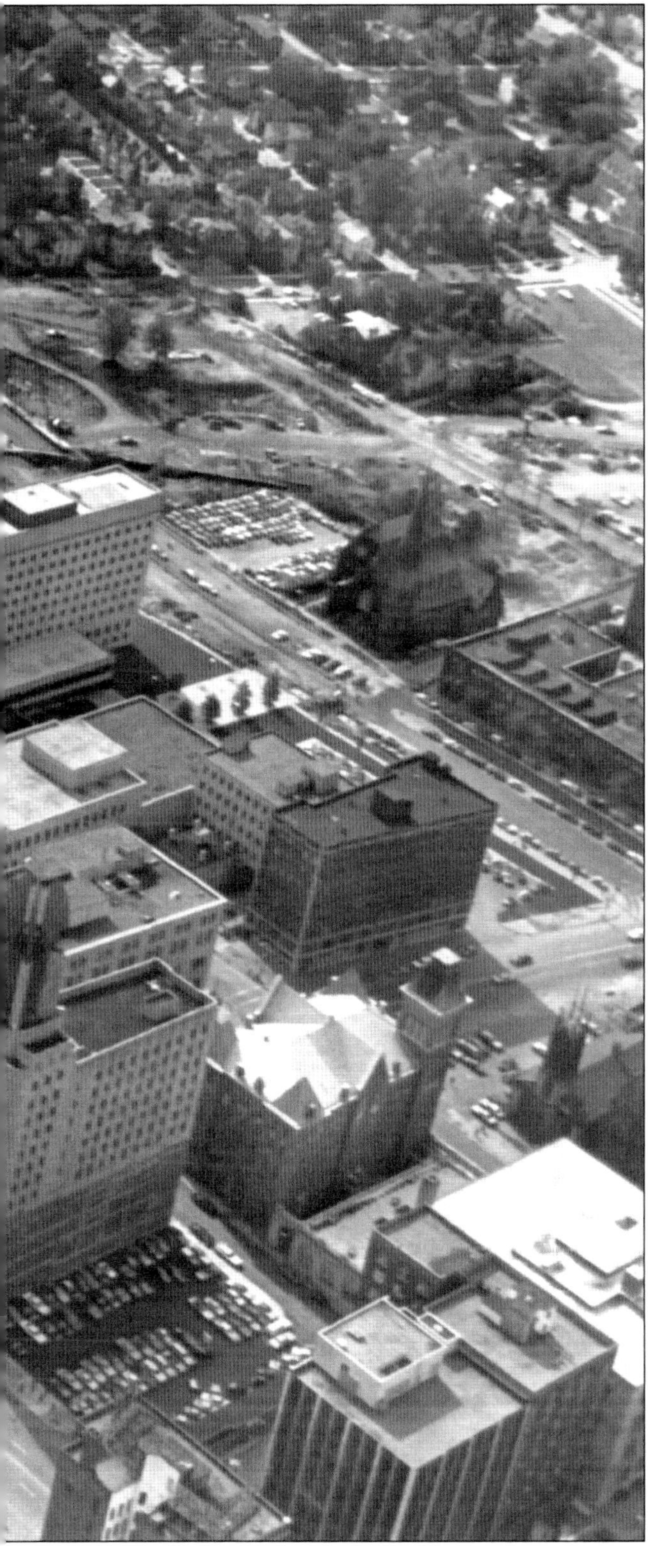

Unlike the earlier proposals, most of the concept from the 1956 plan would be brought to fruition. However, like the previous proposals, this concept would not be completed as designed. The city/county tower was never built over Exchange Street, and with it the river promenade was lost. Mercury would have to wait another decade for placement on another building nearby. The largest building in the complex, the Hall of Justice houses the city and county courts, and is located at the northeast corner of the plaza, across Exchange Street from the Community War Memorial. Four of Rochester's most prominent architecture firms, along with the descendant firm of Ralph T. Walker, architect of the winged Genesee Valley Trust Building, collaborated on the design and planning of the Monroe County Civic Center, with each firm taking on the design of a component of the project. In the late 1990s and early 2000s, a new city public safety building, as well as an expansion of the county jail, was added to the complex, and to this day, buildings continue to be planned and constructed at the civic center. In 2009, ground was broken for a new crime lab that will be used by both city and county police. (RMA.)

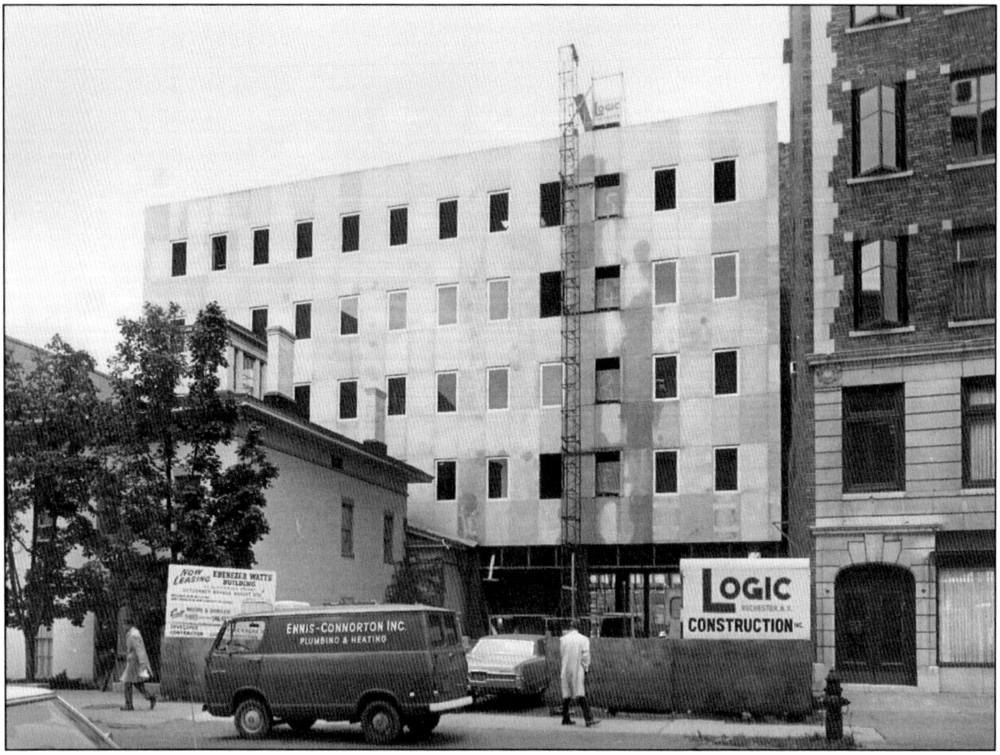

Scheduled for completion in August 1970, the Ebenezer Watts Building on Fitzhugh Street incorporates the 1828 house of the same name. The Ebenezer Watts House is one of the oldest homes in the city and is rumored to have been a stop on the Underground Railroad. (RMA.)

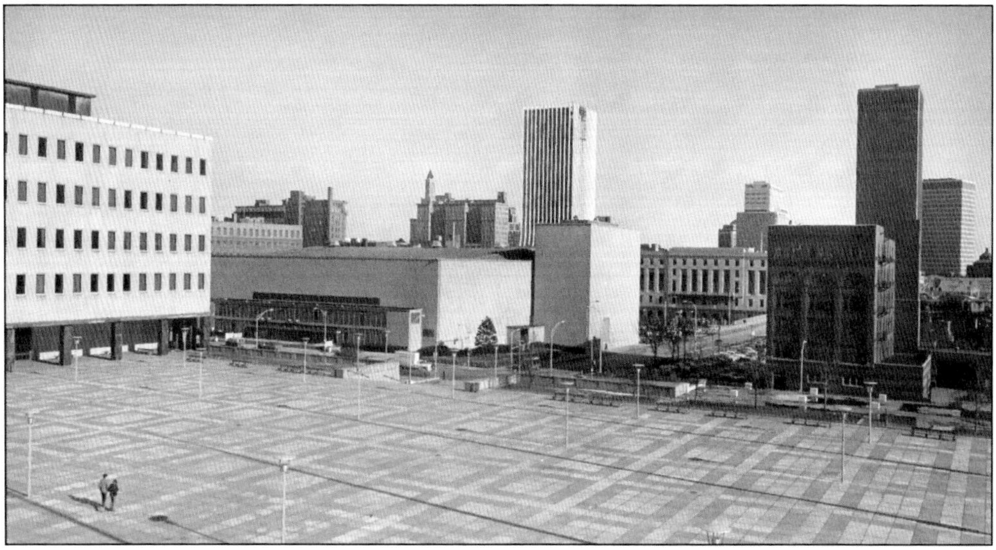

Despite the best efforts of the county to bring events and people to the civic center, the vast plaza continued to be a barren wasteland most days. Over the years, many proposals have been drawn up that would attempt to make the civic center a more inviting space. In 2009, it was announced that the county planned to turn the plaza into a green roof that would enliven the space and have environmental benefits, like rainwater filtration. (RLLHD.)

Three

GENESEE CROSSROADS

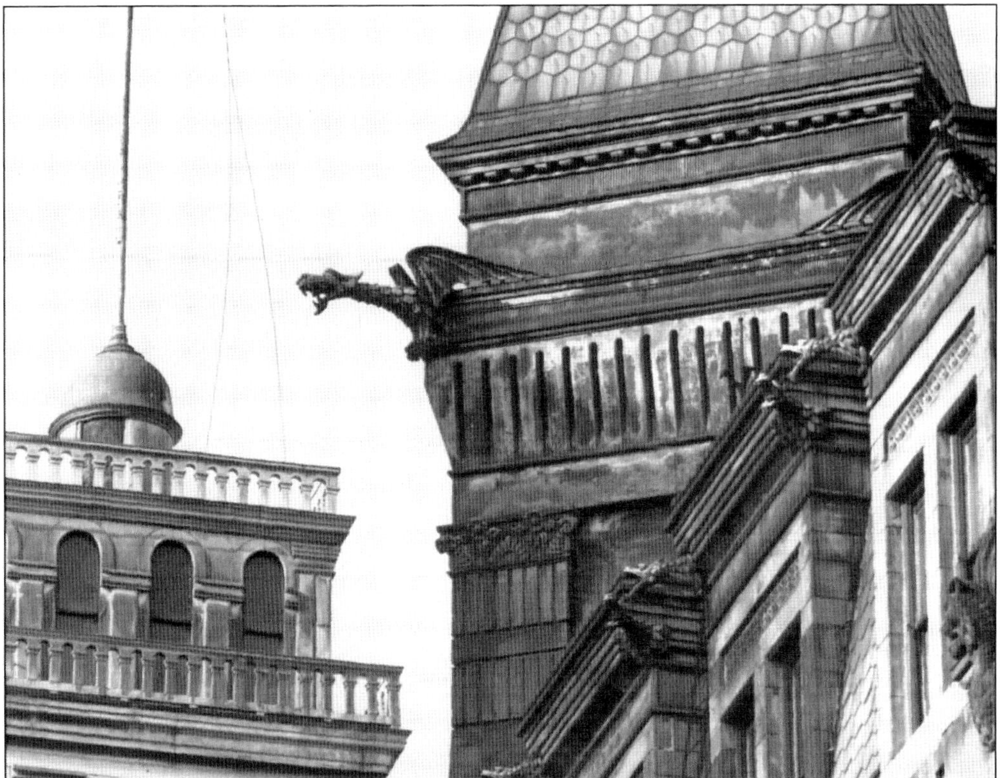

The gargoyles of the Elwood Building roar at their neighbor across State Street, the Powers Block. These structures traded titles as the tallest building in town. The Elwood Building originally outdid its neighbor, but as history would prove time and again, the tower of Daniel Powers would not look up to any other. He added enough height to the Powers Block to surpass the pyramid-topped tower of the Elwood Building. (RLLHD.)

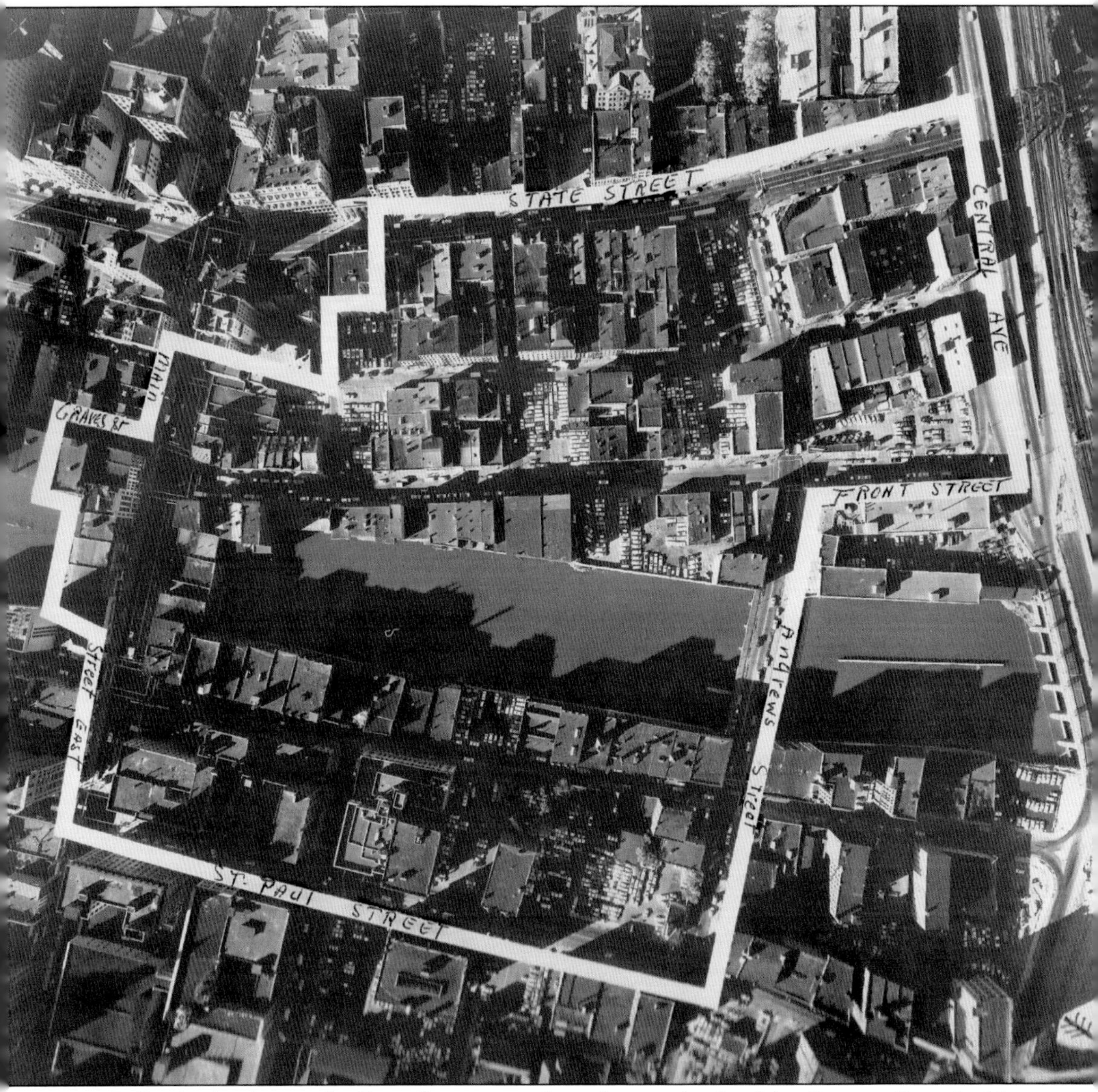

Talk of redeveloping the Front Street area along the west bank of the Genesee River had been heard since the early 1900s. In the 1950s, discourse began heating up about redeveloping both sides of the river between Main and Andrews Streets. In 1959, Victor Gruen, the architect of the Midtown Plaza mall and office complex being built farther up East Main Street, made an early proposal for the east side of the river. I. M. Pei and Partners were hired to create a site plan and design concepts for the new construction in the 13-acre project. Their plan called for a 20-story hotel to straddle the river on the north side of Main Street, as well as offices, housing, and shops. (RLLHD.)

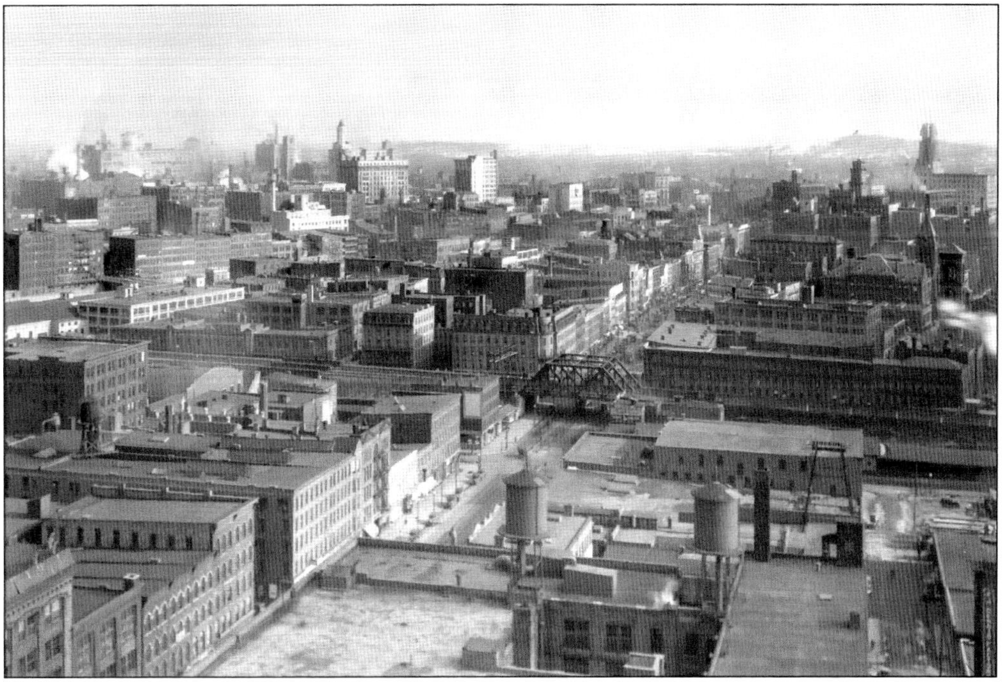

This view of State Street, looking south from the 1930s, shows the western portion of the Genesee Crossroads Project on the left. The area is dense with structures from the early days of Rochester industry and commerce. (RMA.)

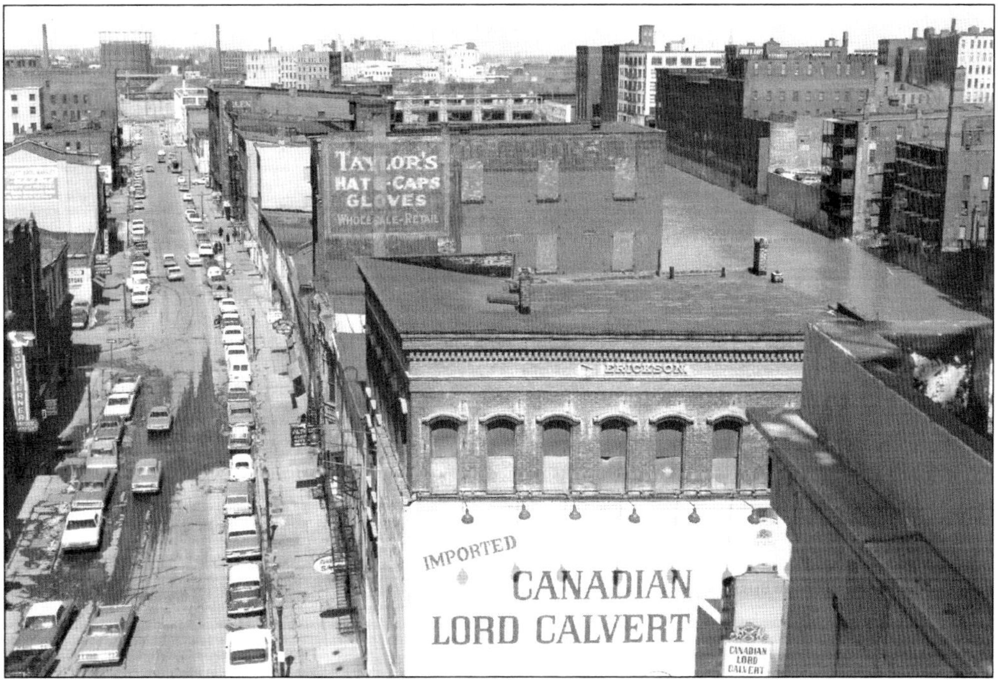

Front Street splits the crowded district in half and runs parallel to State Street. This view looks north toward Andrews Street. By the 1960s, neglect and uncertainty about the neighborhood's future had taken its toll on the 19th-century building stock there. (RMA.)

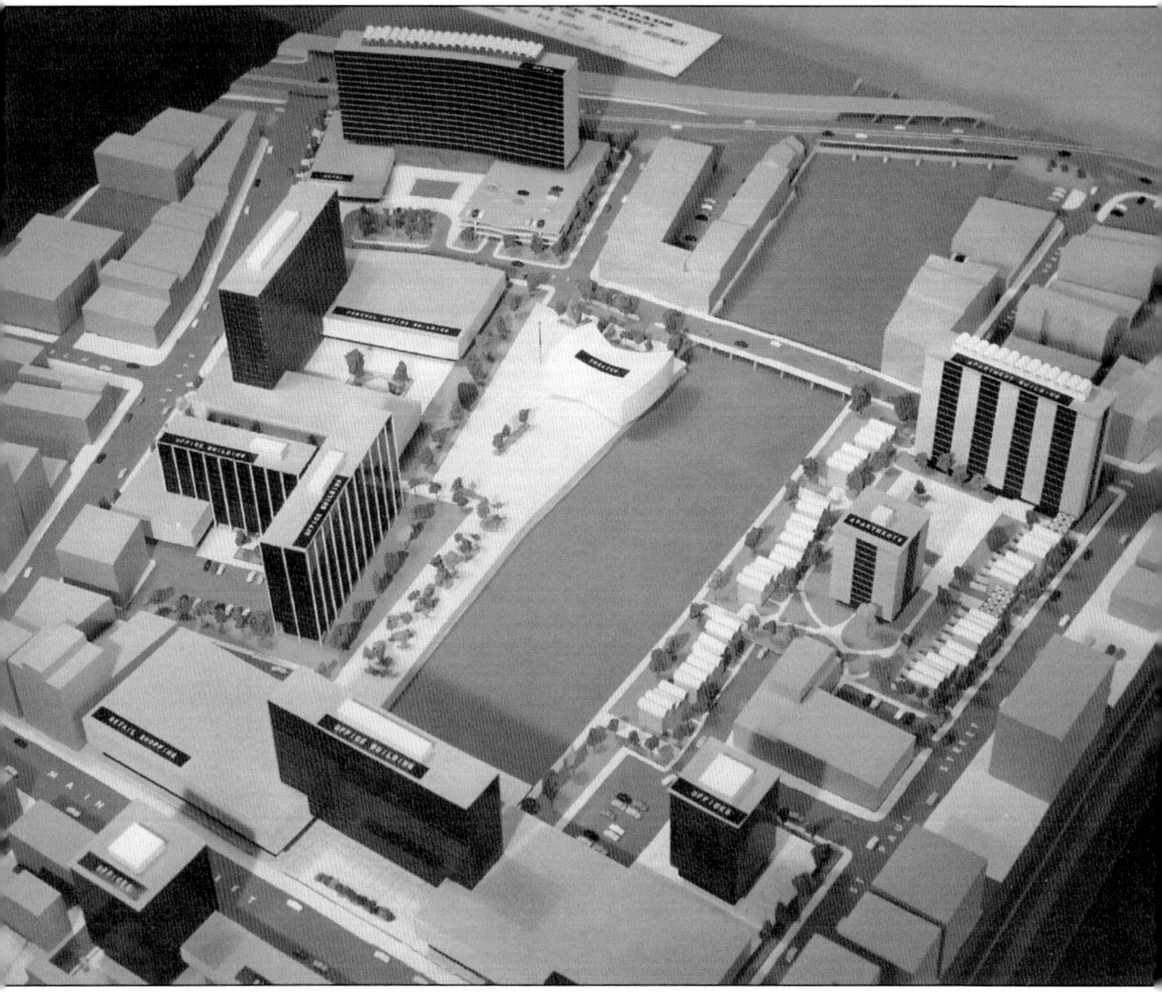

This model, looking northwest with Main Street at the bottom of the image, incorporates a building spanning the river on Main Street from the I. M. Pei study. In this concept, the structure is for offices instead of lodging. Apartments, office space, a riverside park and theater, and a new federal office building were proposed as well. (RMA.)

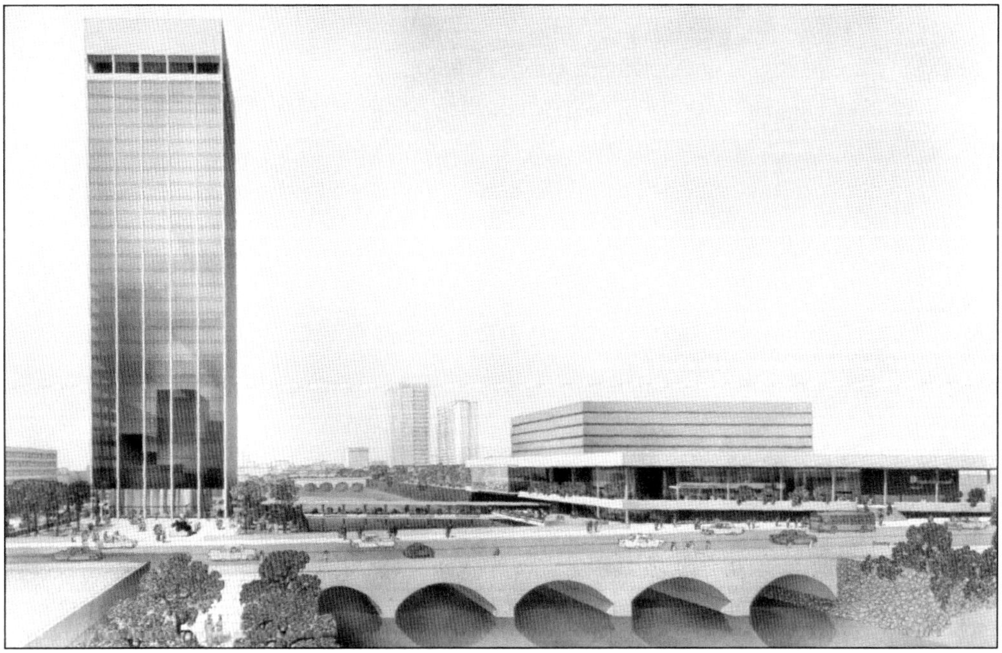

Another proposed development for the Main Street sites included a 30-story tower, sheathed in white marble and tinted glass, as illustrated here. A garage, department stores, and a 372-foot-tall tower would face each other across the river in this rendering by the architects Raymond and Redo of New York City. (RLLHD.)

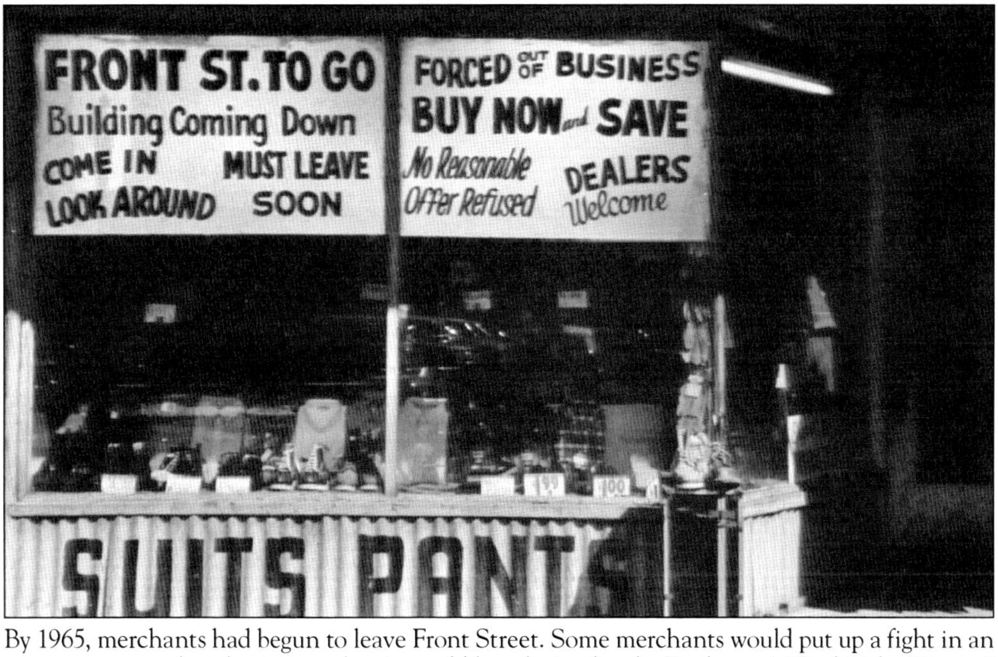

By 1965, merchants had begun to leave Front Street. Some merchants would put up a fight in an attempt to save their businesses, but it would be a losing battle. Rochester's "Red Light District" would be no more within a matter of months. It had been the home of saloons and butcher shops, clothiers and cafes, nightclubs, and the Rescue Mission. Today only a vestigial section of Front Street remains behind the former IBM building. (RMA.)

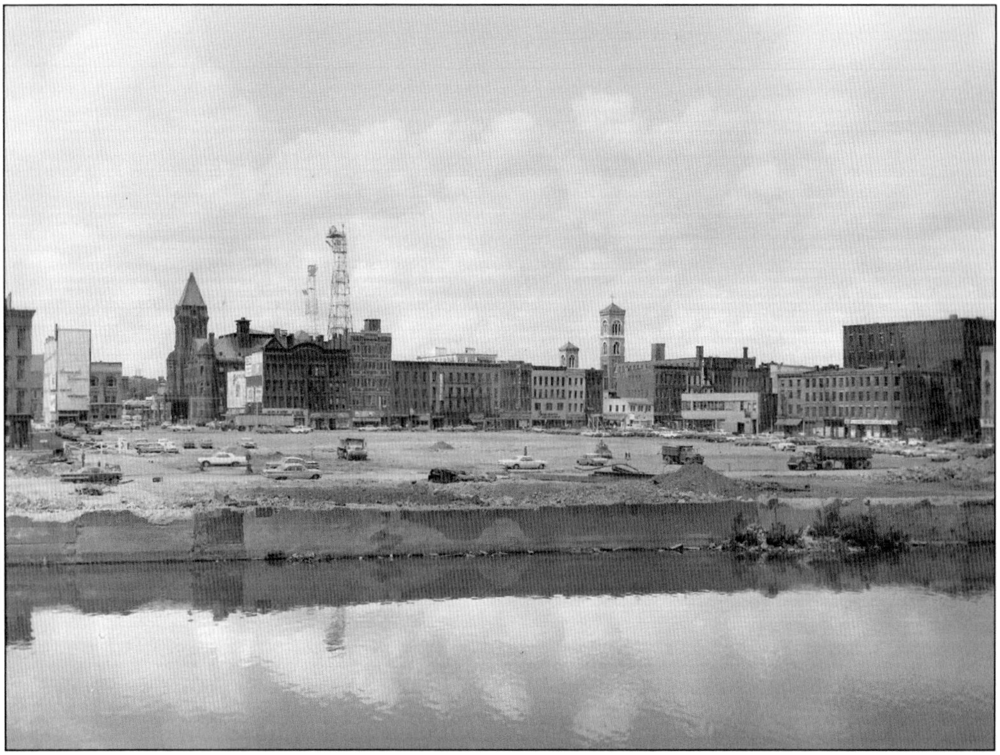

By the fall of 1965, most of the Front Street neighborhood was cleared. It would be more than two years before the first building would begin to rise on the 13-acre site and another decade before it would approach completion. (RMA.)

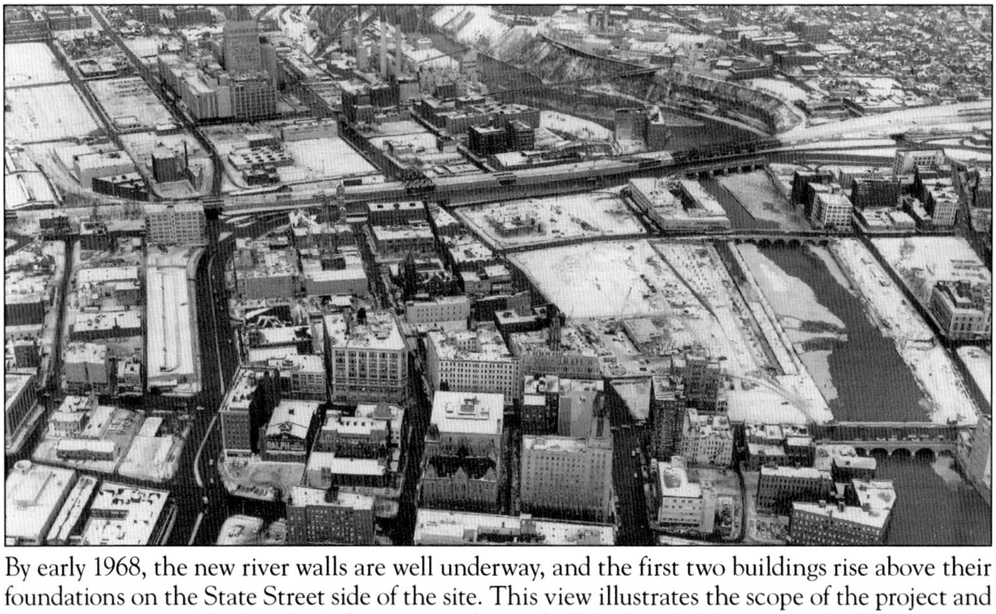

By early 1968, the new river walls are well underway, and the first two buildings rise above their foundations on the State Street side of the site. This view illustrates the scope of the project and how it contrasts with the relatively intact and crowded blocks of 19th-century buildings on the other side of State Street. (RLLHD.)

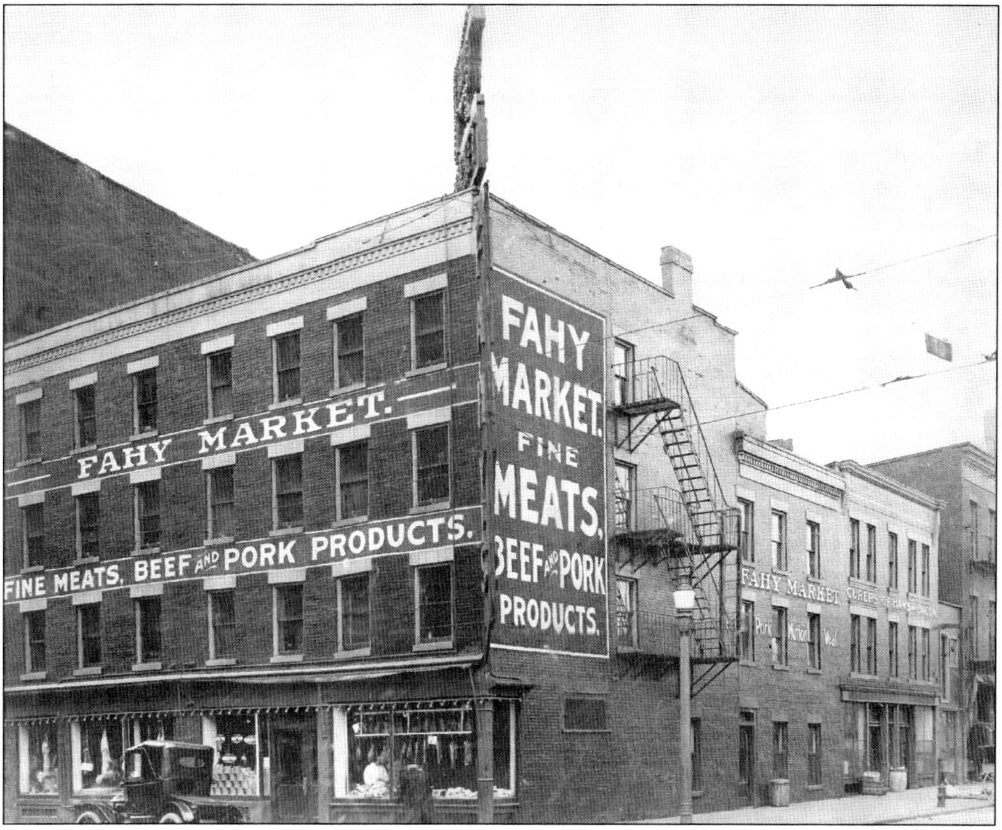

Fahy Market stands on the southwest corner of Front and Andrews Streets in this image from 1915. A sign on the side of the building advertises its cured ham and bacon, while a Model T waits out front for its owner to return. (RLLHD.)

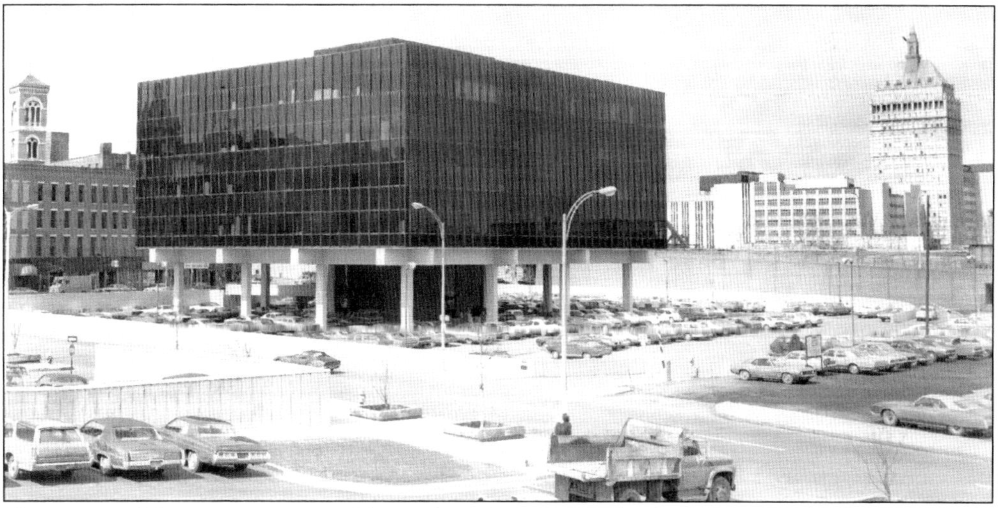

This view is of the same corner over 50 years later. Constructed for the International Business Machine Company (IBM), it was the first building to be completed at the Genesee Crossroads Urban Renewal Project site. Construction began in January 1968 and was completed in September of that year. Four levels of offices were raised on concrete stilts over the depressed parking area below. (RLLHD.)

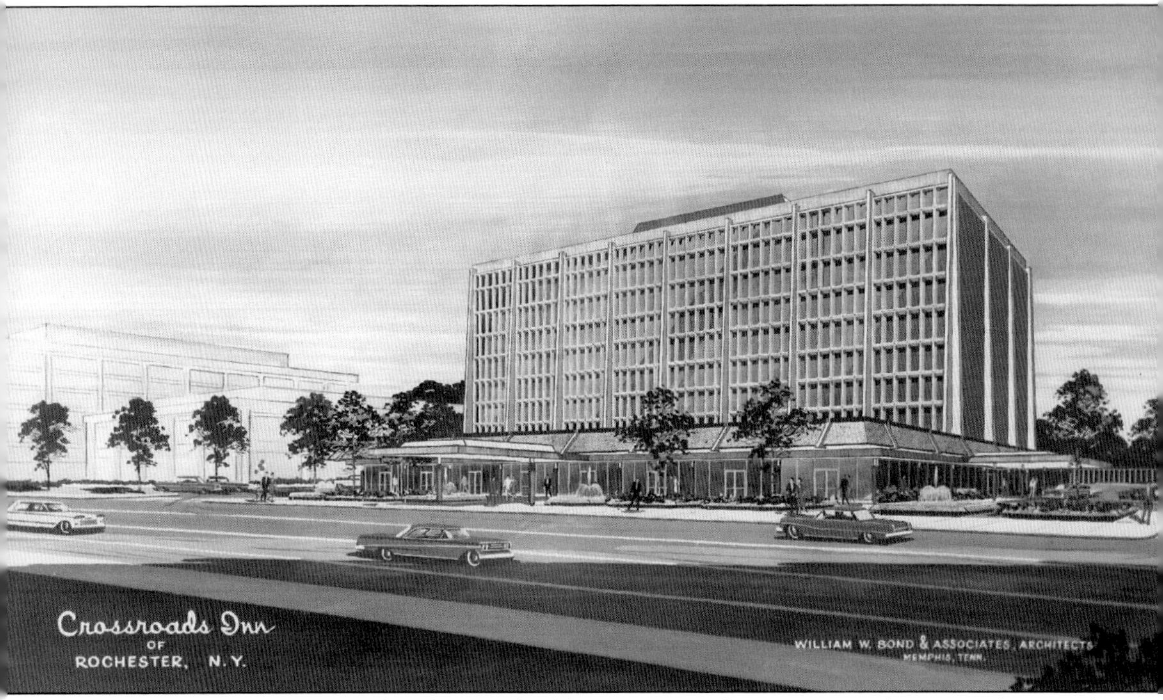

At about the same time that the IBM building was started, construction began on the upscale hotel planned for a parcel on State Street, closer to the Main Street intersection, known as "The Four Corners," than the IBM building. William W. Bond and Associates of Tennessee designed this early rendering, dubbed the "Crossroads Inn." (RMA.)

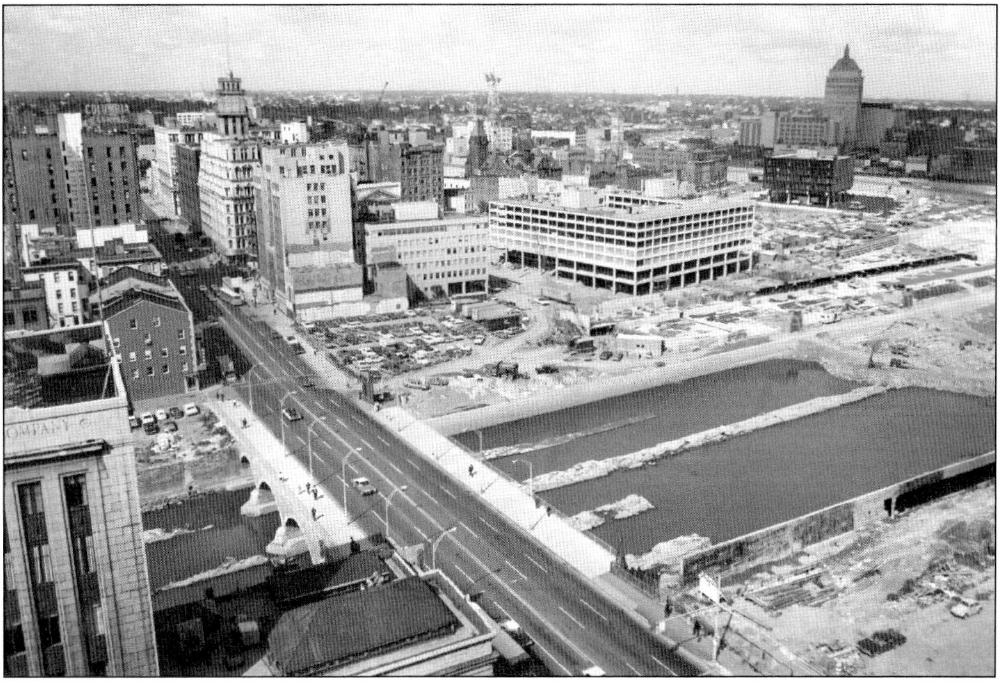

By August 1968, the hotel now called the "Americana" has its concrete structure finished and awaits the completion of the interior and landscaping, before it opens for business in the coming months. The hotel would change owners and names many times. (RLLHD.)

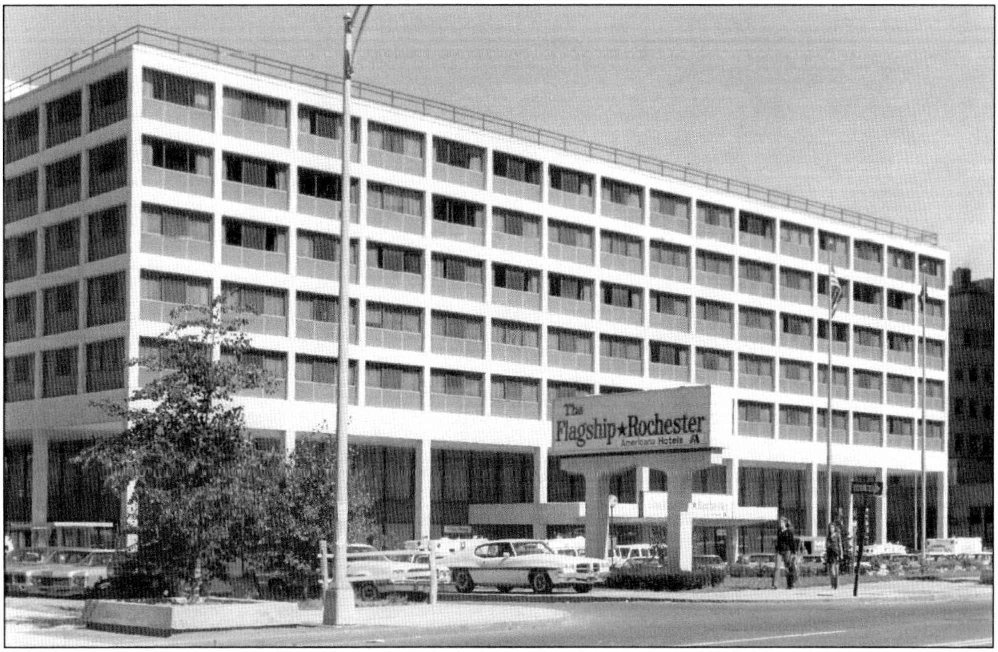

William B. Tabler, who was also responsible for the New York Hilton, among many other hotels across the nation, designed the Americana Flagship Hotel in Rochester. It contains over 300 rooms and features a ballroom that can accommodate crowds of 1,000. A local developer of shopping centers and office buildings, Wilmorite was the main developer of the gigantic project. (RMA.)

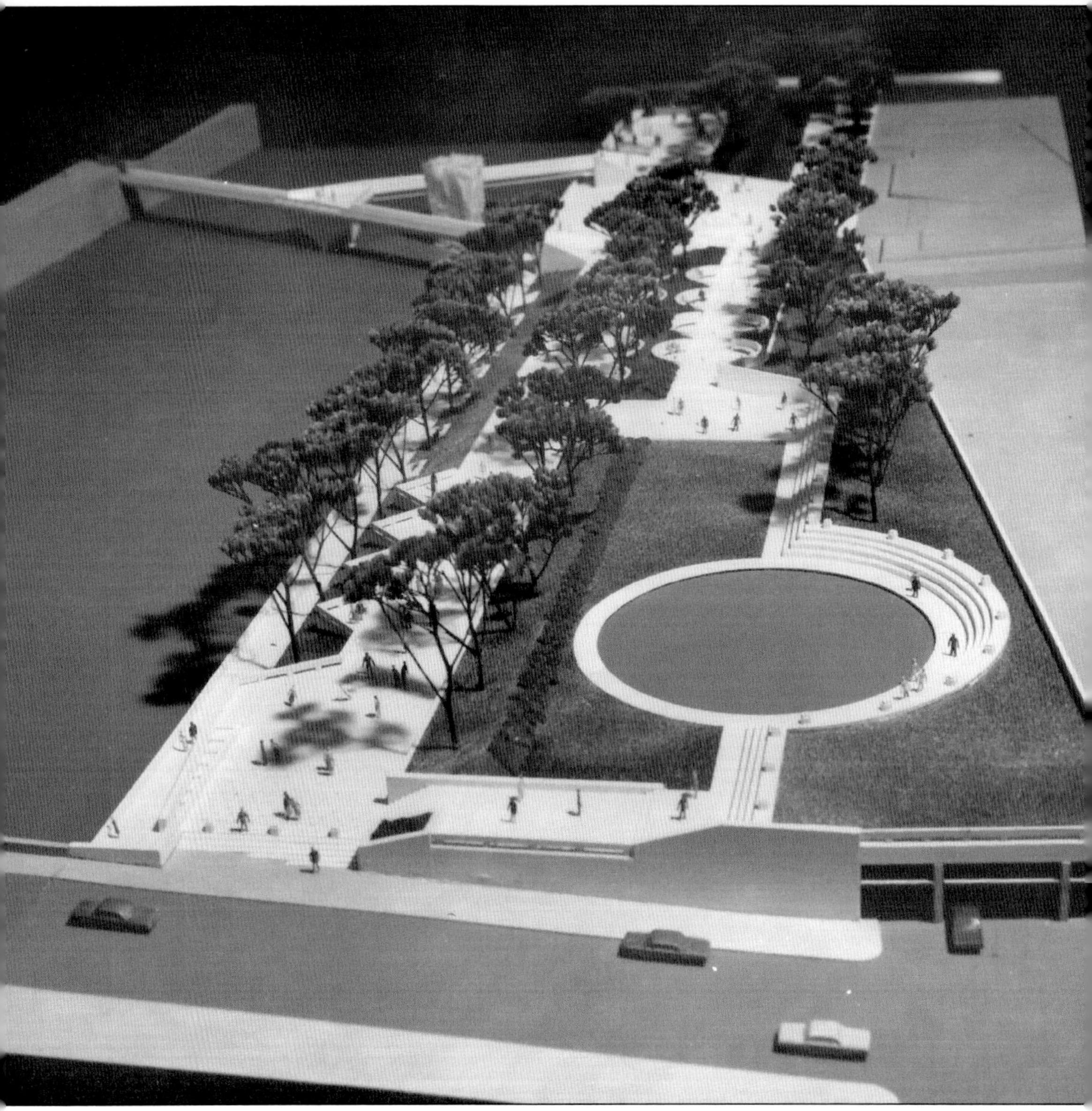

Frank Schlesinger designed the 3-acre rooftop park at the Genesee Crossroads Garage. This view of the park model and garage is looking south from Andrews Street. A 40-foot fountain of water jets would shoot out from the river between the two arms of the pedestrian bridge. The bridge would be named the "Sister Cities Bridge" and would be lined with the flags of its many sister cites' countries. (RMA.)

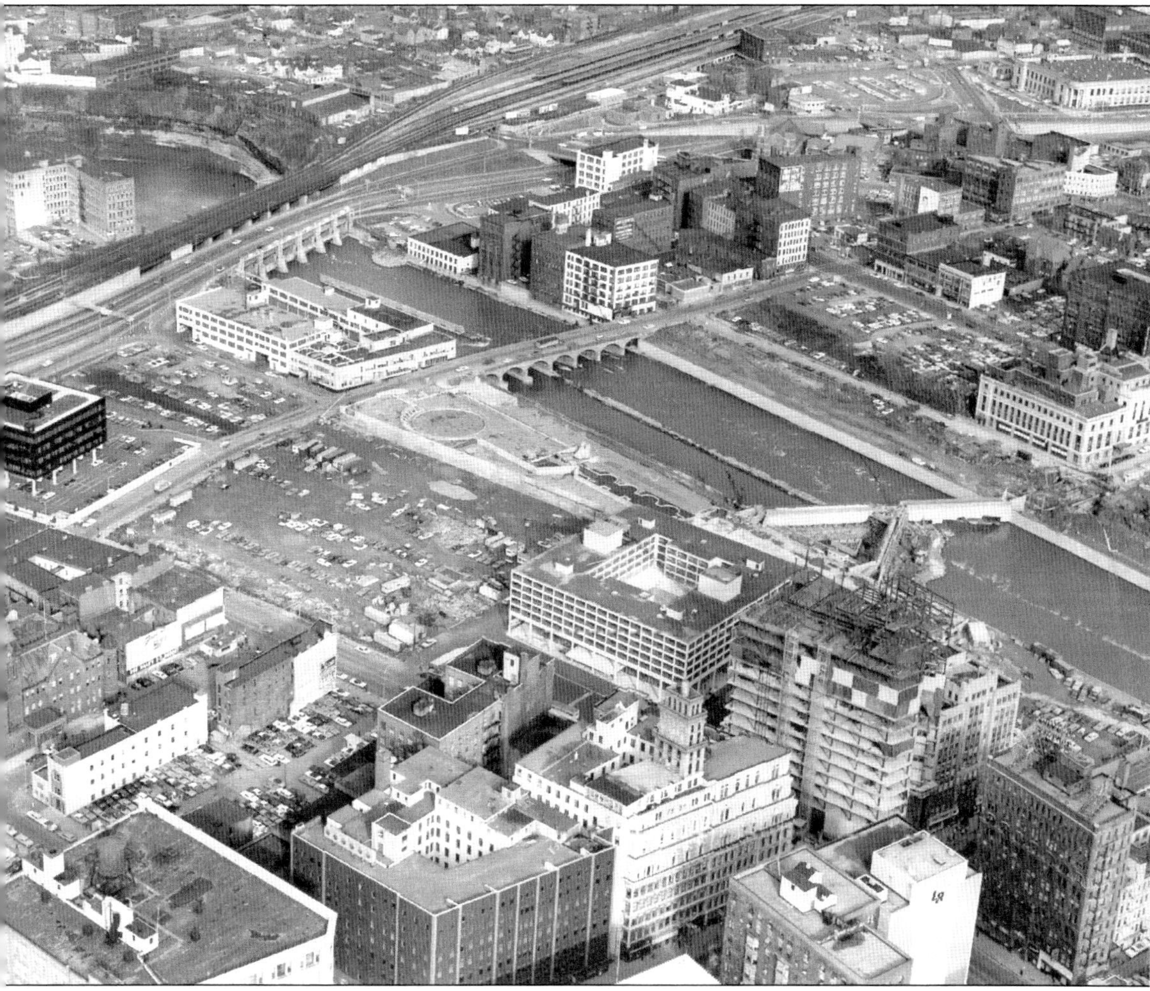

Wahl's photographic service took this aerial picture of the Genesee Crossroads Project in November 1968. The garage and park were nearing completion, and the pedestrian bridge had the triangular fountain installed between its western arms. The building rising at the lower right of the image is the Crossroads Building. (RLLHD.)

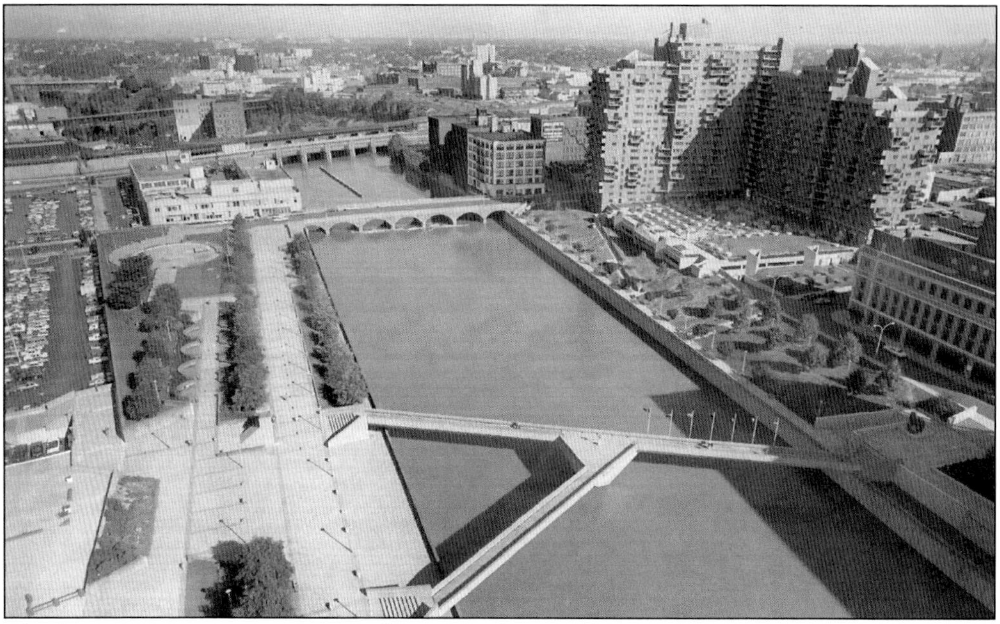

The fountain is conspicuous in its absence in this aerial view of the finished project from the 1970s. It did not work from the start, and efforts were made to adjust the jets' pressure and aim. The desired effect could not be achieved, and it was removed. This was a point of contention in the community for years. The Plaza Apartments, the last building to be built at Genesee Crossroads, can be seen on the right of this image. (RLLHD.)

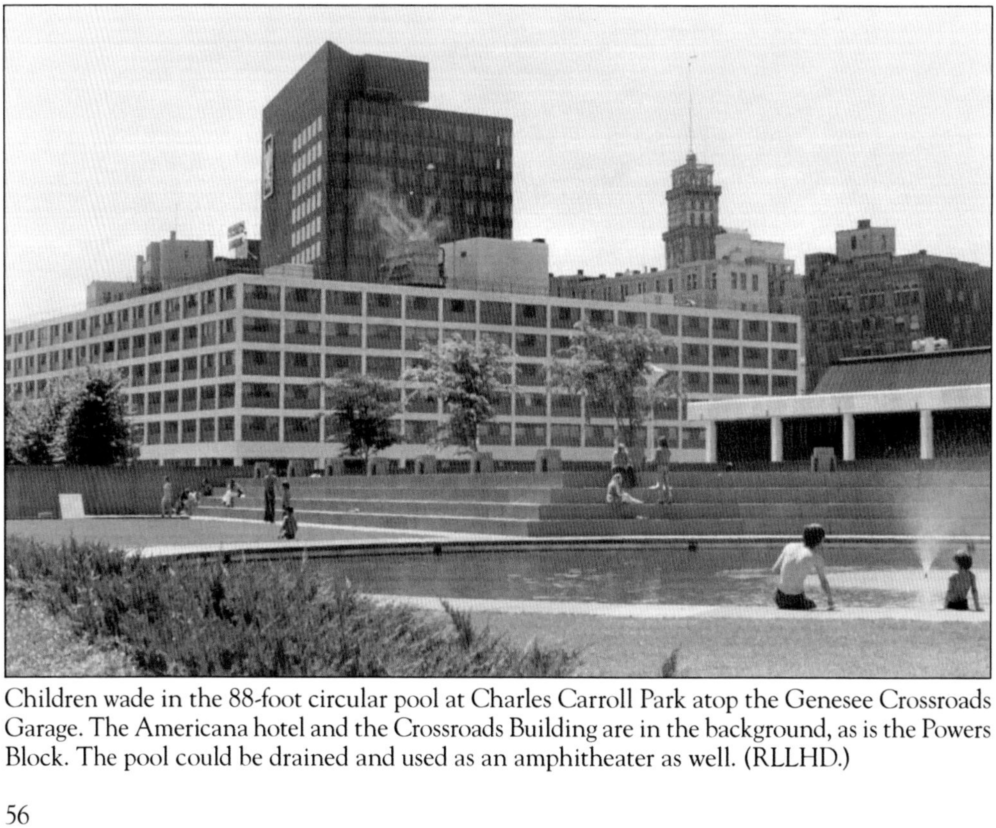

Children wade in the 88-foot circular pool at Charles Carroll Park atop the Genesee Crossroads Garage. The Americana hotel and the Crossroads Building are in the background, as is the Powers Block. The pool could be drained and used as an amphitheater as well. (RLLHD.)

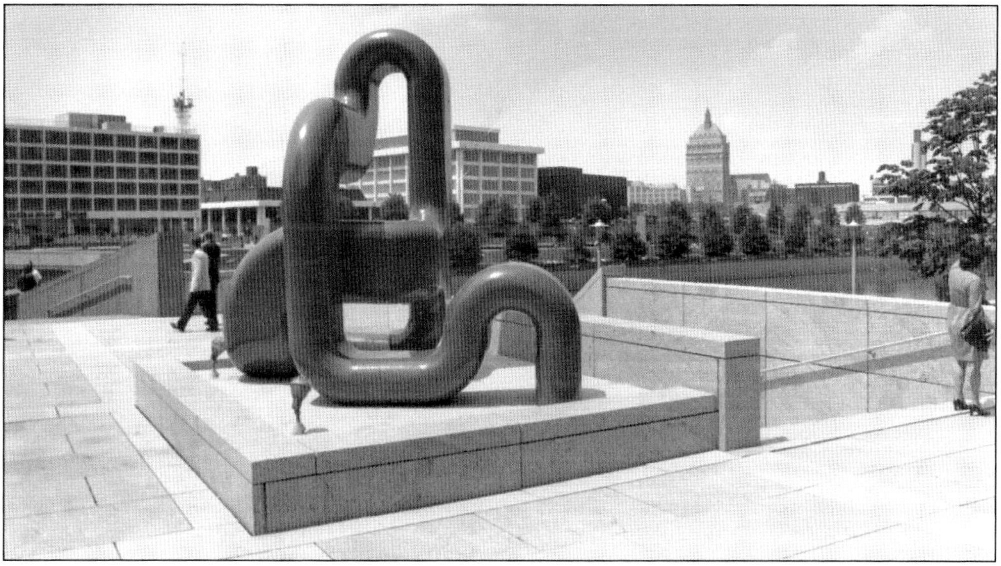

This modern sculpture is called *The Twist*. Created by Wendel Castle, it was a controversial piece when presented to the public but is now an accepted part of the cityscape. (RLLHD.)

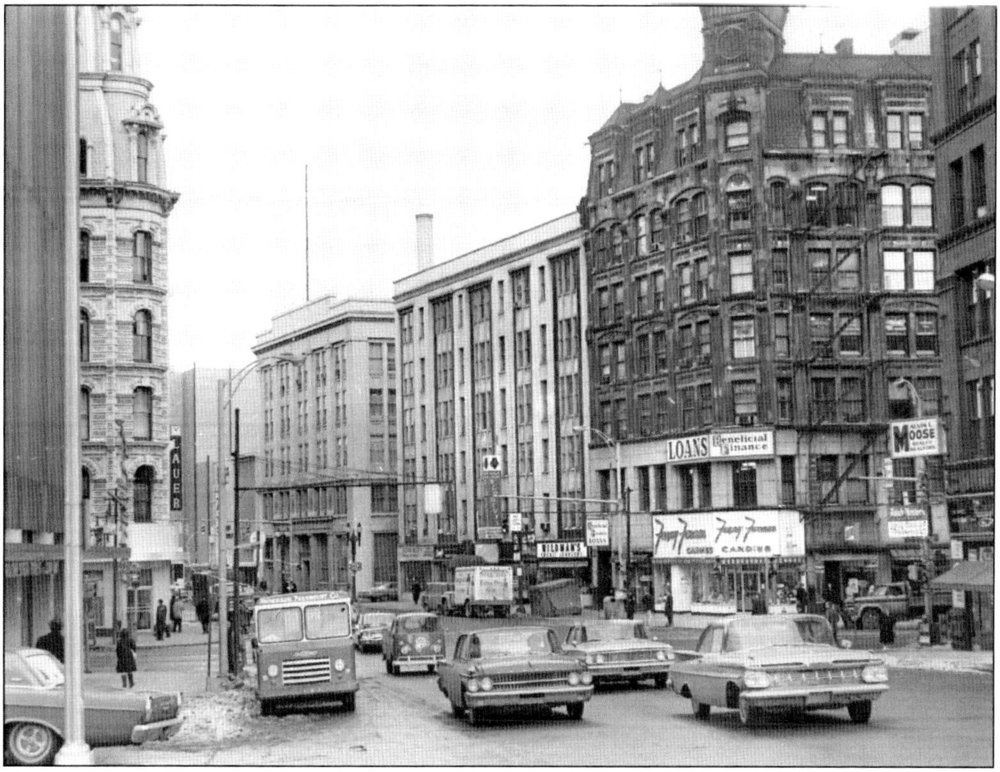

This image from 1967 looks north up State Street at the Four Corners intersection of Main Street. From the times when the city was first settled on the western bank of the Genesee River at the "100 Acre Tract," this intersection has been the heart of downtown Rochester. Within a few years, this view would change dramatically, as the new would replace the old on the east side of State Street, and a local landmark would be lost. (RMA.)

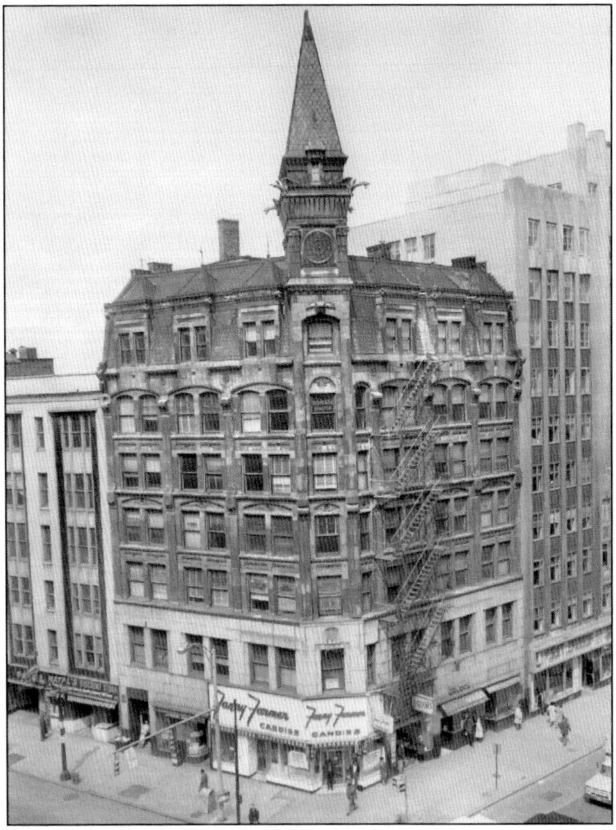

Frank Elwood constructed a building in memory of his father, Isaac Elwood, on the northeast corner of State and Main Streets. Opened in 1879 from designs by James G. Cutler, it featured a corner tower ringed by menacing gargoyles. It was in this building that Cutler would install the world's first mail chute. He later would install his perfected design for the mail chute in the Wilder Building across the street. (RMA)

In December 1965, the corner parcel that was originally left out of the plans for the Genesee Crossroads Project was added to the master plan. An office building that would house a branch of the Security Bank and Trust Company, as well as lawyers and banking offices, was designed by New York City architects Kahn and Jacobs. In this image from 1968, the first five floors of the 17-story building's steel structure are complete. (RLLHD.)

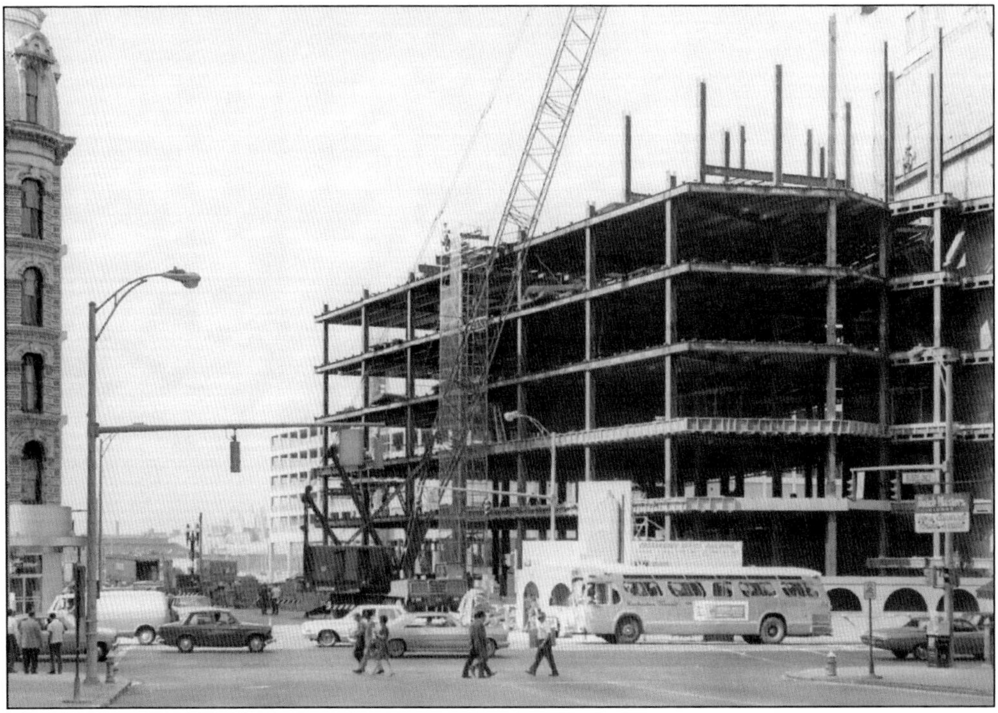

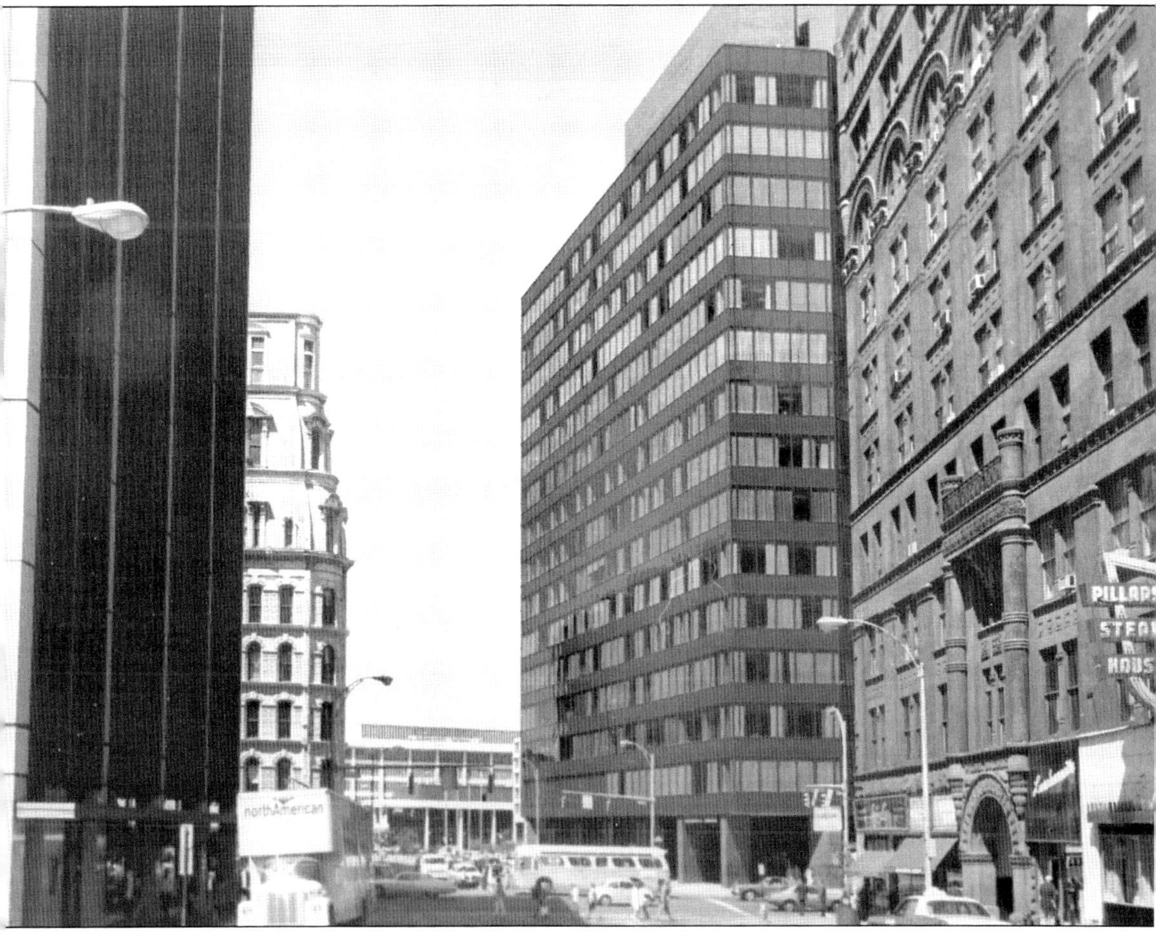

This view from the 1970s of the Four Corners intersection is very similar to the one on the previous page in terms of perspective. However, the view has changed. Where the Elwood Building once stood is the sleek and vertical Crossroads Building. The department stores north of the intersection have been replaced with the Americana hotel and the new Federal Building, seen in the background. The Powers Block and the Wilder Building survive to this day. (RMA.)

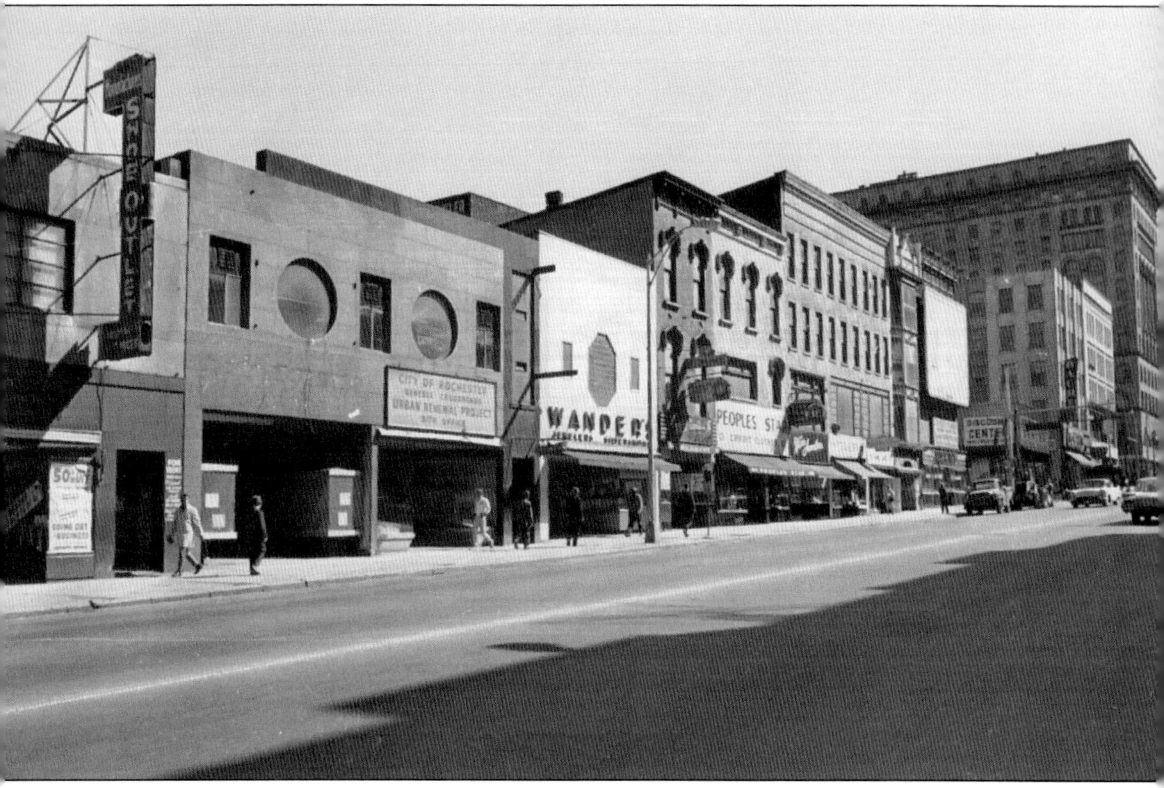

The block of East Main Street pictured here is home to the Urban Renewal office for the project. Ironically it would be demolished in the name of urban renewal, when the largest hotel in the city was built on its site. (RMA.)

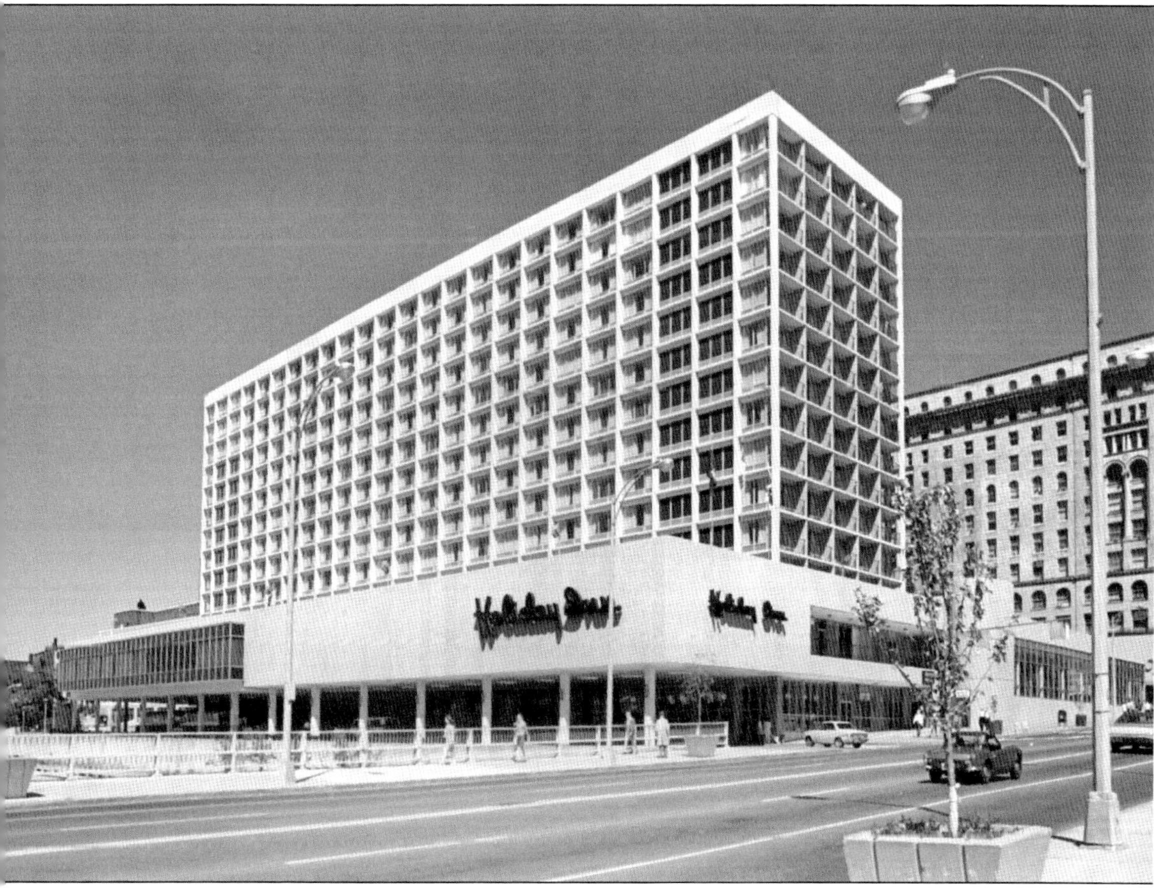

With over 500 rooms, a rooftop pool, enclosed parking, restaurants, ballrooms, and shops, the Holiday Inn opened to positive reviews in 1970. Due to its narrow shape and 15 stories of height, guests of the hotel enjoyed gorgeous views of the river and downtown. (RLLHD.)

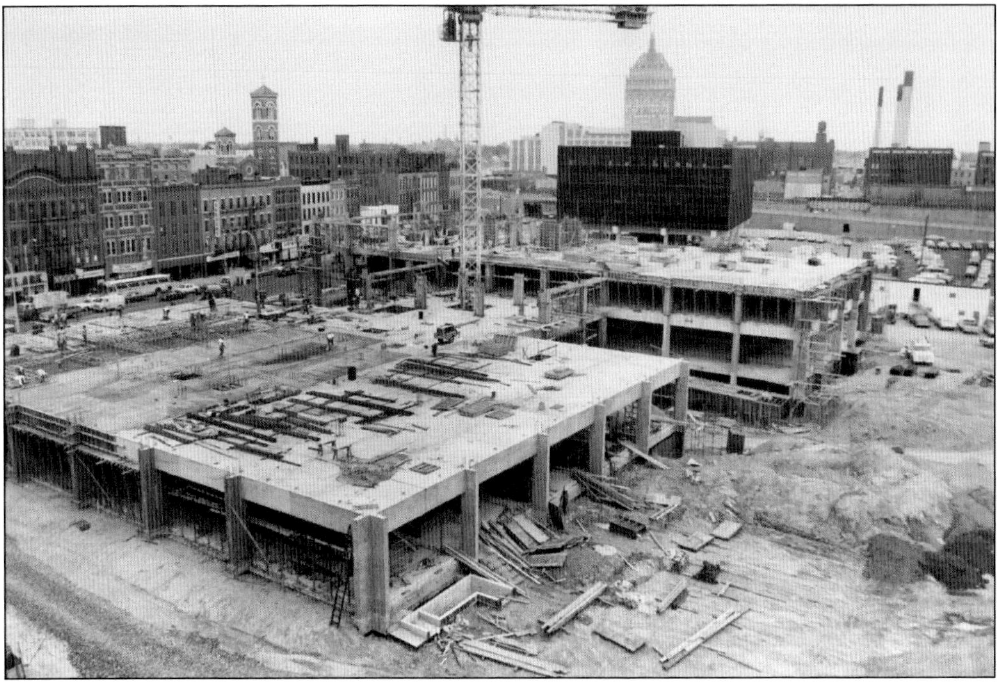

The reinforced concrete structure of the Federal Building slowly rises from State Street in 1971. When completed, the federal government would move its local offices here from a Romanesque building on Church Street, a block away. In 1978, the former Federal Building would reopen as Rochester City Hall and annex. (RMA.)

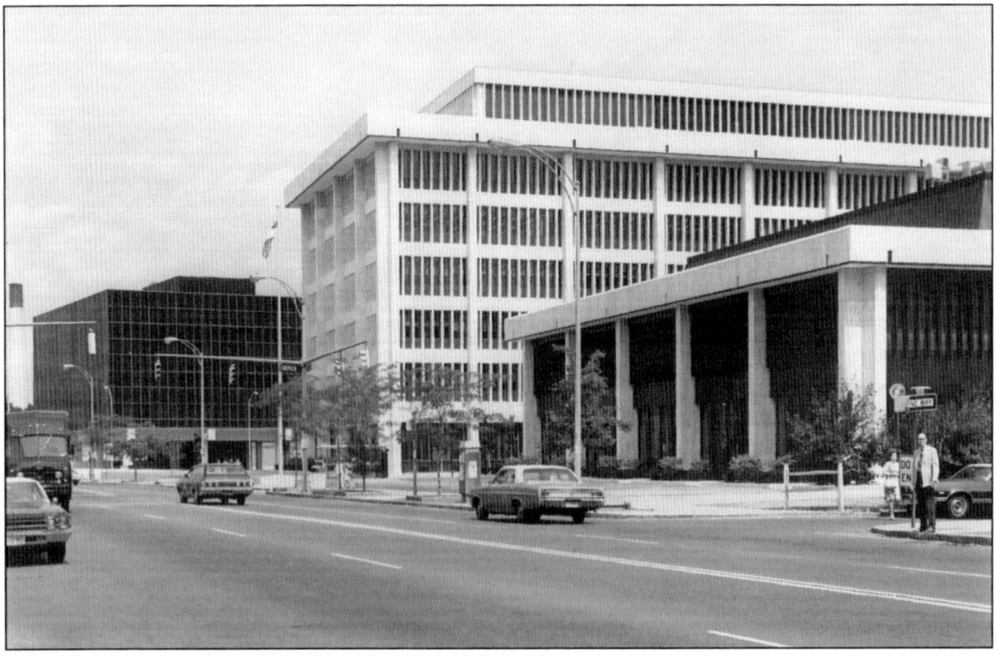

A modern take on the monumental and marble-clad temple style of governmental architecture, the Federal Building and its adjacent courthouse can be seen in this view of State Street looking north. The IBM building is in the background. (RMA.)

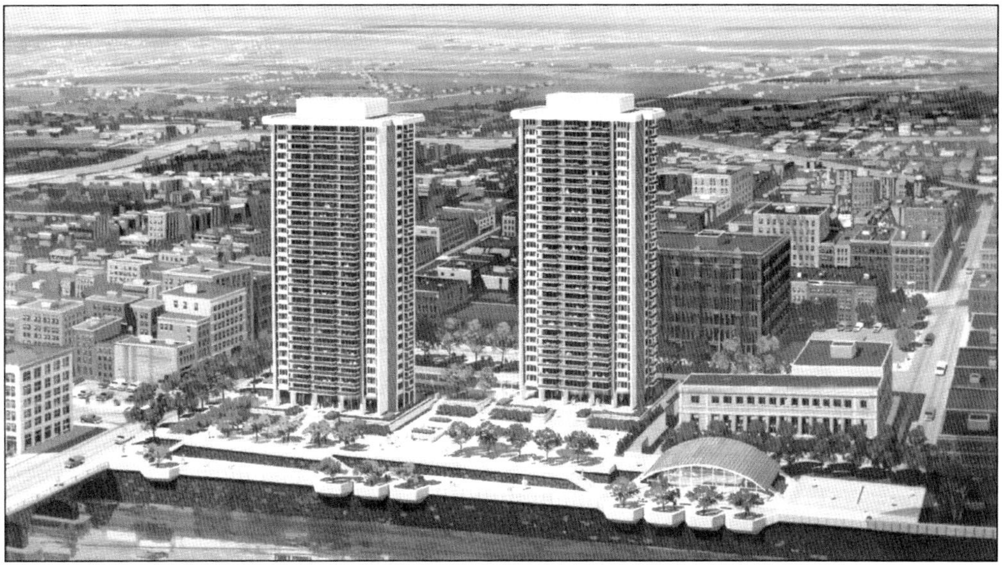

Officially referred to as "Parcel 2," this site on Andrews Street and the eastern banks of the river was designated for senior housing. This early concept features twin high-rise apartment towers set on a tiered riverside plaza. An enclosed pool and tennis courts appears to the bottom right of the image, and tree planters cantilever over the river. (RLLHD.)

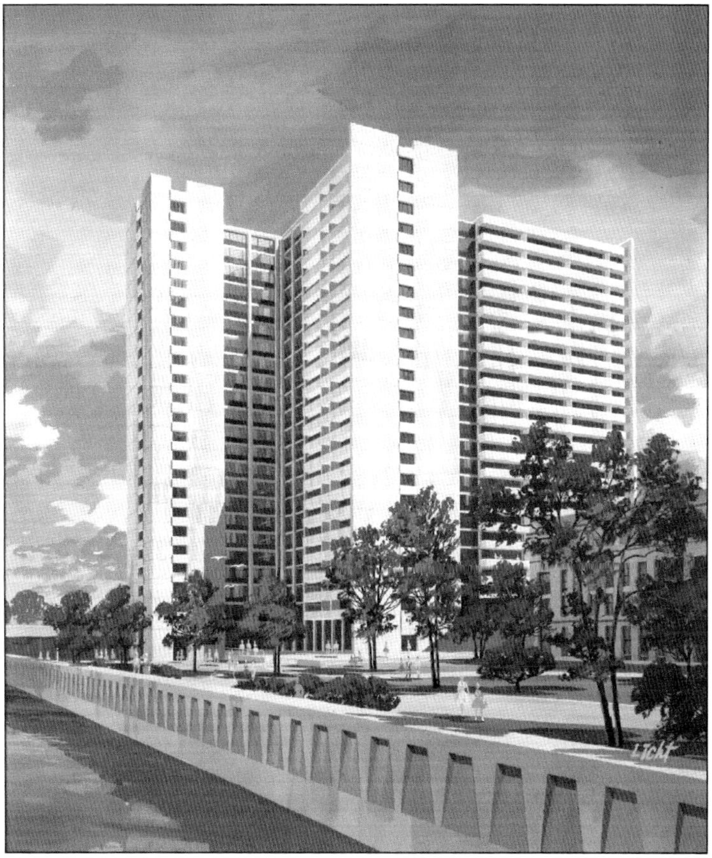

Another proposal for Parcel 2 also includes a river walk plaza and high-rise senior apartments. In the place of twin towers, this concept would provide a single, irregularly shaped tower of concrete. (RLLHD.)

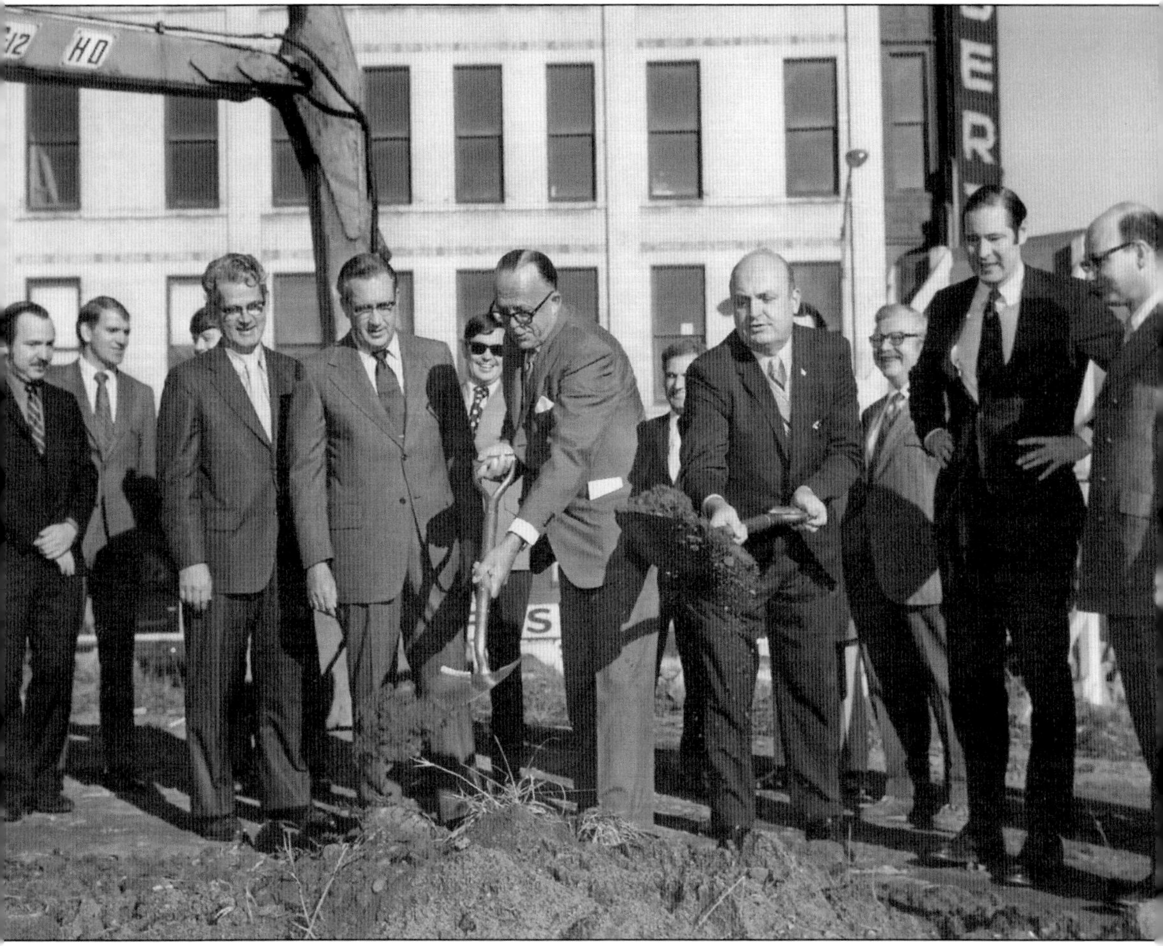

In October 1971, the senior housing at Parcel 2 was underway. Neither of the two previous concepts would be built. Instead, the apartment tower would be L-shaped and would feature unfinished reinforced concrete balconies in its Brutalist design. Here local leaders attend the ground-breaking ceremonies. (RMA.)

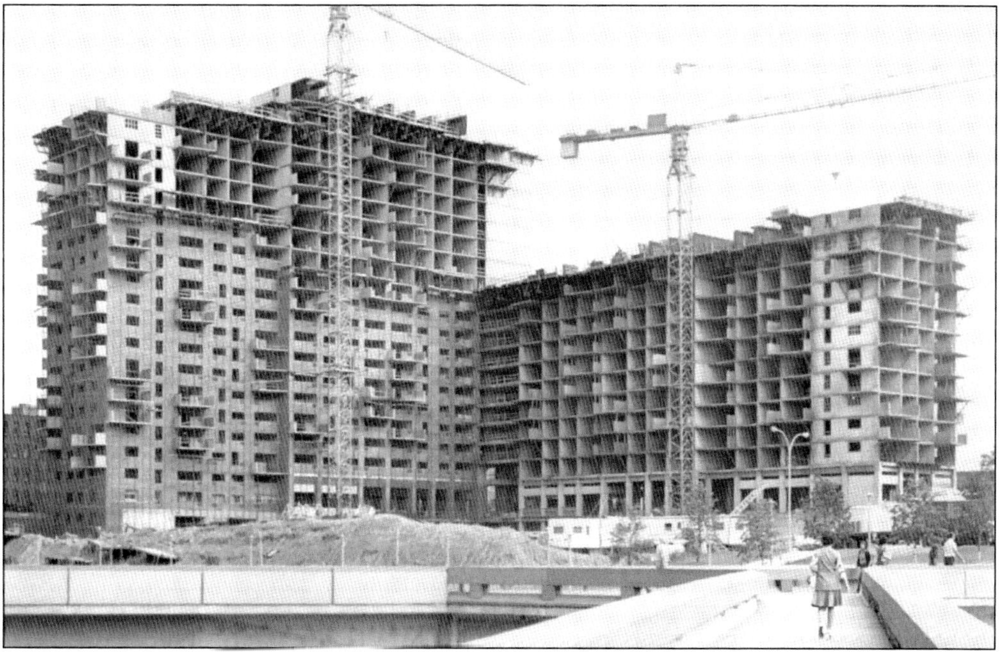

Almost three years later, the Plaza Apartments' reinforced concrete structure continues to rise to its eventual height of 22 stories. The apartments are actually two buildings connected at each level with balconies. It would be at least two more years before the Plaza Apartments would be completed. (RLLHD.)

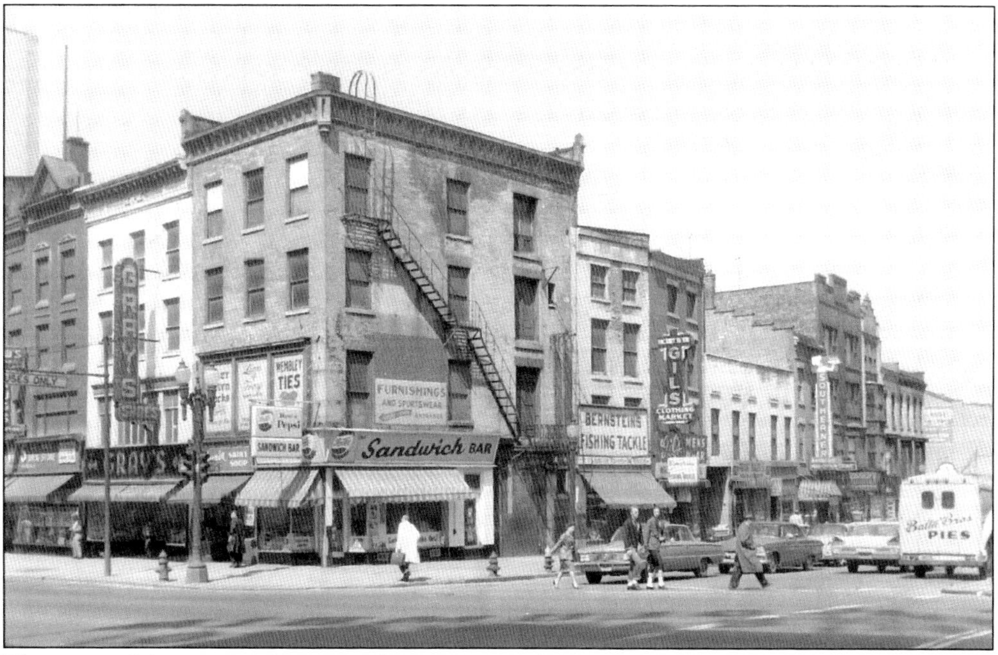

This view of the corner of Front and Main Streets from 1965 illustrates the scale and density of the neighborhood of small buildings and narrow streets. Within a year, the entire neighborhood would disappear. This corner would become the site of the tallest building at Genesee Crossroads, the First Federal Plaza. (RMA.)

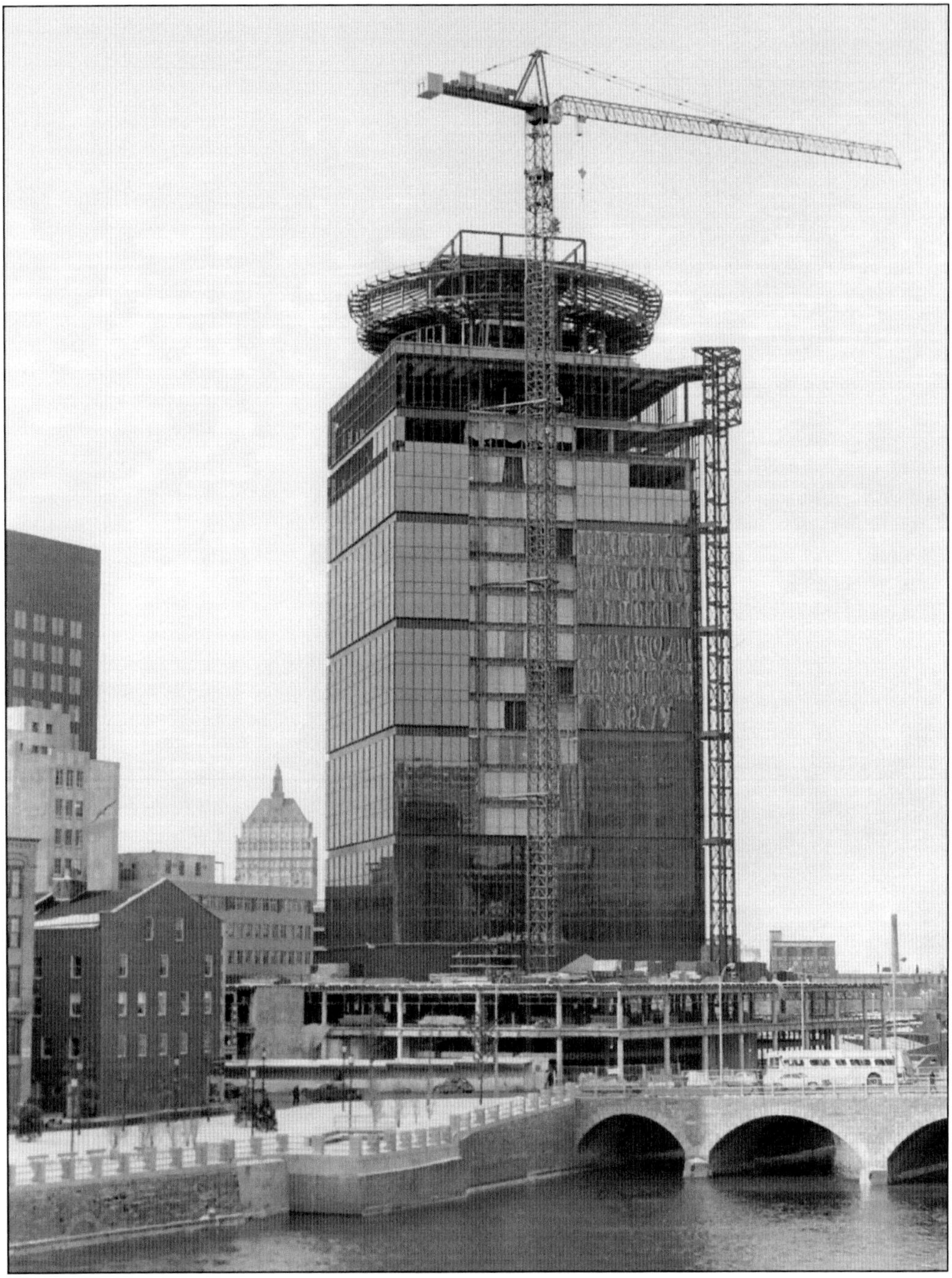

Three hundred feet tall, with a revolving restaurant on the top floor that fully rotates every 45 minutes, the First Federal Plaza rises from the rubble of the buildings seen in the previous image. The 19th floor of the tower would be home to the First Federal Savings and Loans "Statesman's Club," where VIP members of the bank could hold social gatherings and business meetings. (RLLHD.)

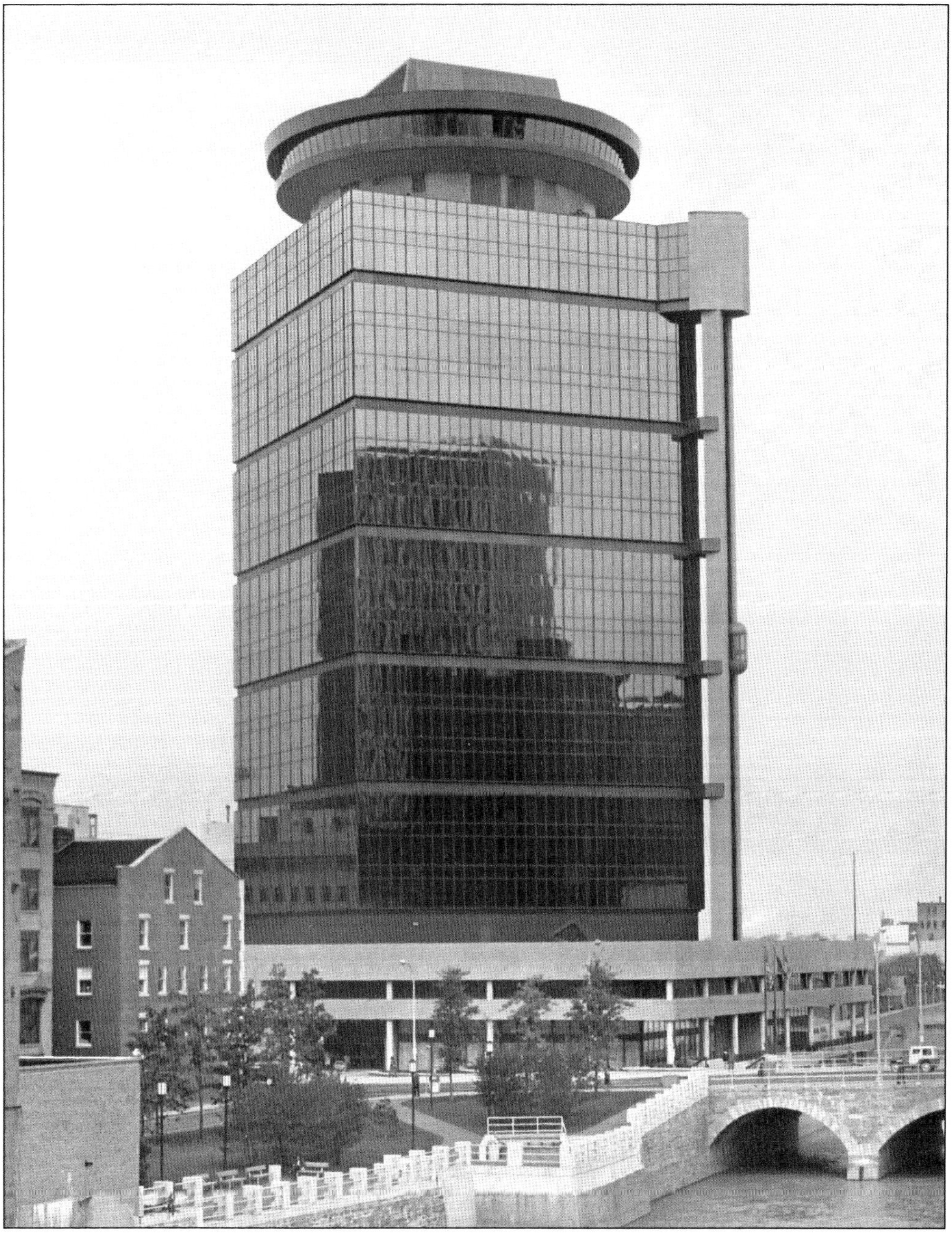

Completed in 1977, the First Federal Plaza won awards for its architects Corgan, Balestiere, and Leaper from the local chapter of the American Institute of Architects and the Real Estate Board of Rochester. An external glass elevator brought patrons to the restaurant on the 21st floor for unrivaled views of Rochester. (RLLHD.)

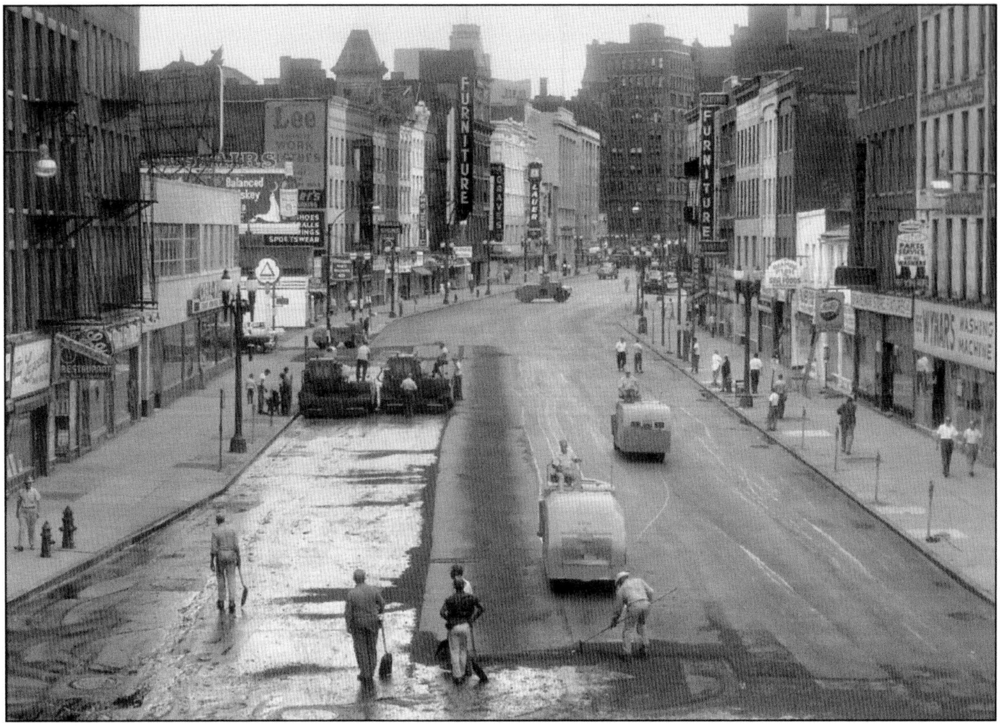

State Street is shown here as it appeared in the early 1960s. The street wall curves to meet Main Street at the Four Corners. Ornate stone and brick buildings frame the view and draw the eye toward the Elmwood and Wilder Buildings at the center of the image. Workers on steamrollers and with shovels repave a State Street lined with stores in this image. (RMA.)

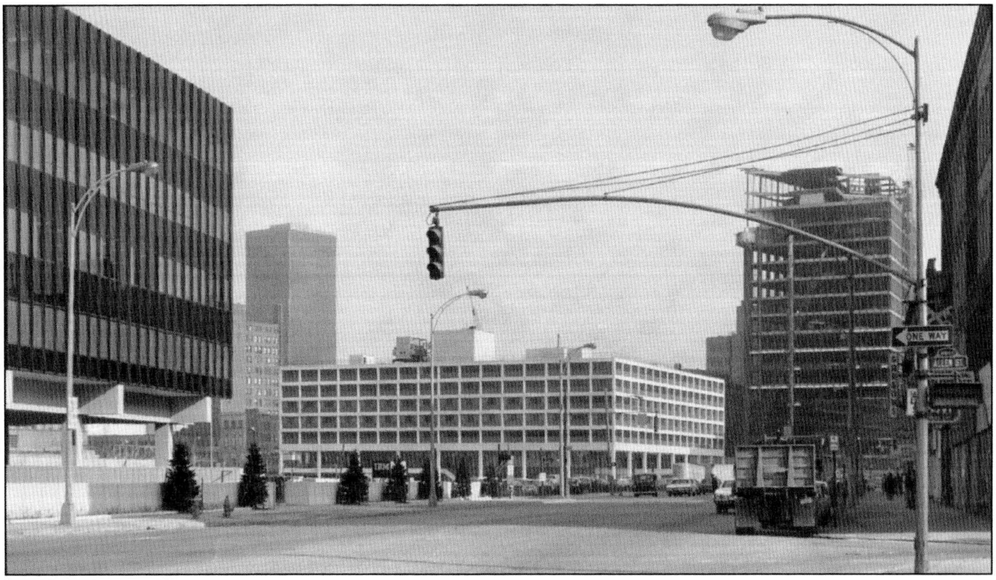

Don Eddy took this 1969 photograph of the same section of State Street less than 10 years later. This stretch of road has changed to the point of being unrecognizable. The IBM building, the Americana hotel, Xerox Square, and the skeleton of the Crossroads Building are visible in this view looking south. (RLLHD.)

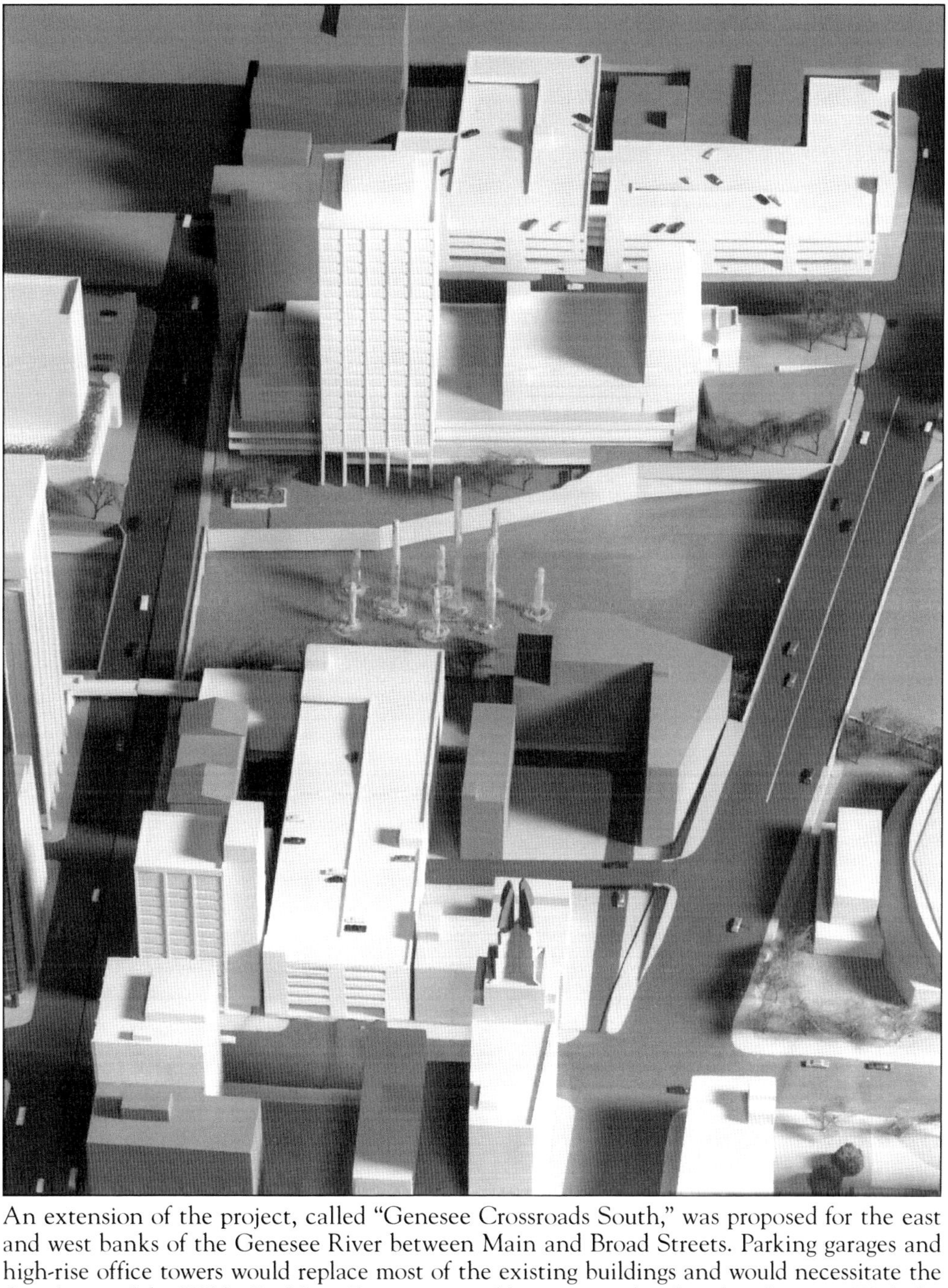

An extension of the project, called "Genesee Crossroads South," was proposed for the east and west banks of the Genesee River between Main and Broad Streets. Parking garages and high-rise office towers would replace most of the existing buildings and would necessitate the demolition of the Wilder Building. Fountains would once again be placed in the river. With the exception of the South Street Garage at the upper right of the image, this project would not be realized. (RMA.)

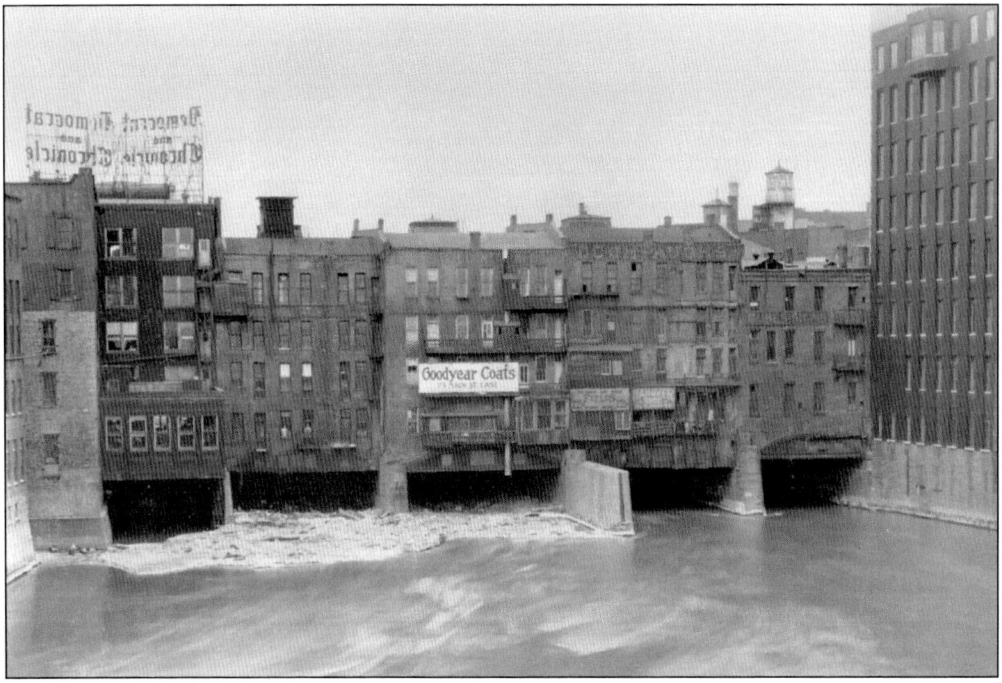

Buildings line the north and south sides of the Main Street Bridge, as they have for more than 100 years. Visitors to the city would often cross this bridge unaware that a river ran beneath their feet. (RMA.)

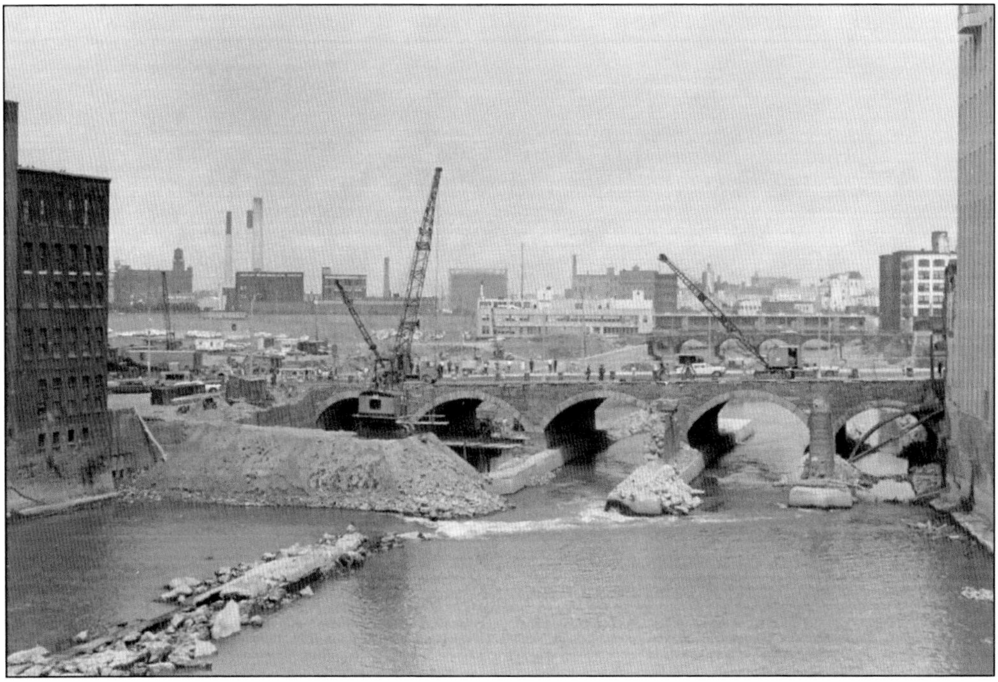

In the late 1960s, the buildings were removed, and the view of the river opened up for those walking across the Main Street Bridge. In this image, work continues on the support structure of the bridge. (RMA.)

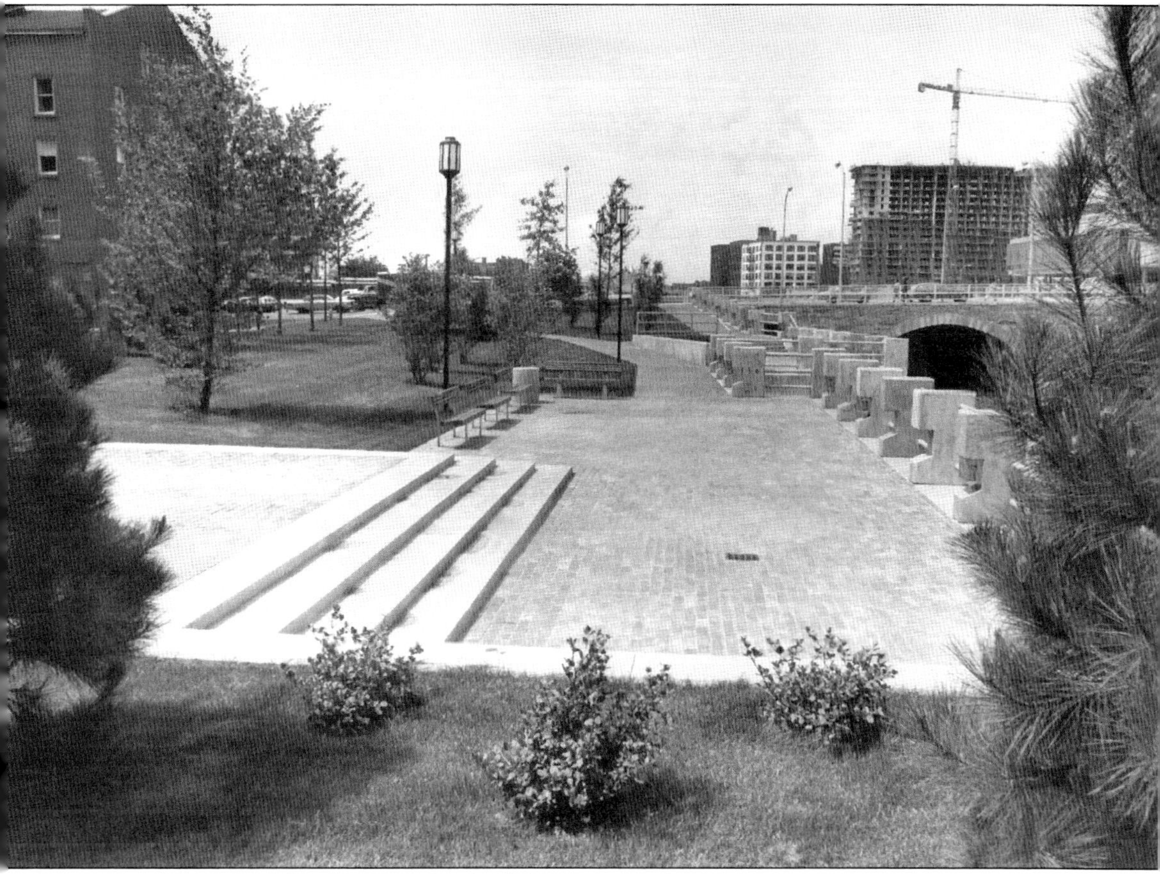

Aqueduct Park opened on the west bank of the river, south of the Main Street Bridge, in 1974. Intimate and comfortable, it would prove to be more popular than the 3-acre plaza to its north and remains a favorite lunchtime destination. (RLLHD.)

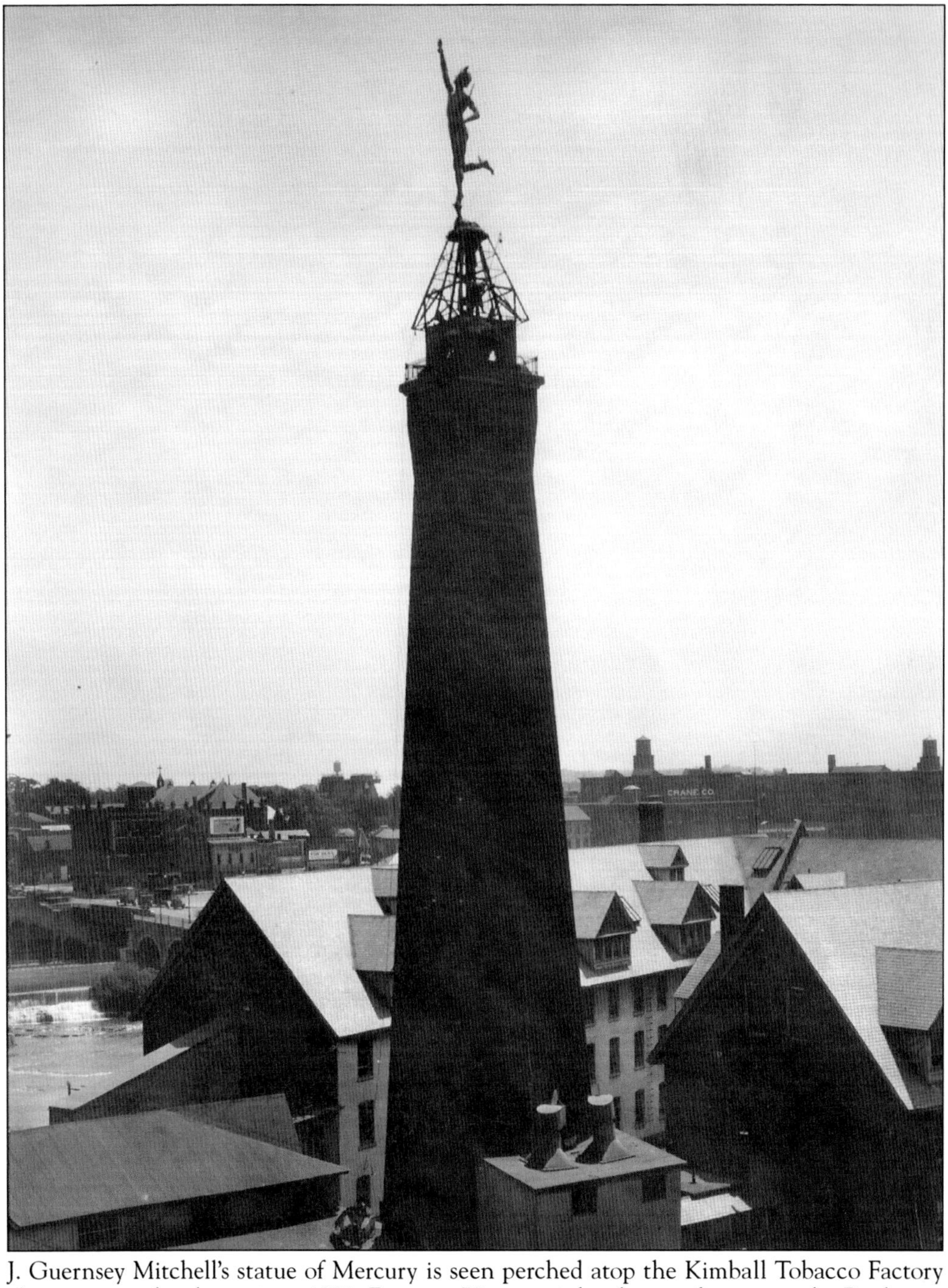

J. Guernsey Mitchell's statue of Mercury is seen perched atop the Kimball Tobacco Factory chimney, as it has been since 1880. For over 70 years, it has been a fixture on the Rochester skyline. (RLLHD.)

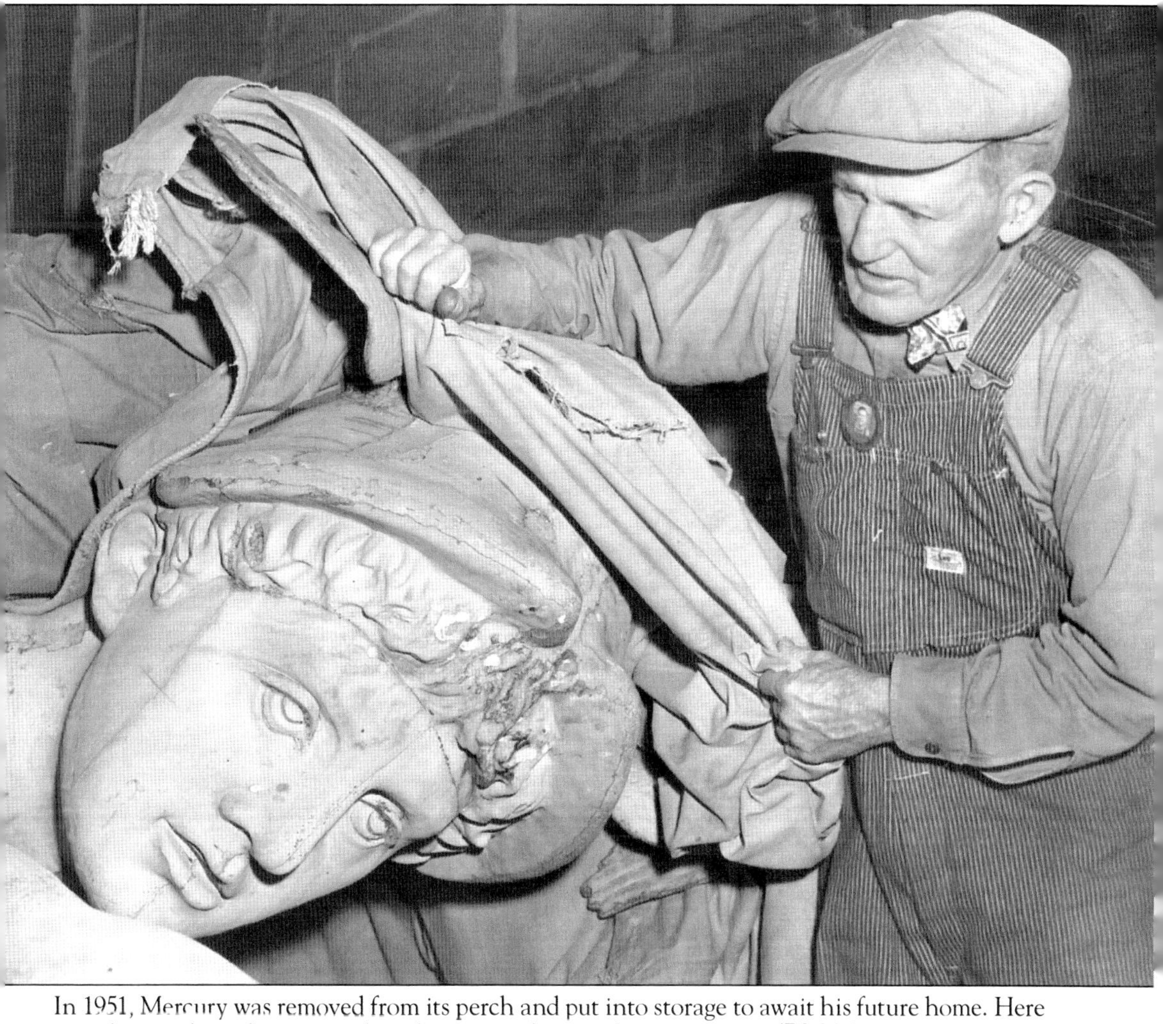

In 1951, Mercury was removed from its perch and put into storage to await his future home. Here a worker tends to the seemingly sad statue and covers him in canvas. (RMA.)

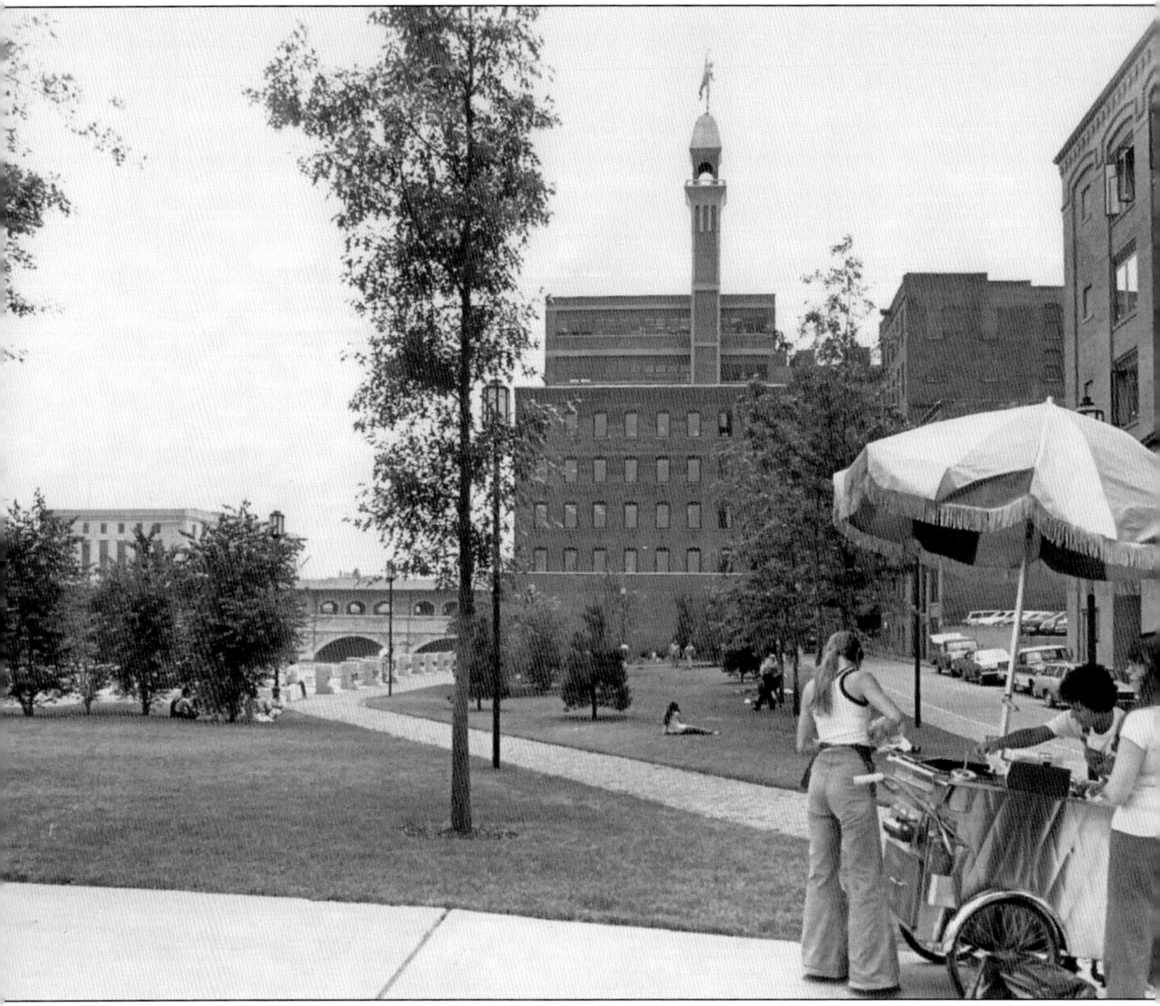

Mercury once again took his rightful place on the Rochester skyline in 1974, when the Lawyers Cooperative Publishing Company renovated its offices and added a slender tower that resembled Kimball's chimney as a new home for Mercury. This view from Main Street looks south across Aqueduct Park. (RLLHD.)

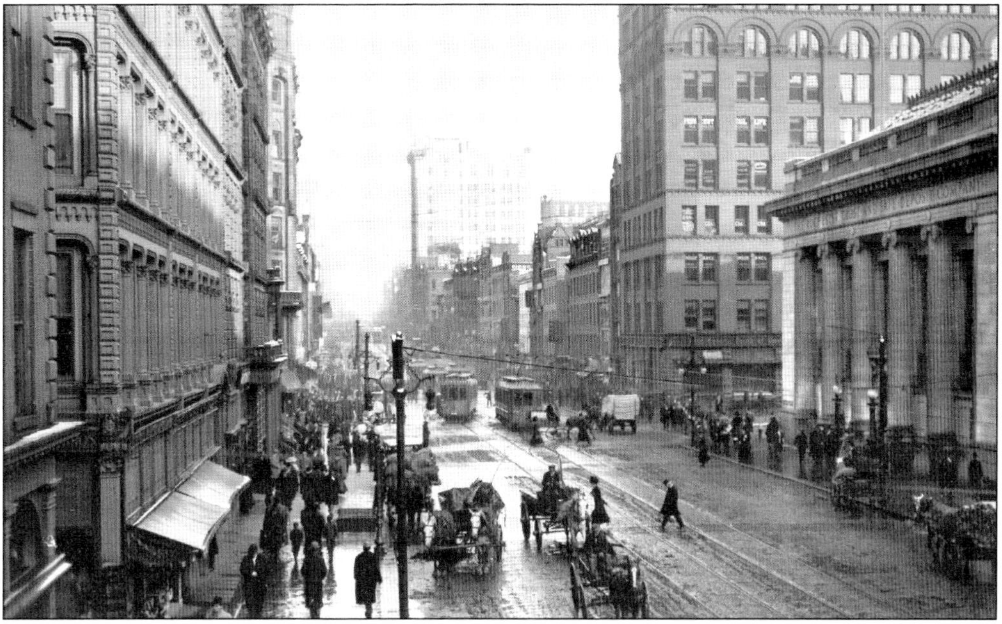

Main Street is seen here in an image from the late 19th century. The view is to the east from the Four Corners. Just beyond the Four Corners is the Main Street Bridge, lined with buildings as if the river is not there. The Powers Block can be seen on the left. The high-rise in the distance is the Commerce Building. (RMA.)

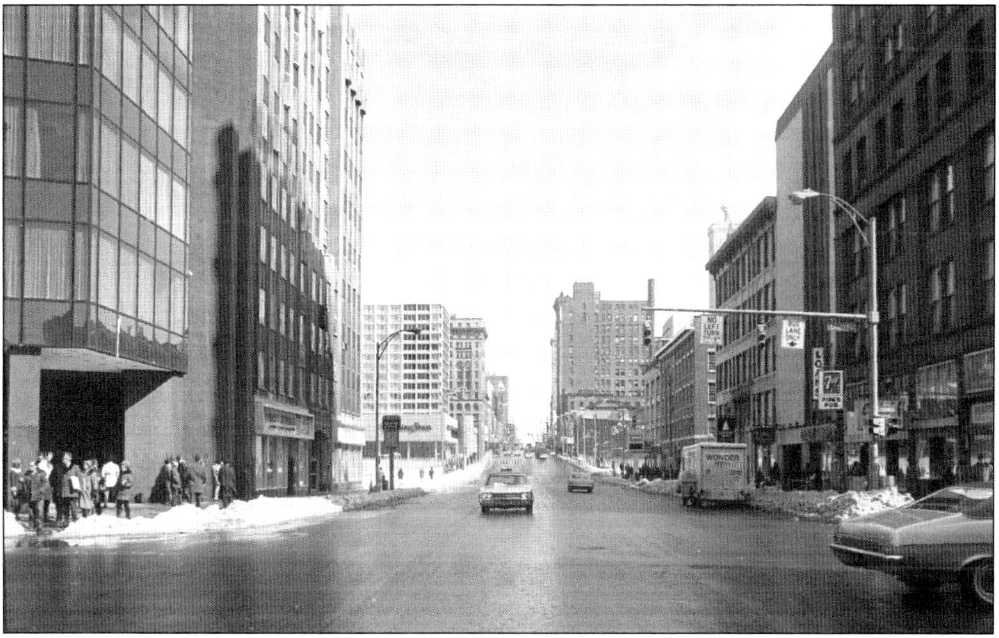

The same view is seen in this image from the 1970s. The crowded blocks of old have been replaced with wide-open vistas and gleaming towers set back from the street. The buildings of Genesee Crossroads line the left side of Main Street. The clock tower of the Sibley department store appears in the distance. (RMA.)

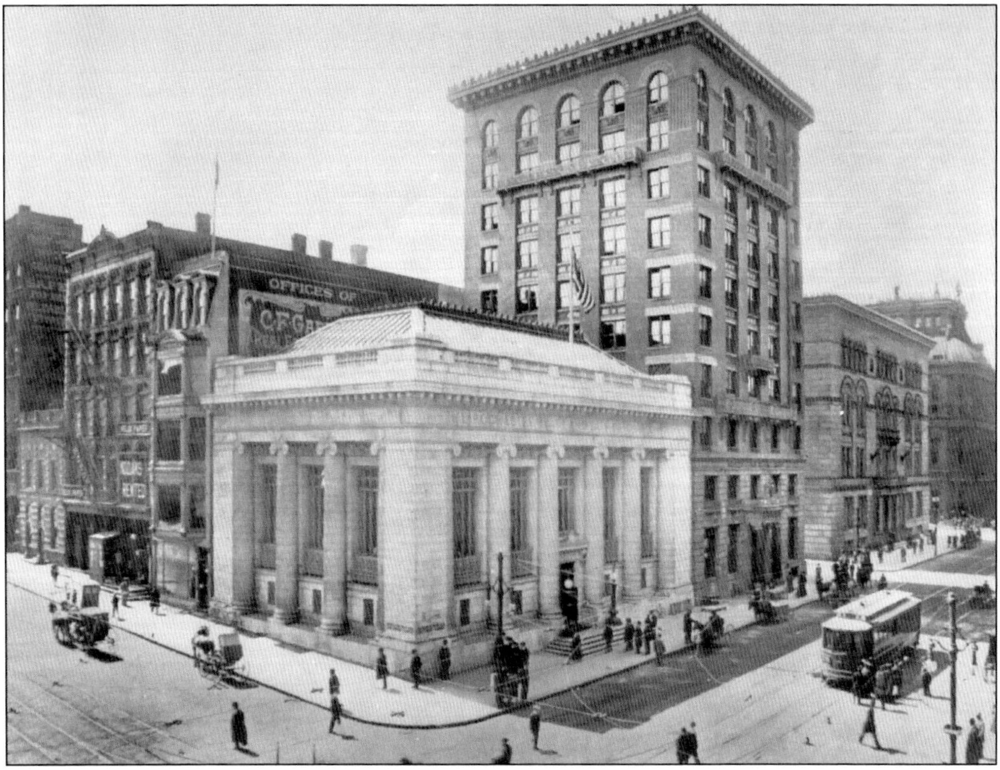

The Greek temple of the Rochester Trust Company anchors the southwest corner of Main and Exchange Streets at the Four Corners. In the background, the German Insurance Company Building and the third Monroe County Courthouse can be seen. (RMA.)

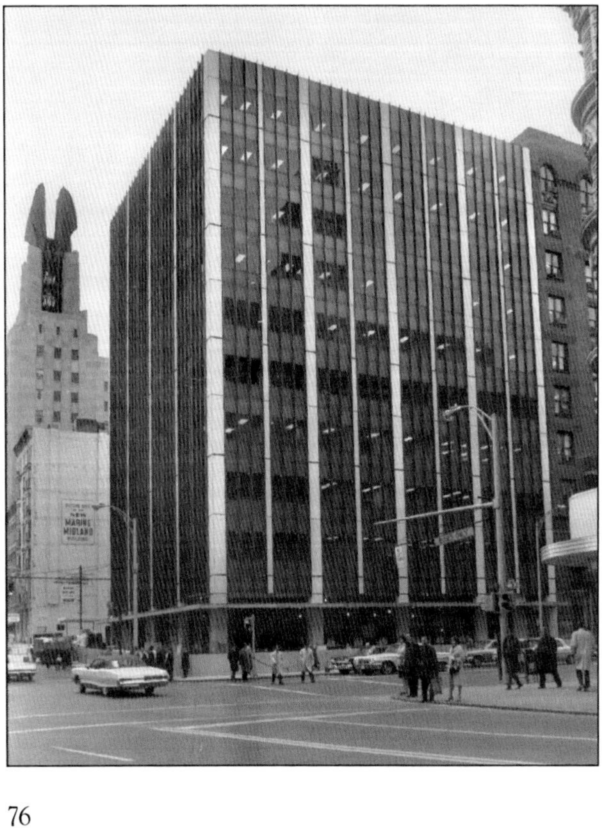

The Four Corners Building was the first new structure to be erected at the Four Corners in decades. Lincoln Rochester Bank opened a branch on the first floor, while the rest of the building was used for financial and legal offices. Local architects Faragher and Macomber designed the Four Corners Building. (RLLHD.)

Four

MIDTOWN PLAZA

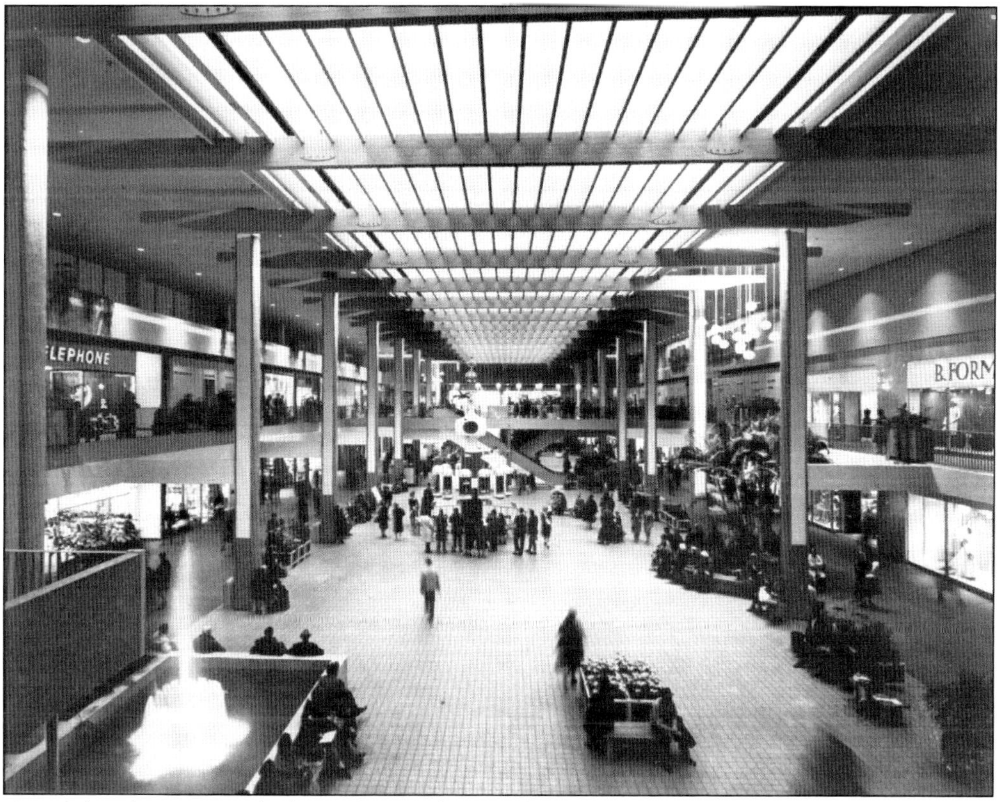

A crowd gathers to watch the Midtown Plaza's "Clock of the Nations" perform its hourly show. Midtown Plaza was a joint venture between local retail families, the McCurdys and Formans, and the City of Rochester. Completed in 1962, it is considered the first enclosed downtown shopping mall in America. It remained open until 2008. (RMA.)

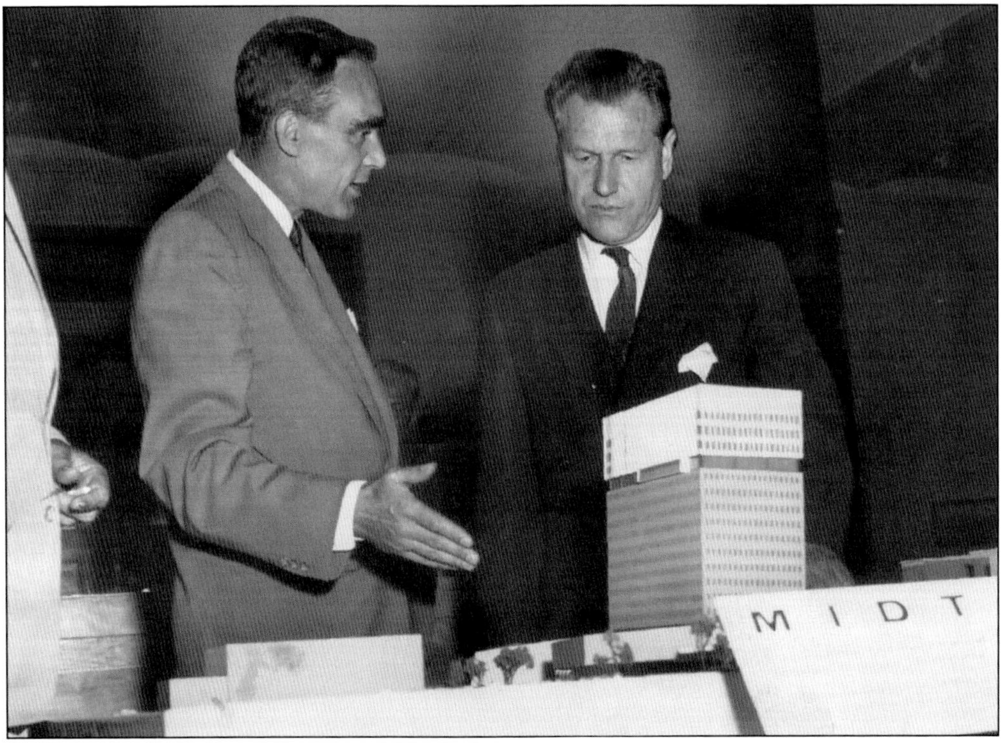

Mayor Barry (left) shows Gov. Nelson Rockefeller the model of the Midtown Plaza complex. Rockefeller was no stranger to large urban building complexes, having run the main operations of Rockefeller Center in New York City for years. He would later be the driving force behind the massive Empire State Plaza development at the state capitol in Albany. (RLLHD.)

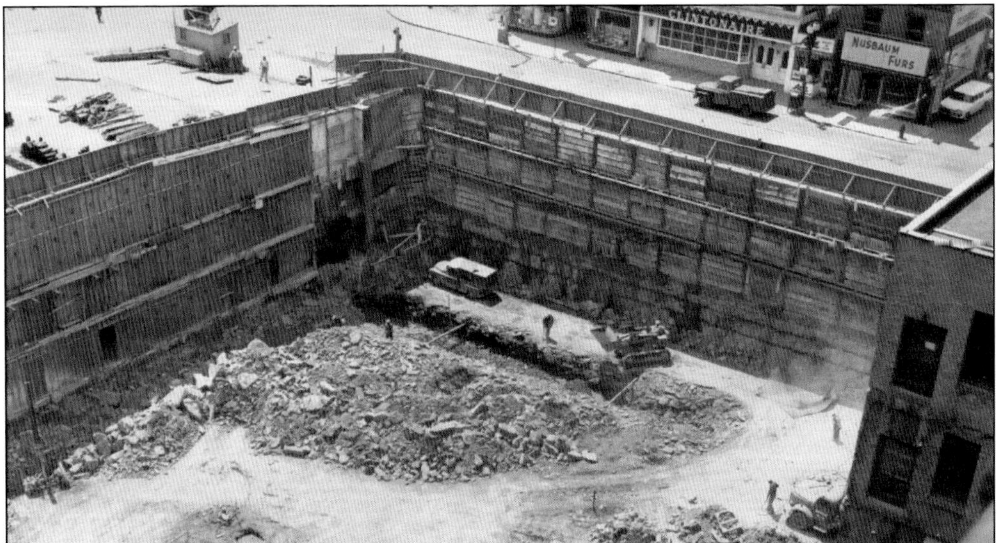

Three levels of underground parking, with a combined capacity of 1,800 cars, are being excavated in this image of Midtown Plaza's construction. The City of Rochester paid for the garage as proof of their commitment to the project. The McCurdy and Forman families would pay for the construction of the mall and tower. (RLLHD.)

Two "sidewalk superintendents," in this case Gov. Nelson Rockefeller (left) and city manager F. Dow Hamblin, peek through a porthole on Clinton Avenue to watch the progress being made on the Midtown Plaza complex. This was a common pastime for Rochesterians during this era, as multiple projects would simultaneously be in the process of construction and would draw the interest of passersby. (RMA.)

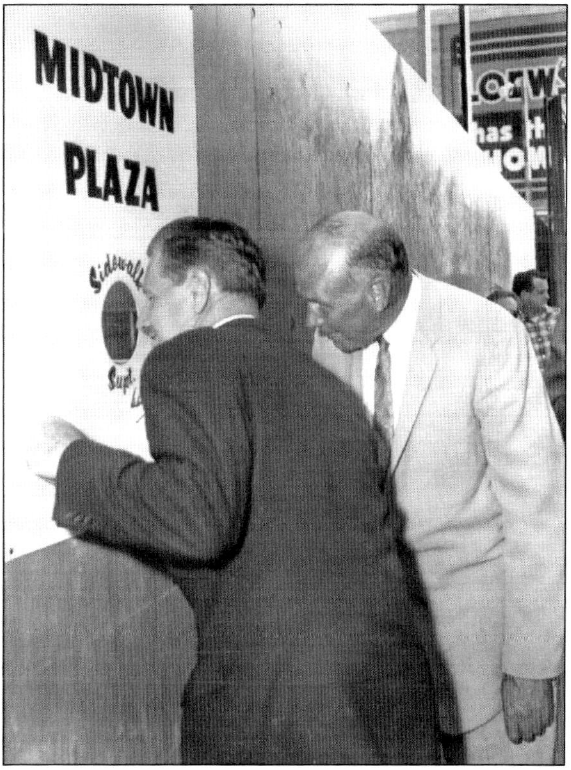

The Broad Street extension is complete, and the steel structure of the Midtown Plaza's hotel and office tower is almost ready to be covered by its facade of brick and aluminum. The narrow section toward the top of the tower will house a high-end hotel and restaurant with impressive views of the river and the surrounding city. (*Democrat and Chronicle*.)

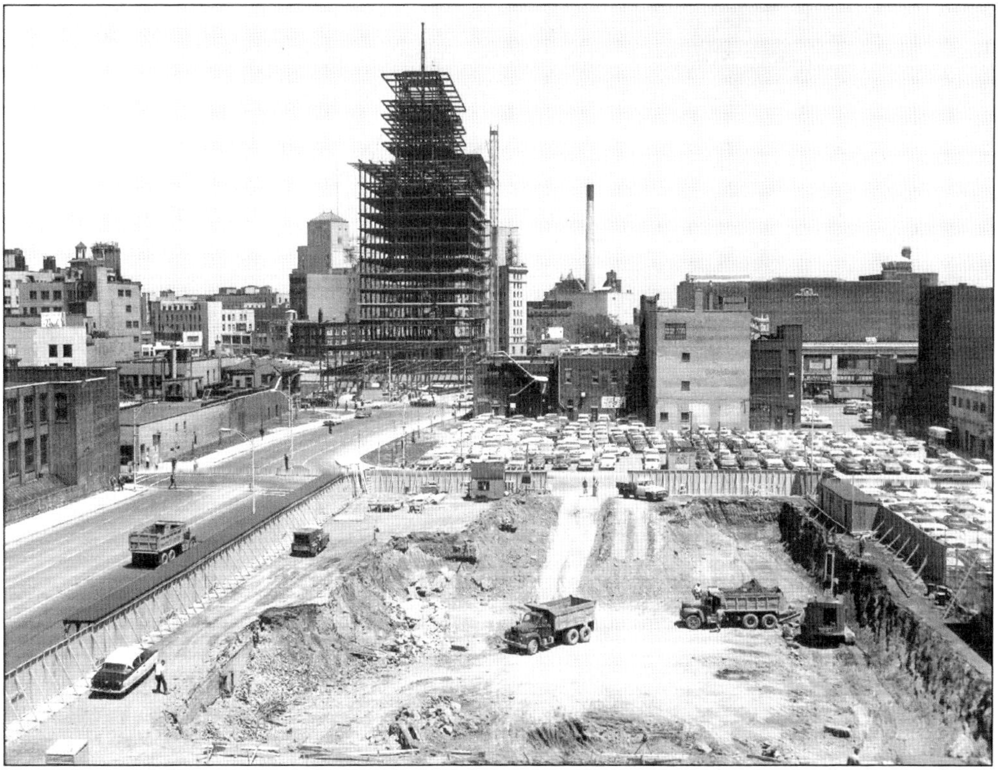

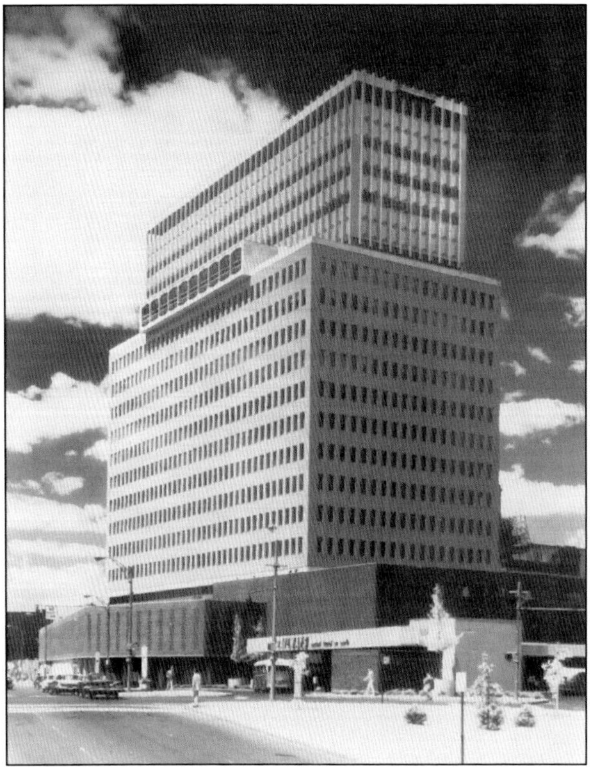

Facade in place, the Midtown Tower is ready for occupation. The tower would be clad in gray brick on its lower floors and prefabricated, diamond-shaped aluminum panels on its upper floors. The type of cladding also denotes the two main functions of the tower. Brick was used on the floors reserved for offices, while the aluminum panels denote the hotel portion of the building. (RLLHD.)

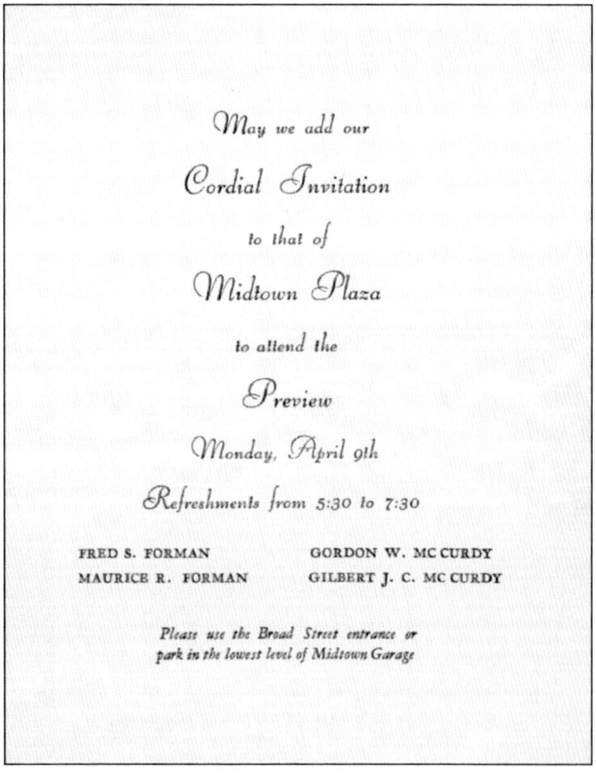

May we add our

Cordial Invitation

to that of

Midtown Plaza

to attend the

Preview

Monday, April 9th

Refreshments from 5:30 to 7:30

FRED S. FORMAN — GORDON W. MC CURDY
MAURICE R. FORMAN — GILBERT J. C. MC CURDY

Please use the Broad Street entrance or park in the lowest level of Midtown Garage

The Forman and McCurdy families invited their friends and associates to preview Midtown Plaza in the spring of 1962. Soon after, the complex would open for business. Architects and planners from around the world would visit Rochester in the early 1960s to see the innovative complex and to learn from its design. Initially the mall was open to the public 24 hours a day but was eventually closed for the overnight hours. (RMA.)

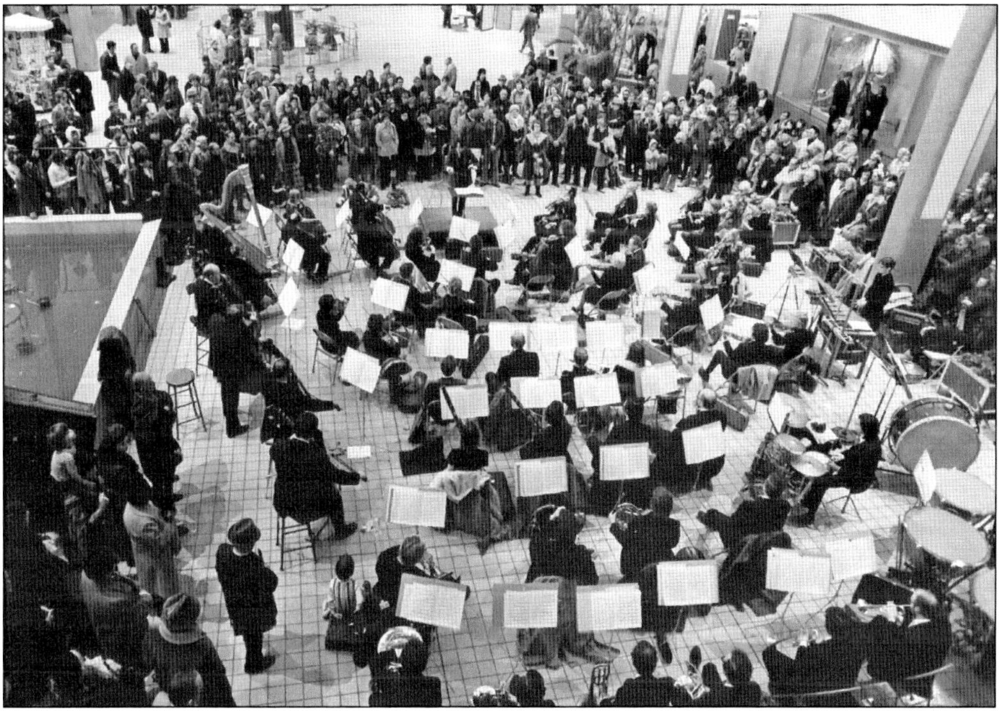

A crowd gathers on opening day to attend the festivities and to take in a free concert. Midtown Plaza was intended to function not only as a mall and office complex, but also to serve as Rochester's meeting place. It would be the home of the city's Christmas tree and "Magic Mountain" display. (RLLHD.)

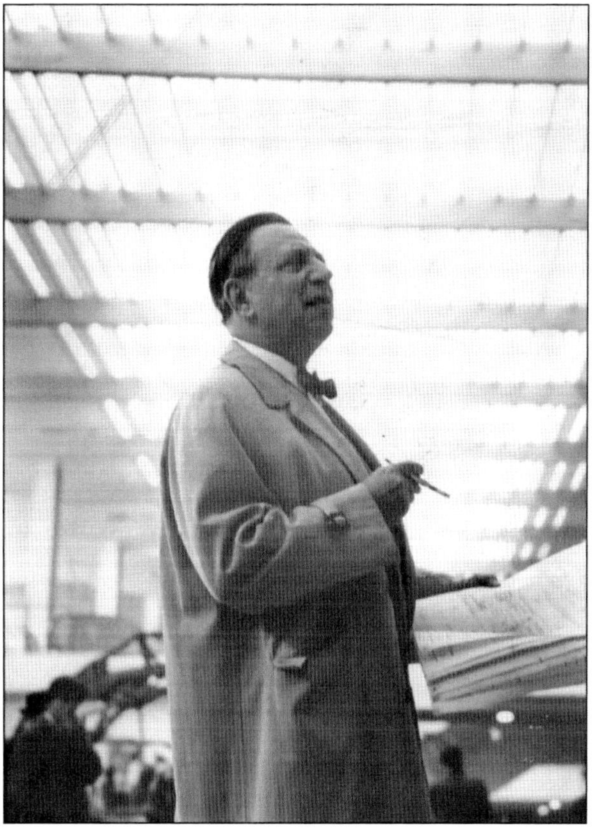

Architect Victor Gruen evaluates the finished product of his labors in 1962. Although he is credited as being the inventor of the modern shopping mall, Gruen was most pleased with his work in the downtowns of American cities. Midtown Plaza was one of his most cherished works. (RLLHD.)

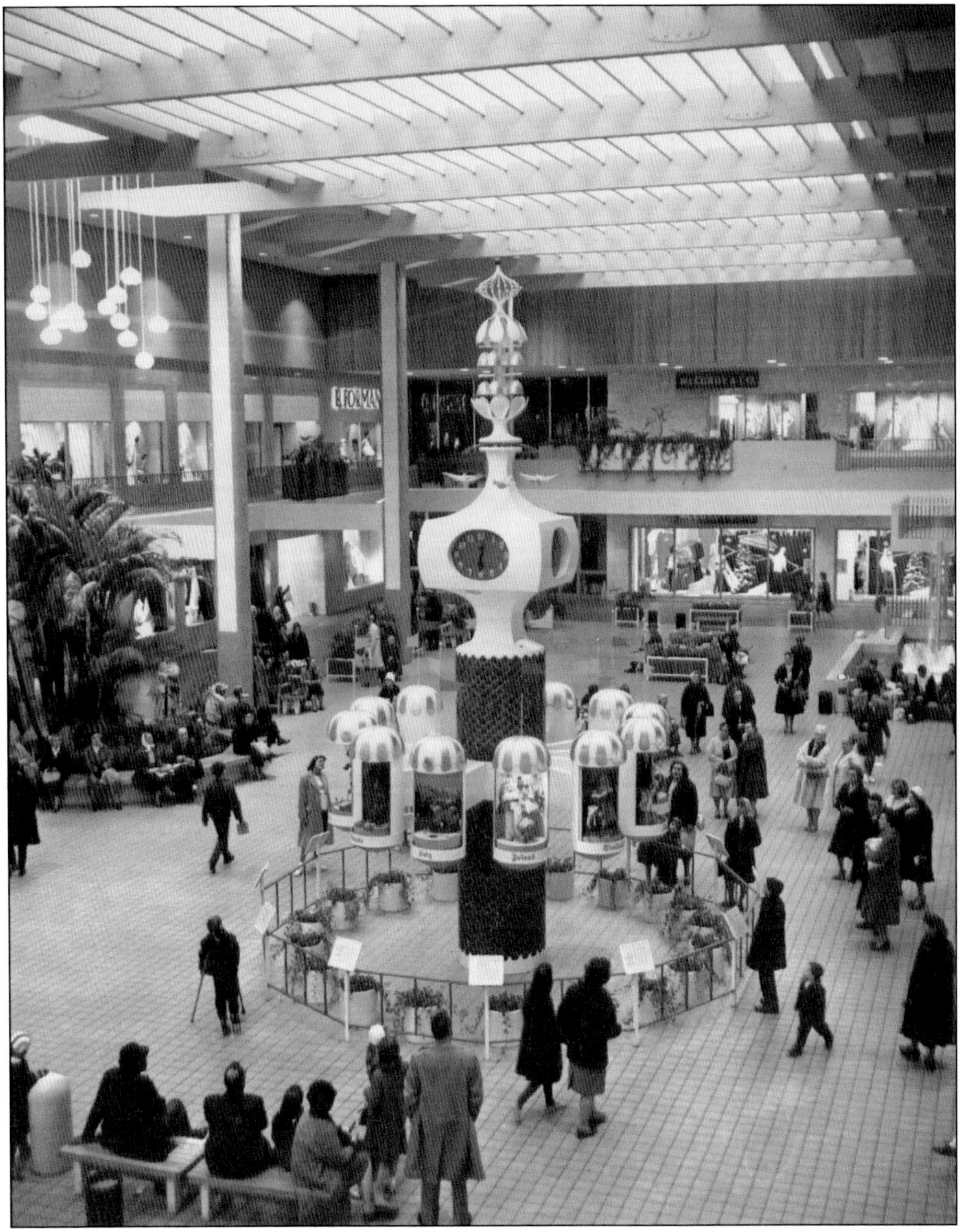

The Clock of the Nations was the centerpiece of the mall portion of Midtown Plaza. After plans were announced in the 2000s to demolish most, if not all, of the complex, the clock was restored and moved to the concourse of the Rochester International Airport, where it continues to fascinate and entertain the public. (RMA.)

Five

Towers, Parks, and Banks

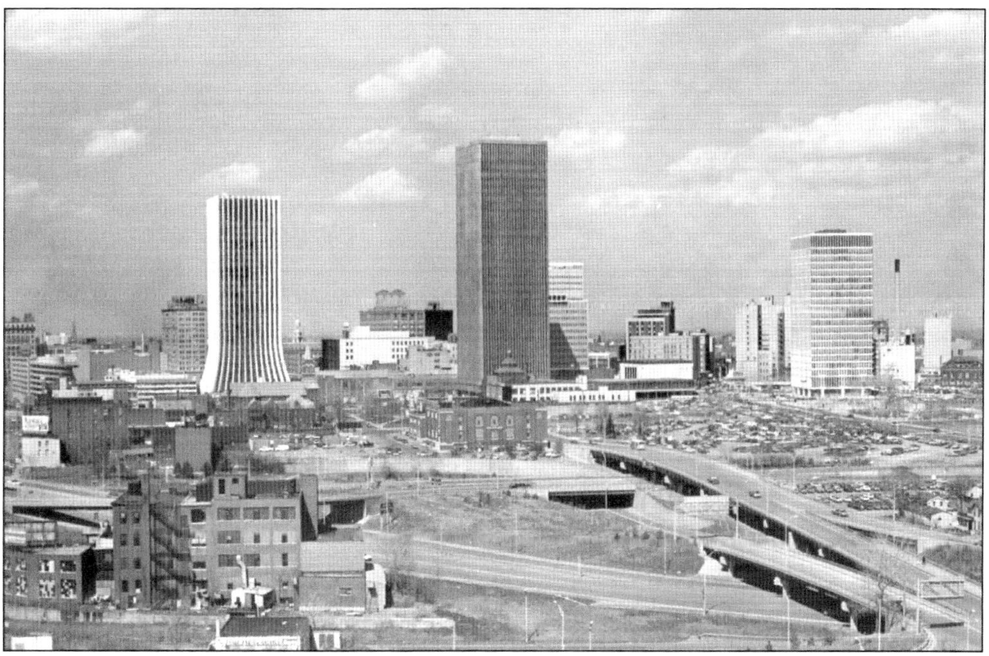

Three giants of the Rochester skyline, Lincoln First Tower, Xerox Square, and Marine Midland Plaza, dominate this view of downtown Rochester from the 1970s. All three would incorporate load-bearing exterior walls in their engineering and a kind of sculptural expressionism to their architecture. These towers were built at the end of the modern period, when architects attempted to create more lively designs while staying true to the functional ethic that modern architecture required. (RMA.)

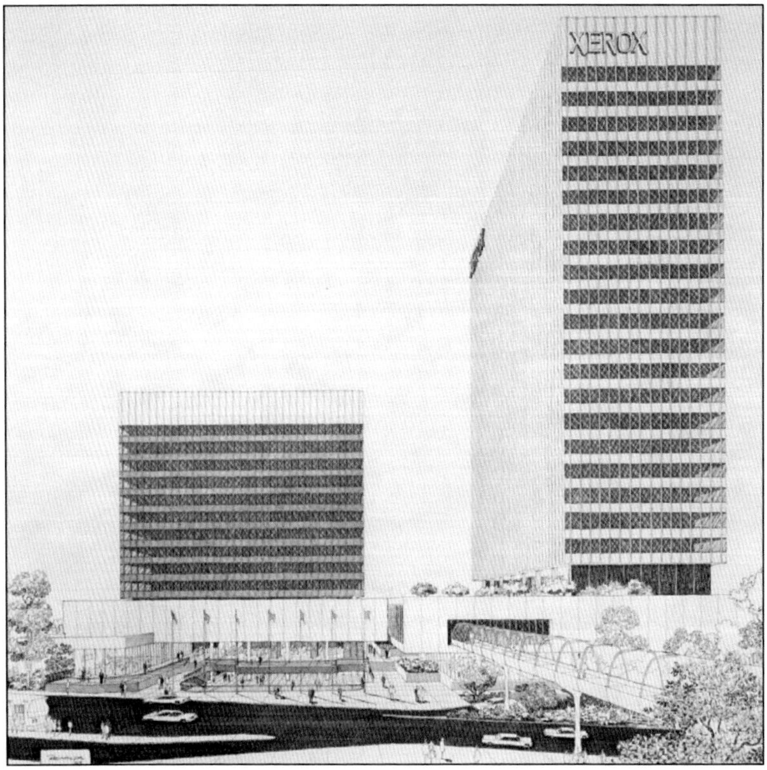

Due to the excitement surrounding the opening of Midtown Plaza, Xerox officials decided against moving their headquarters to the suburbs and made a commitment to build their office tower across Broad Street from the mall. A sky bridge would connect the two complexes. Two office towers on an L-shaped base would face a tiered plaza lined with shops and eateries in this early concept. (RMA.)

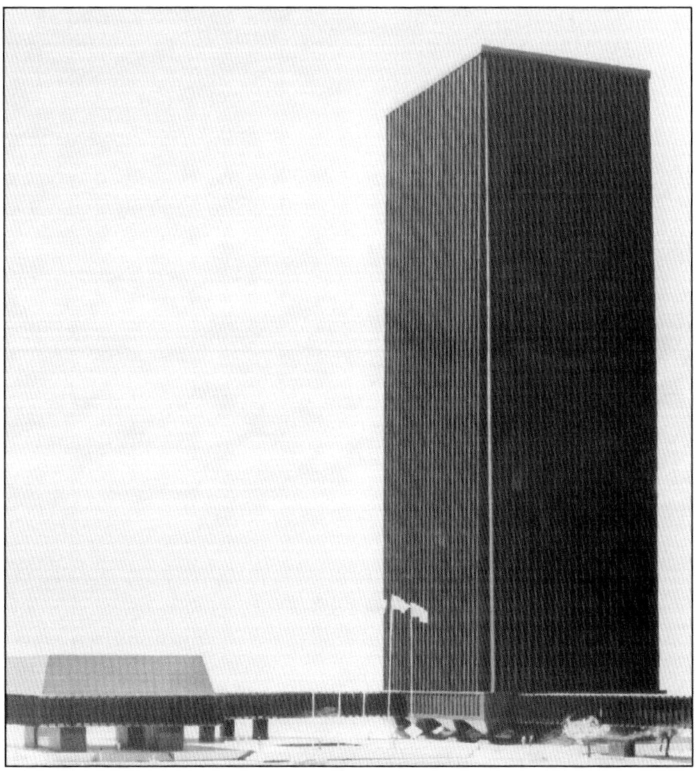

The eventual shape of Xerox Square is displayed in this model from architect Welton Becket. The shops and restaurants have disappeared, and the office space has been combined into a singular, gradually tapering tower of reinforced concrete and granite. A smaller building is connected to the tower by a sky bridge. (RMA.)

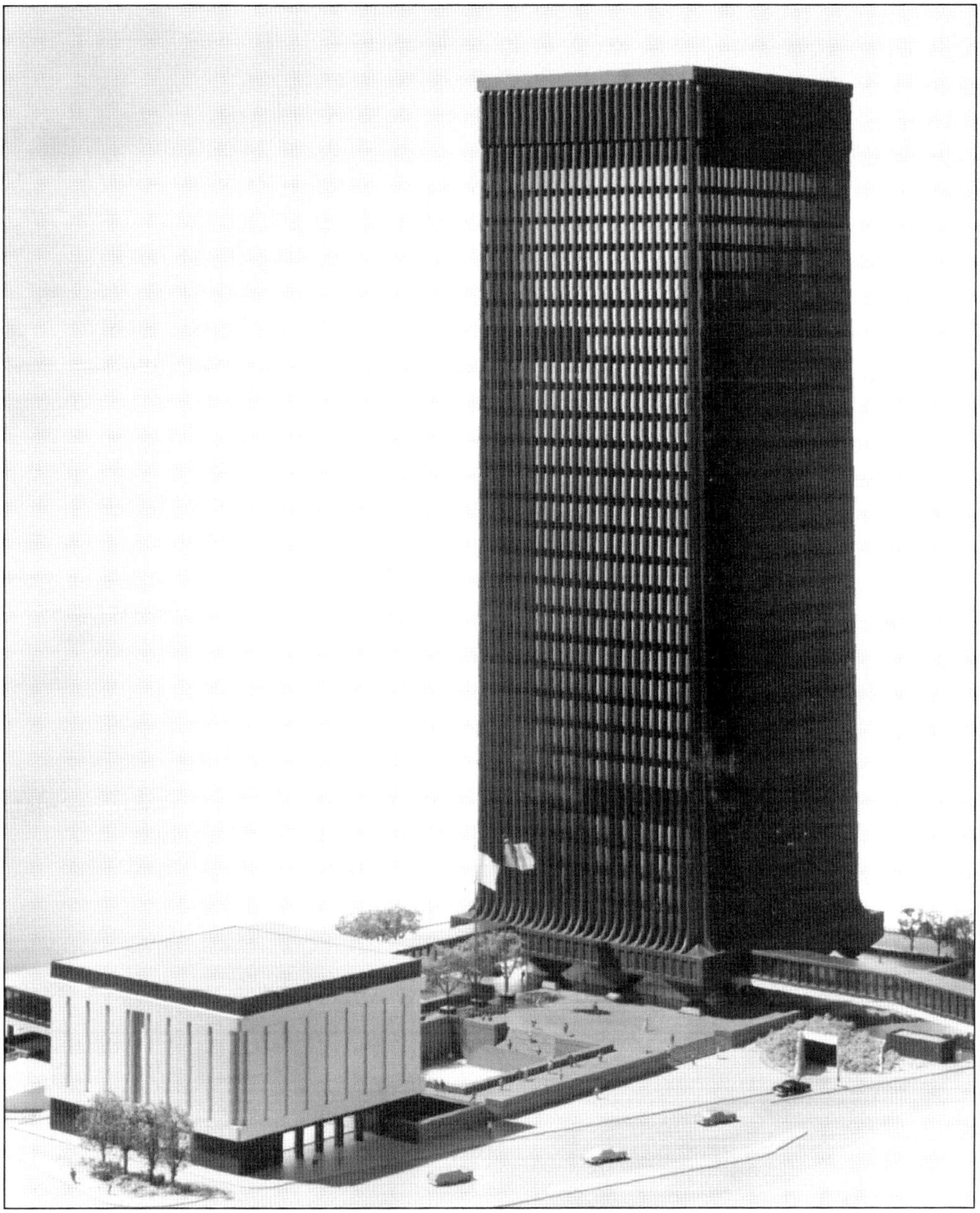

Xerox Square reaches its final design phase in this model. The plaza has been enlarged and features a sunken area that will be used as a skating rink in the winter months. A large auditorium building, clad in white marble, has been added to the plan, and the tower's look has been refined. Its form now evokes a classical column with a distinct base, shaft, and capital. (RMA.)

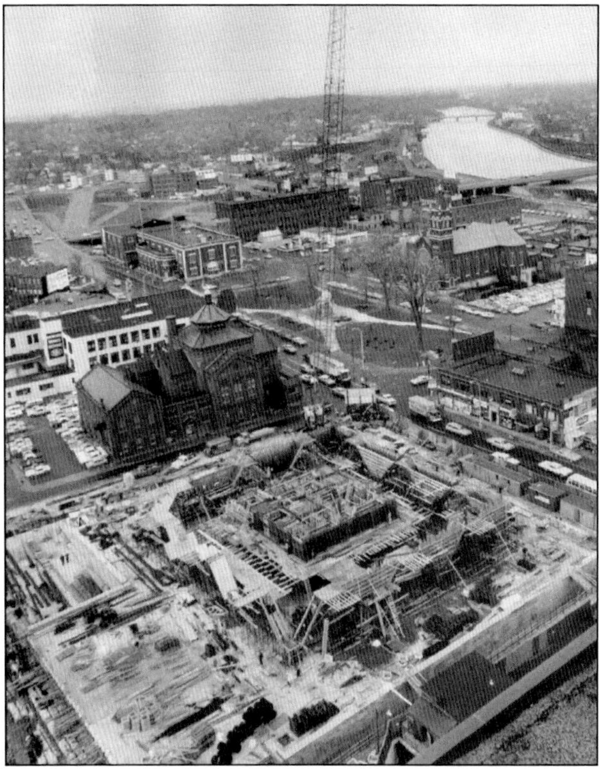

Wooden forms cover the reinforced concrete structure as it hardens. Xerox Square was built on the site of one of Rochester's most beloved and opulent movie palaces, the Loews-Rochester Theater. Claude Bragdon's First Universalist Church stands across Court Street from the new project. (RLLHD.)

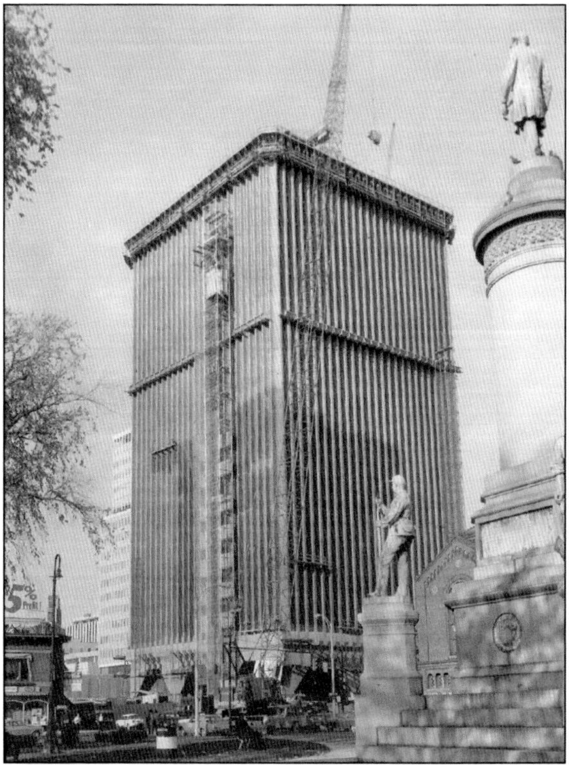

In this view from Washington Square Park, the innovative structure of the tower can be seen. Note the massive base columns and the deep concrete beams above them. These beams transfer the gravity load of the building from the slender columns of the main shaft of the tower to the 12 tapering base columns at plaza level. (RMA.)

Xerox Square's exterior is sandblasted in this night image. It was hoped that the sandblasting would reveal the aggregate rock embedded in the building's structure, to give it a sparkling facade. It did not work out as planned, and the tower retained its dark and somewhat dull gray color. The coffered undersides of the tower's floor plates can be seen here as well. (RLLHD.)

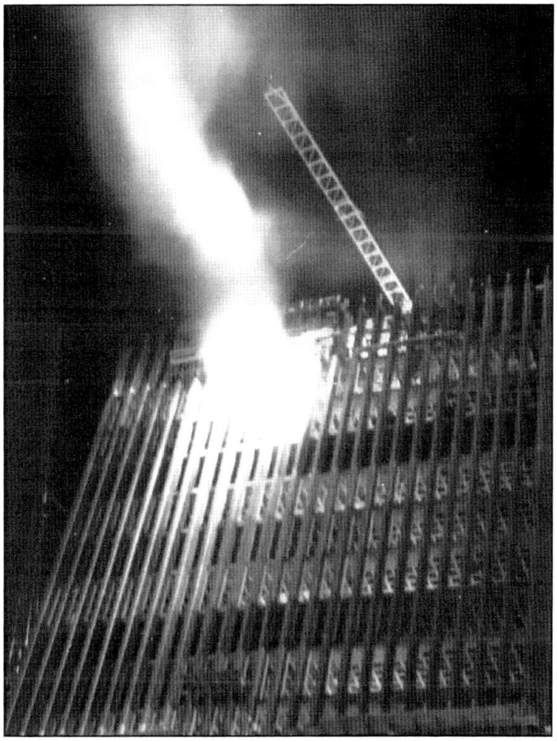

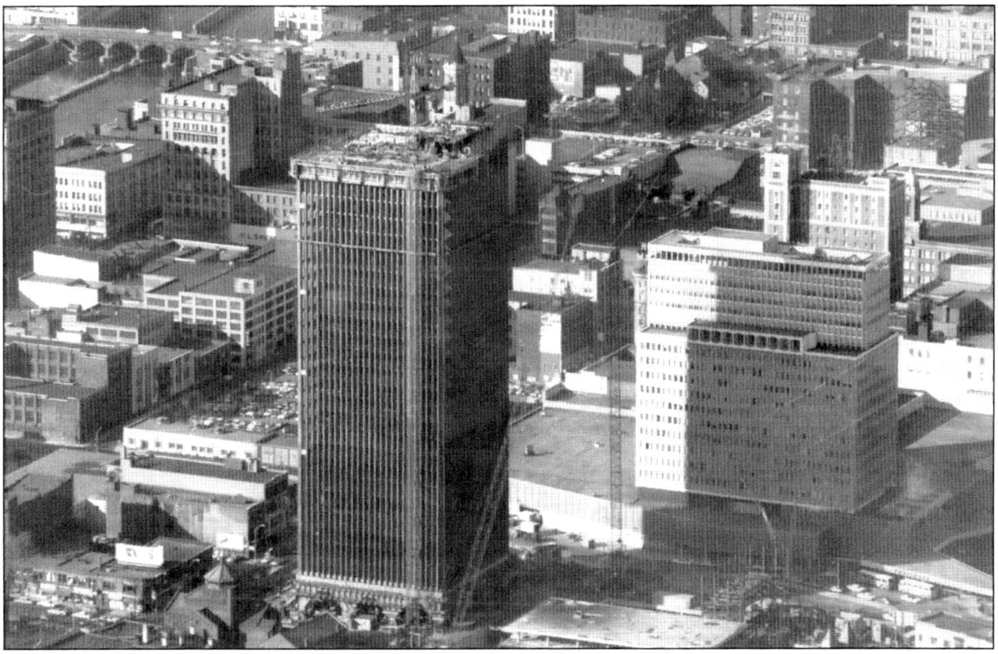

Xerox Square is not yet topped out but already has overtaken the Midtown Tower. The relative thinness of the building's structure can be seen as sunlight passes through the corner of the tower. There were no internal columns to carry the tower's weight. Instead, the slender exterior columns bear the weight of the building. This was a common practice during the 1960s and 1970s, as engineers attempted to create the easily adaptable floor plans that developers preferred. (RLLHD.)

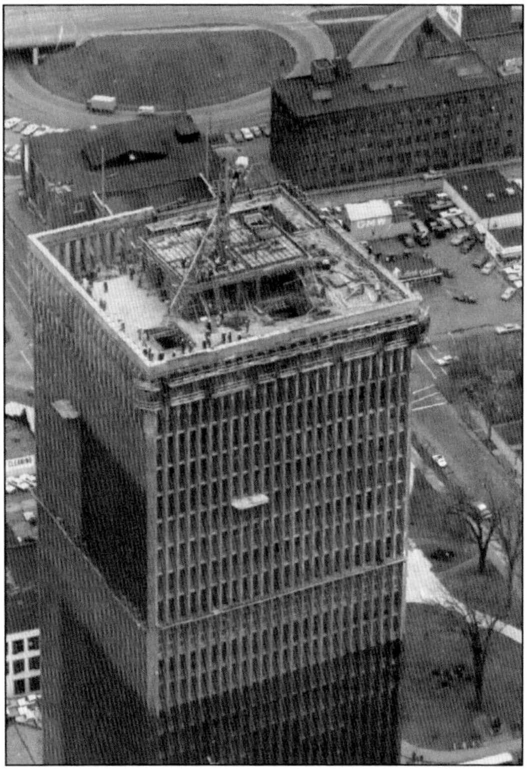

This aerial view allows one to understand the structure of Xerox Square. The exterior columns carry the weight of the building, while the service core and the concrete floor plates provide stiffness and resistance to lateral forces. No interior columns are needed, allowing customizable office layouts. (RMA.)

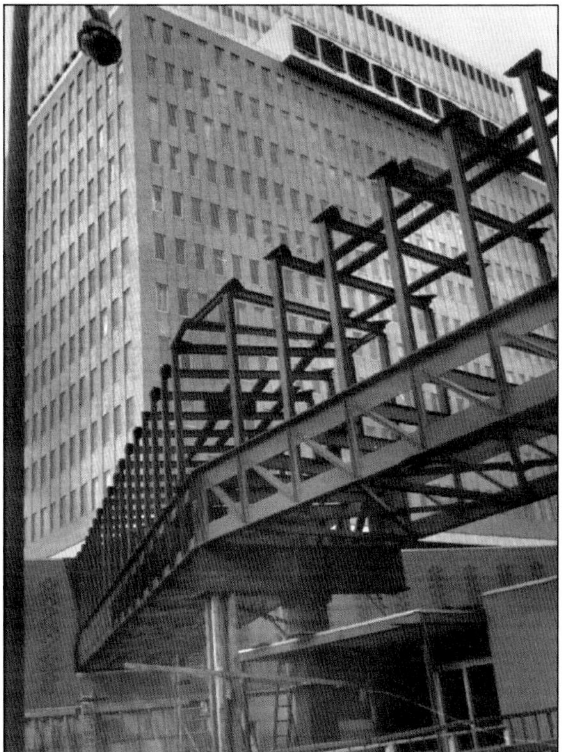

The sky bridge to Midtown Plaza spans Broad Street as Xerox Square nears completion. Later additional bridges would link Xerox Square to a parking garage a block away and an entrance structure for Rochester's "Skyway system" of pedestrian sky bridges and tunnels. (*Democrat and Chronicle*.)

Three Forms, a stainless-steel sculpture, graces the plaza in front of the tower. Artist Roy Gussow was the creator of the artwork. (RMA)

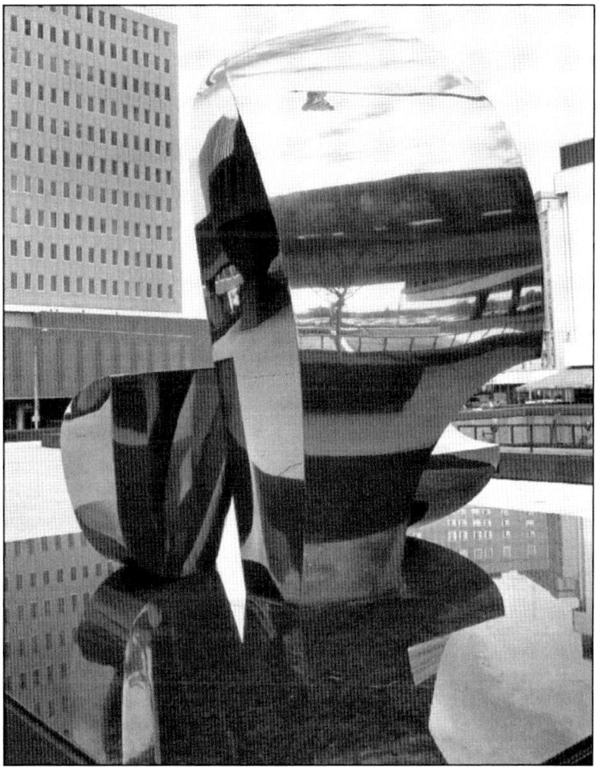

Xerox Square, standing at 443 feet tall, has been the tallest building in Rochester since its completion in 1968. Other towers were built that approached its height, but none matched it. In the early 2000s, a local businessman announced his plan to build a tower that would top Xerox Square. Alas, it was not meant to be, and the proposed building's height design was reduced to 10 floors. (RMA.)

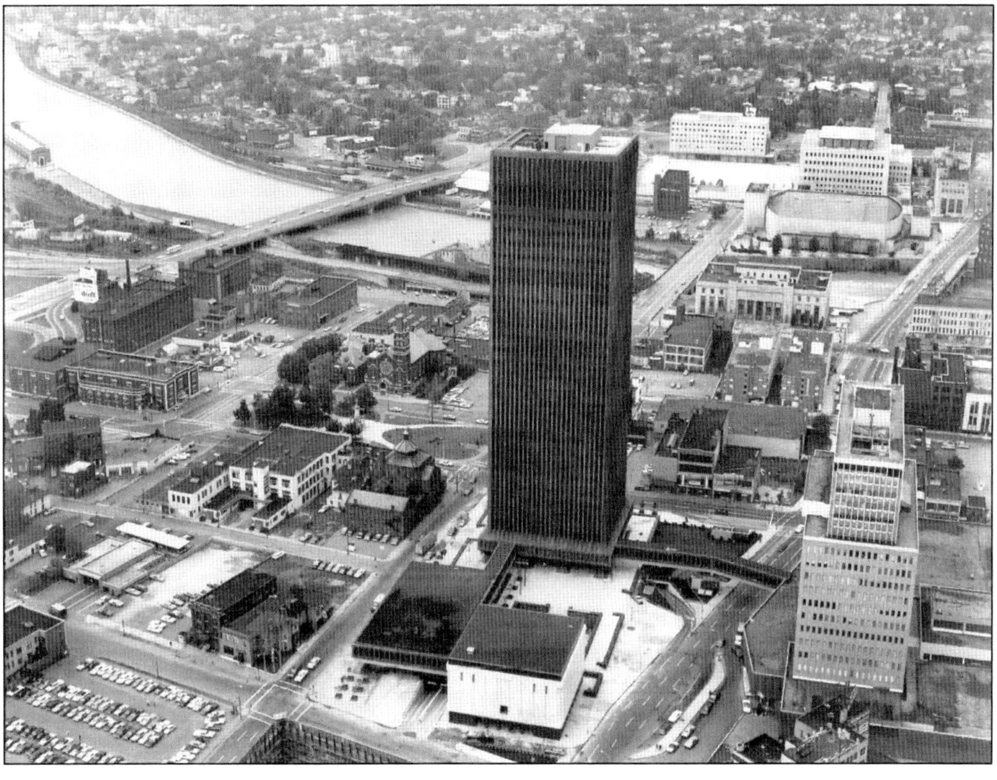

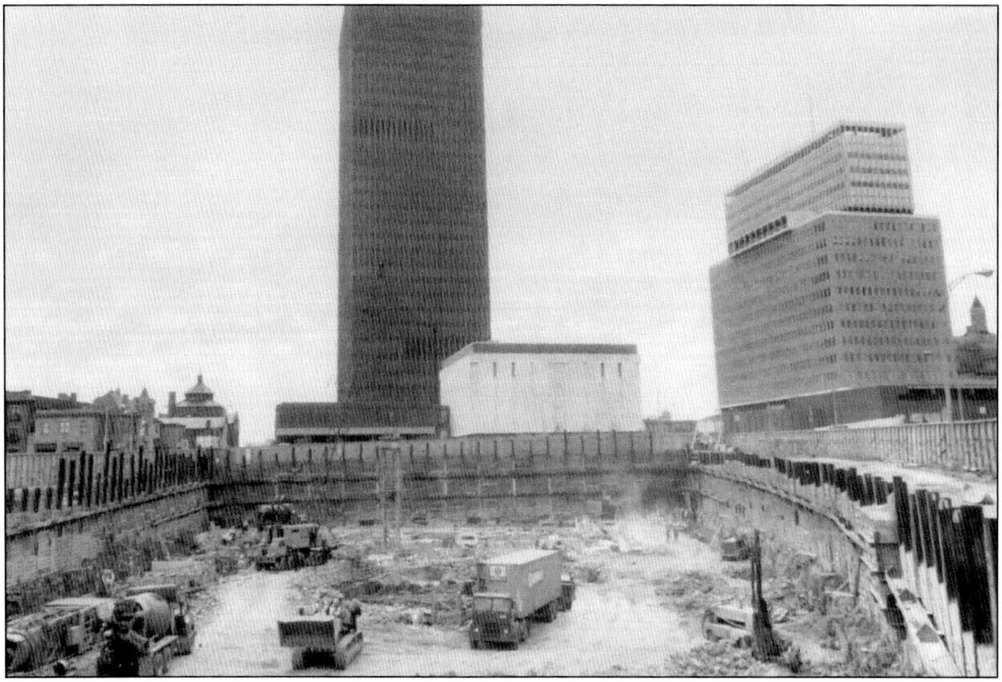

With Xerox Square looming in the background, excavation proceeds for the next great tower that will rise on the skyline, Marine Midland Plaza. Midtown Tower is on the right. Designed to be a counterpoint to Xerox Square, Marine Midland Plaza's concrete structure would be painted white and would be floodlit in the evenings, becoming a 290-foot-tall beacon that was visible for miles. (RLLHD.)

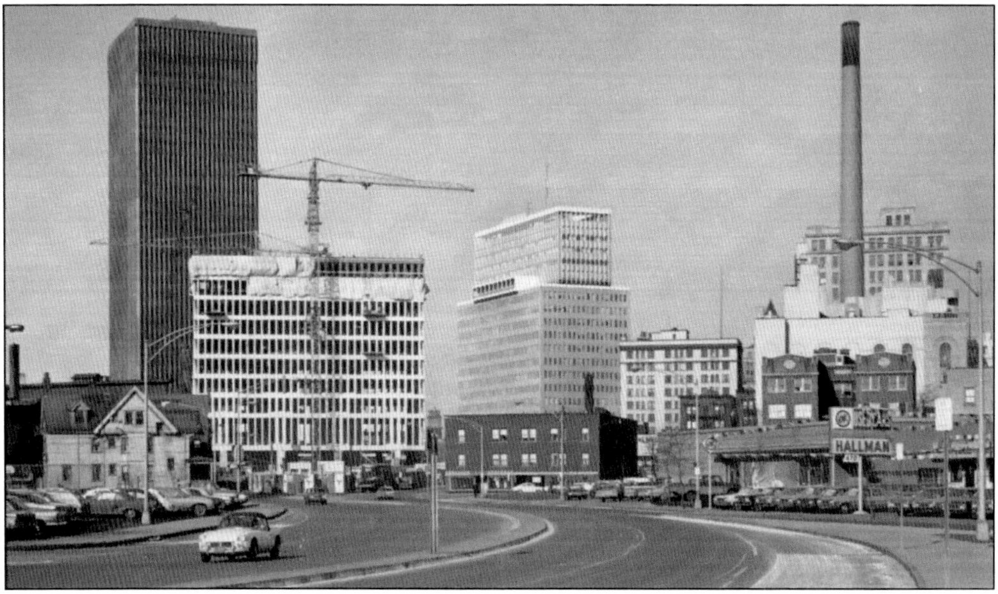

Marine Midland Plaza, like Xerox Square, employs a structural system of load-bearing exterior walls connected to a concrete service core by coffered, reinforced concrete floor plates. Unlike Xerox Square, Marine Midland Plaza's structure gradually widens as it reaches the ground, thereby negating the need for a thick transfer beam above the building's 14 base columns. (RMA.)

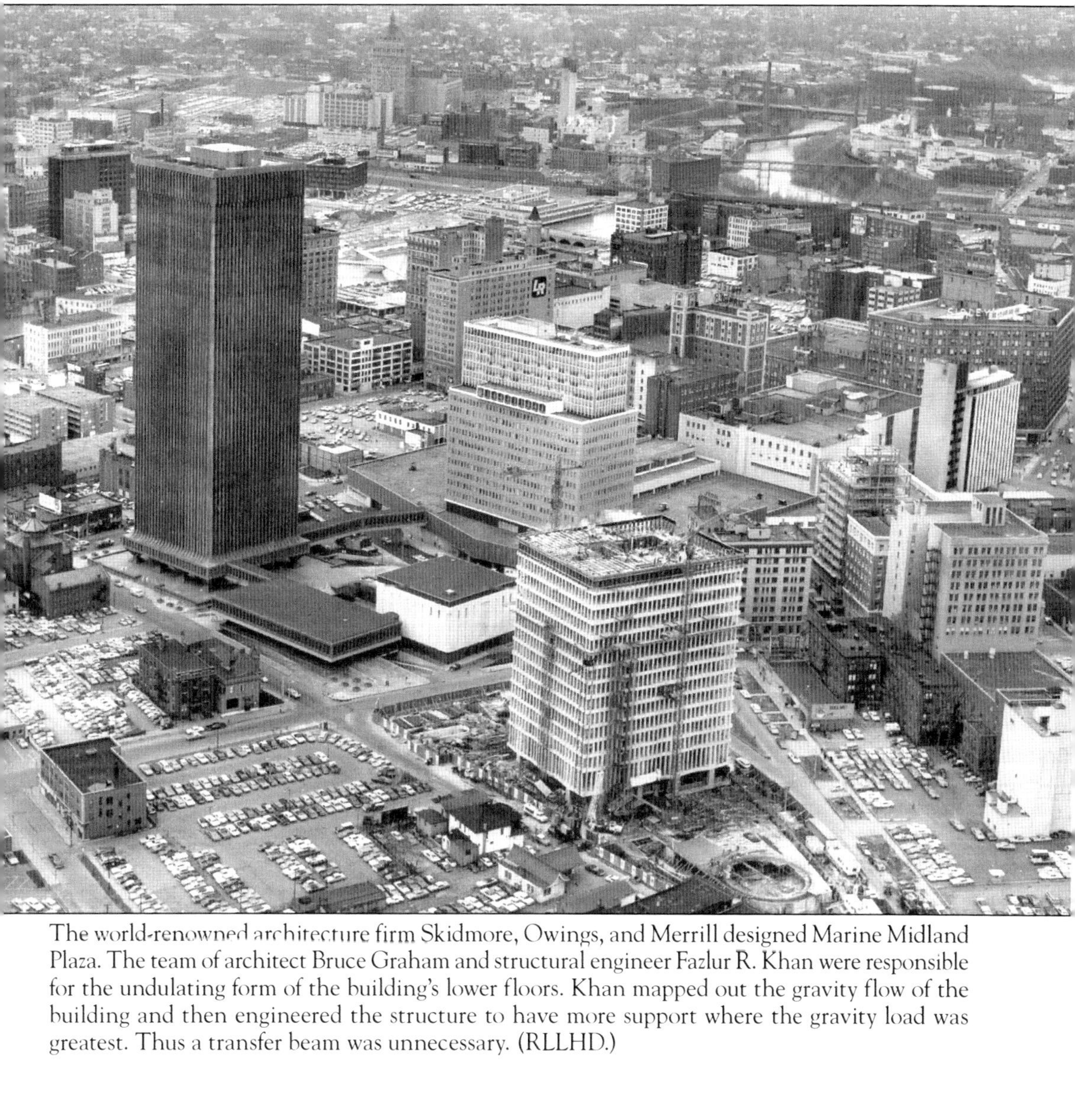

The world-renowned architecture firm Skidmore, Owings, and Merrill designed Marine Midland Plaza. The team of architect Bruce Graham and structural engineer Fazlur R. Khan were responsible for the undulating form of the building's lower floors. Khan mapped out the gravity flow of the building and then engineered the structure to have more support where the gravity load was greatest. Thus a transfer beam was unnecessary. (RLLHD.)

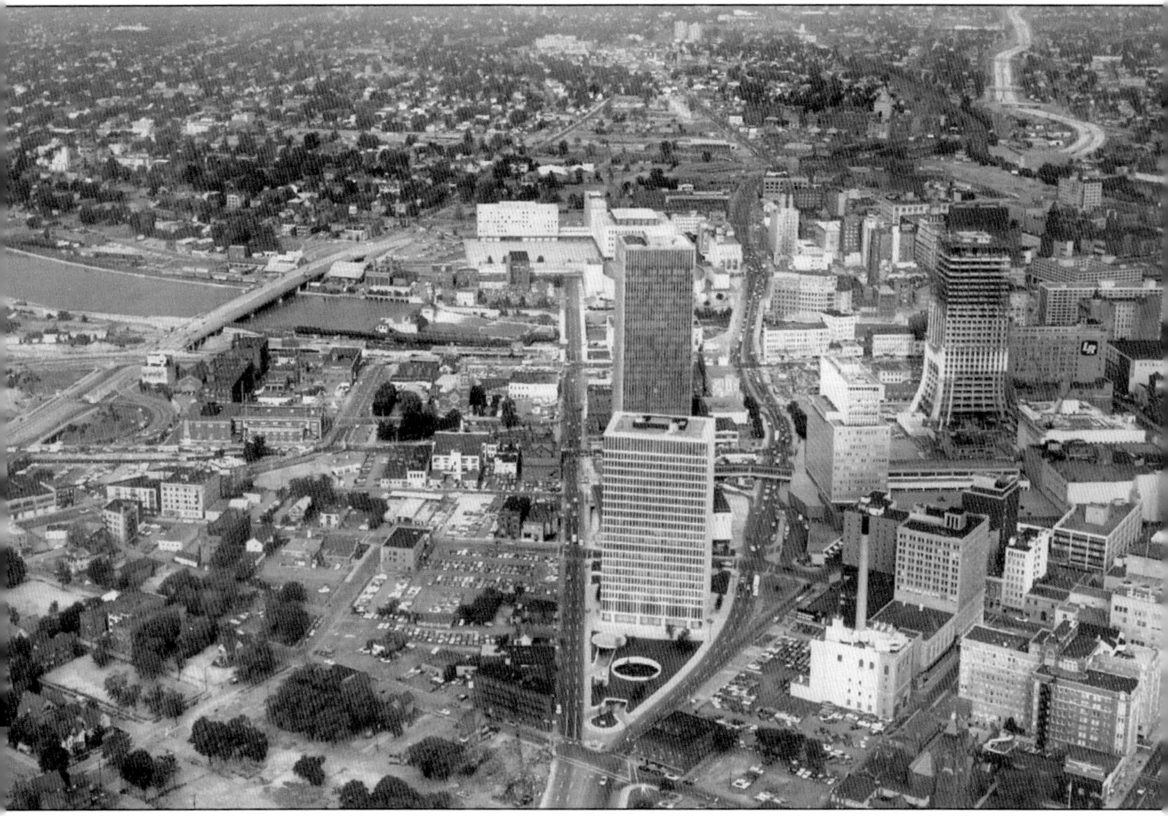

Marine Midland Plaza opened in 1970. The circular forms in front of the building denote a sunken garden on the concourse level and the underground garage's entrance for service vehicles. The banking floors, as well as all shared areas of the building, were sheathed in Italian travertine. Travertine was used extensively by modern architects and was a favored material of Marine Midland Plaza's designers. (RLLHD.)

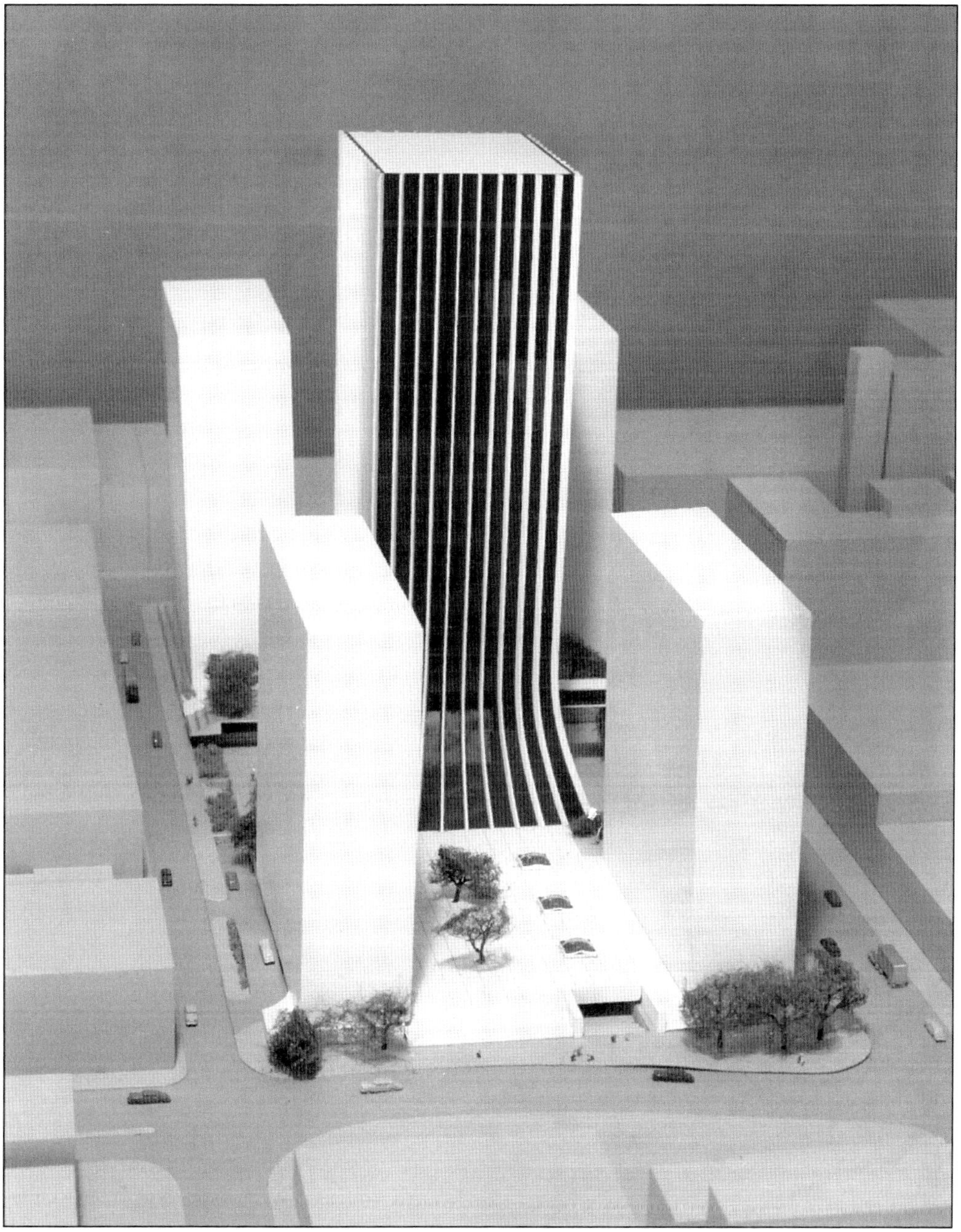

The final expressionist tower to be built downtown was the Lincoln First Tower of 1973. This model depicts a dramatically tapering 400-foot tower surrounded by four identical, but shorter, towers. It is a design reminiscent of Rockefeller Center in New York City. The contrast of the white columns and the black windows would create a "tickertape" effect on the facade that is reminiscent of an early modern masterpiece, the Daily News Building in New York City. (RMA.)

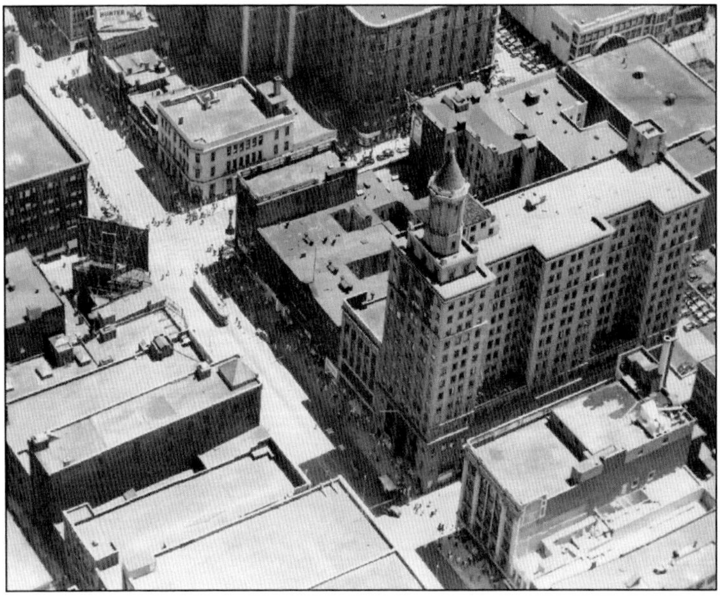

Lincoln First Tower would be built on the southwest corner of Clinton Avenue and East Main Street, seen here in this aerial view from the 1940s. The new tower's predecessor, the Lincoln Alliance Building, is in the foreground. It was constructed in the 1920s from a collaborative design of local architect J. Foster Warner and the famed early-20th-century firm McKim, Mead, and White of New York City. (RLLHD.)

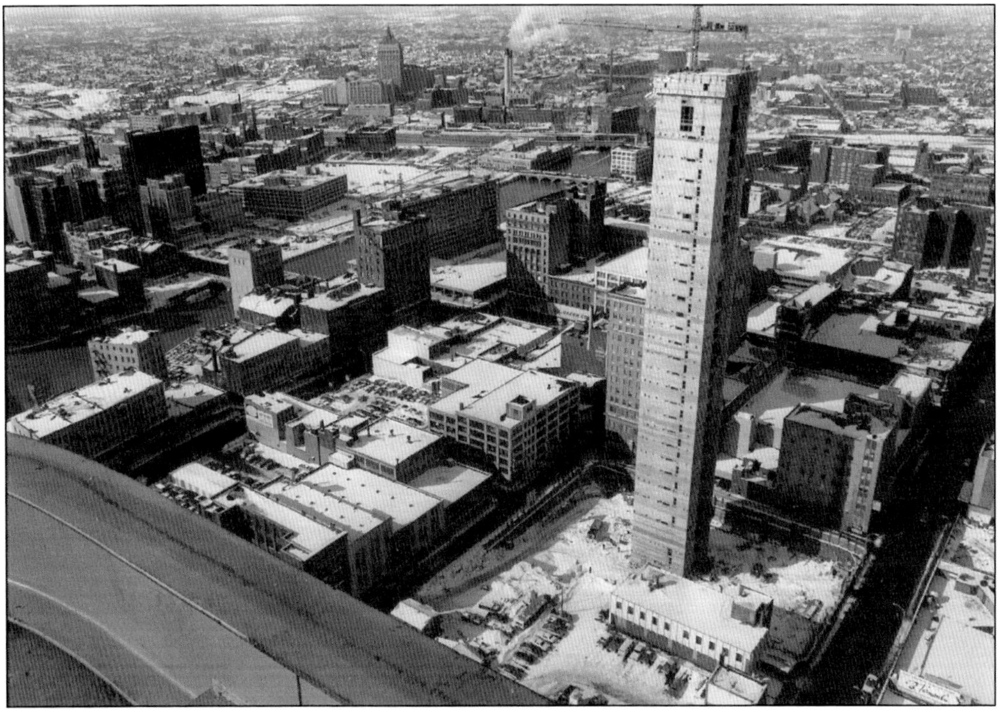

As seen from the top of Xerox Square, the concrete core of the Lincoln First Tower nears completion. The steel of the floor plates and the exterior columns would complete this, the third major "tube" structure to be built downtown. Tube structures, unlike the conventional "rigid frame" of interlocking columns and beams, are hollow and are relatively free of interior columns. The World Trade Center utilized a similar type of structure in its twin towers. (RMA.)

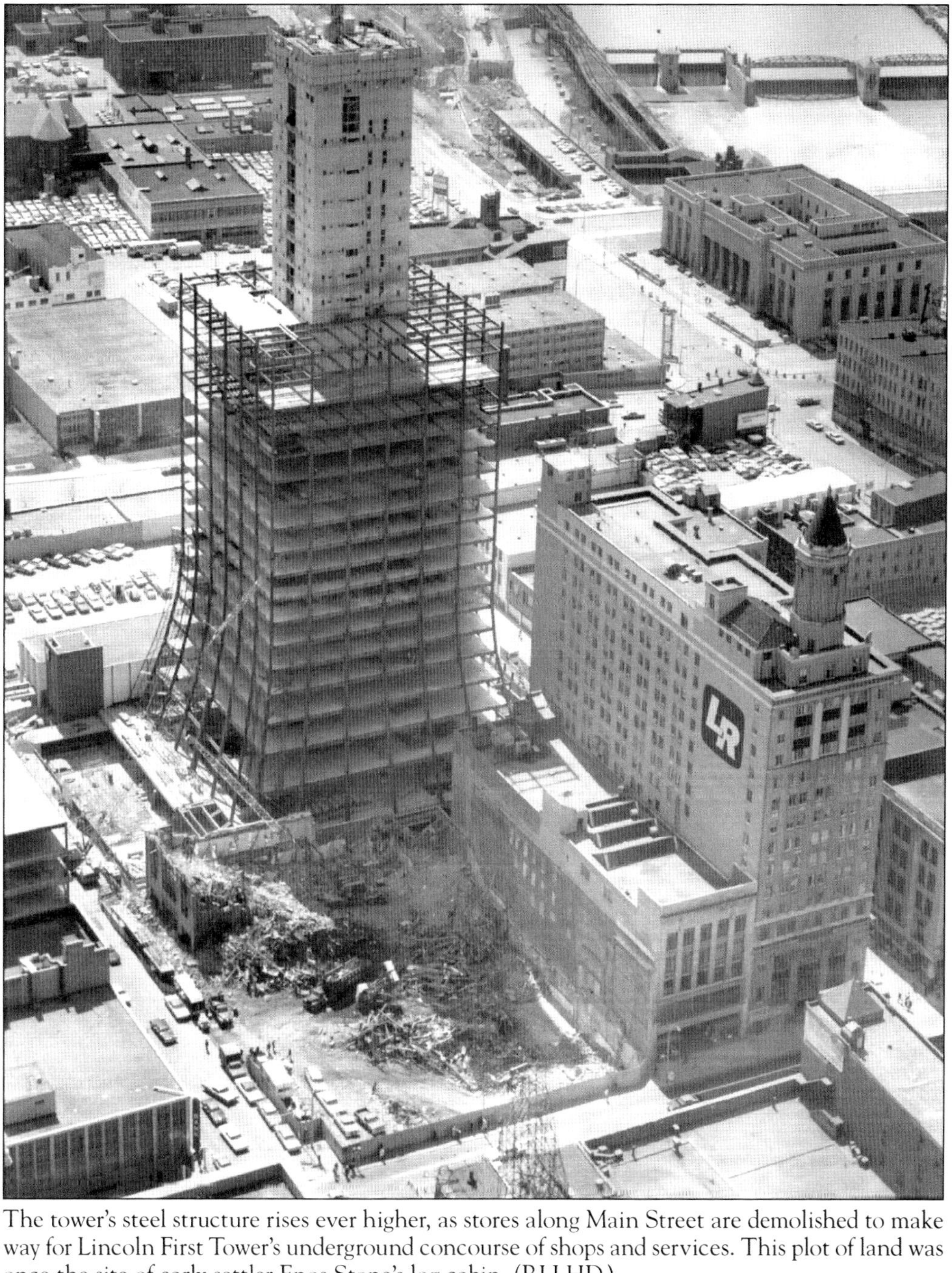

The tower's steel structure rises ever higher, as stores along Main Street are demolished to make way for Lincoln First Tower's underground concourse of shops and services. This plot of land was once the site of early settler Enos Stone's log cabin. (RLLHD.)

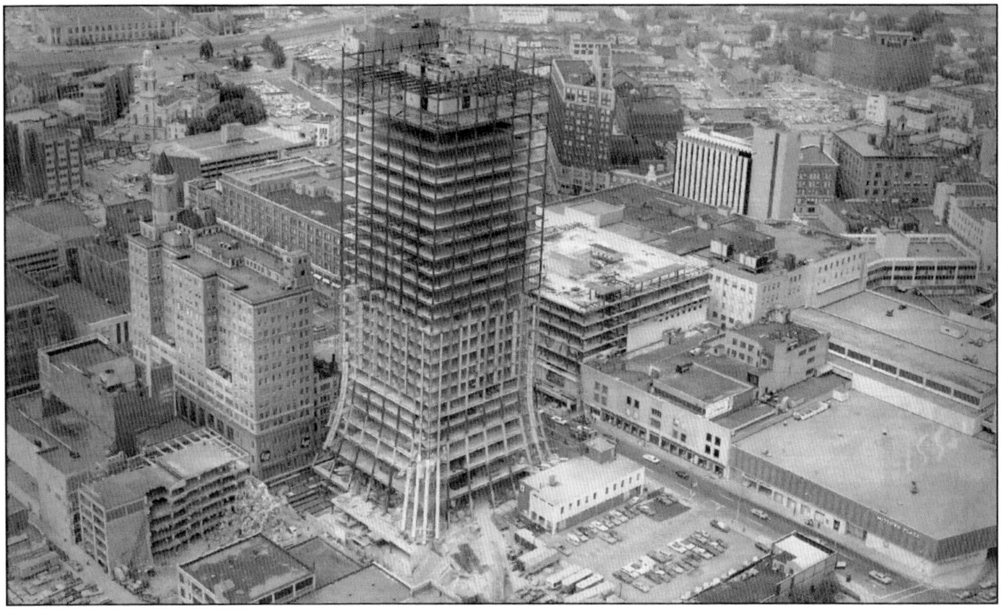

With the structural steel complete, the marble cladding is being applied to the exterior columns in this aerial view from 1971. The panels of Carrera marble would have to be removed in the 1980s. The panels were thinner than the architect specified and began to warp. The underlying metal supports for the marble began to fail, and it was feared the panels would fall off and injure bystanders. (RLLHD.)

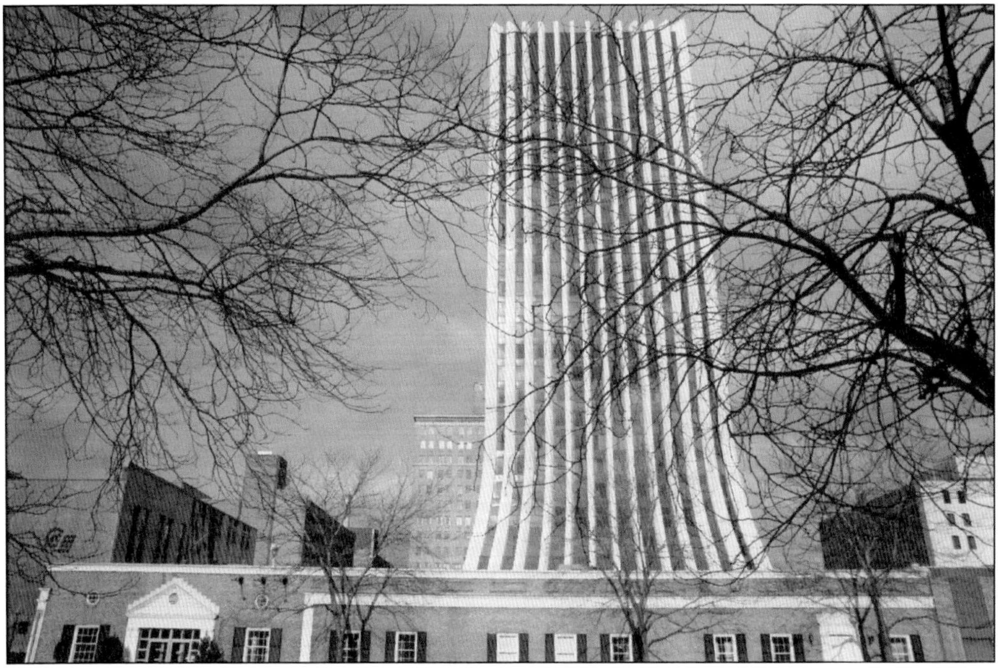

The completed Lincoln First Tower is seen from Broad Street in this image. Half of the swooping columns of the tower are functional and carry the building's weight, while the rest of the marble-clad columns are hollow and contain the building's utility lines. The edifice in front of the tower is a recent structure draped in colonial garb. (RLLHD.)

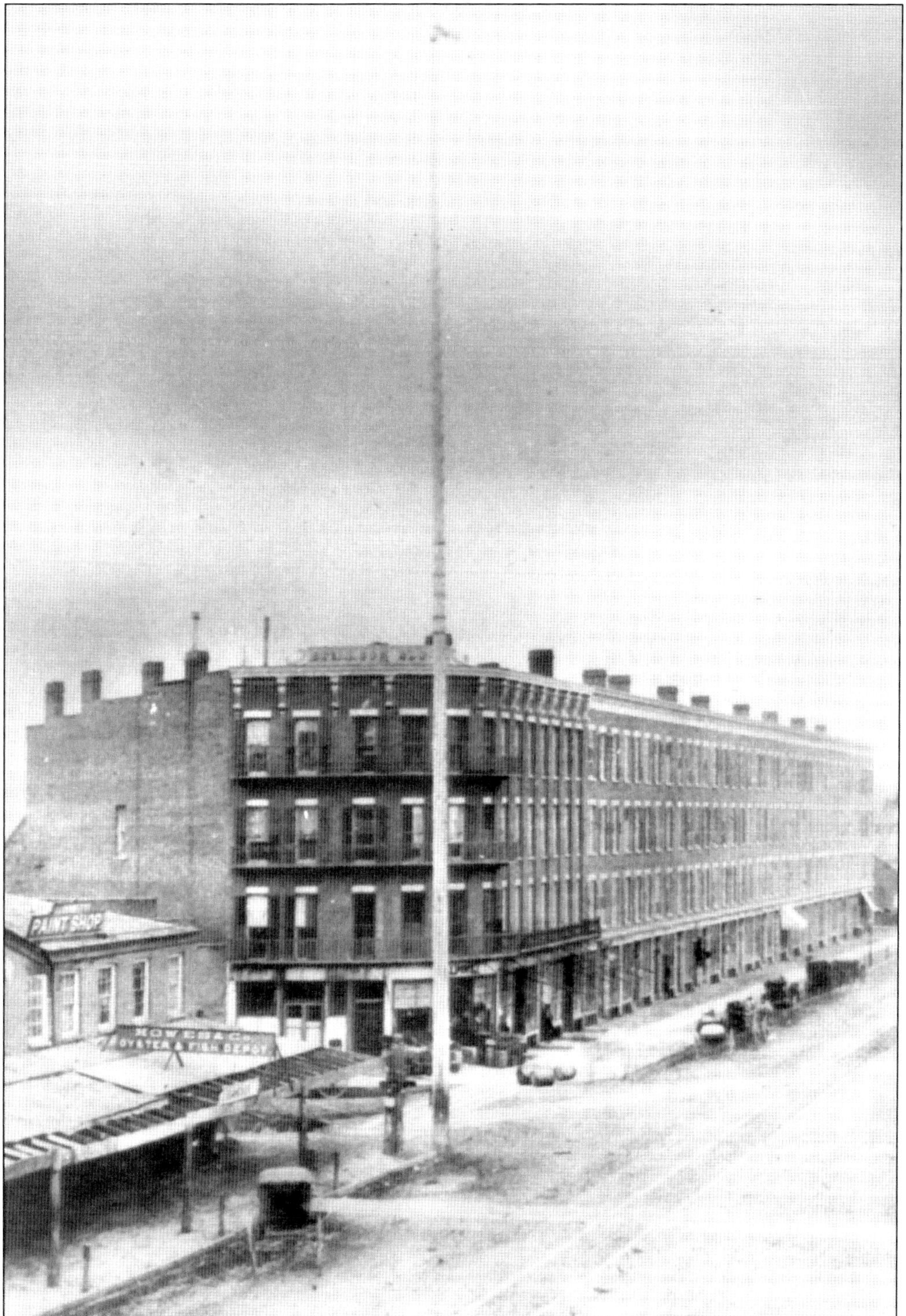

Rochester's second Liberty Pole stood along Main Street until it was toppled by high winds in 1889. The Liberty Pole symbolized this country's independence. (RLLHD.)

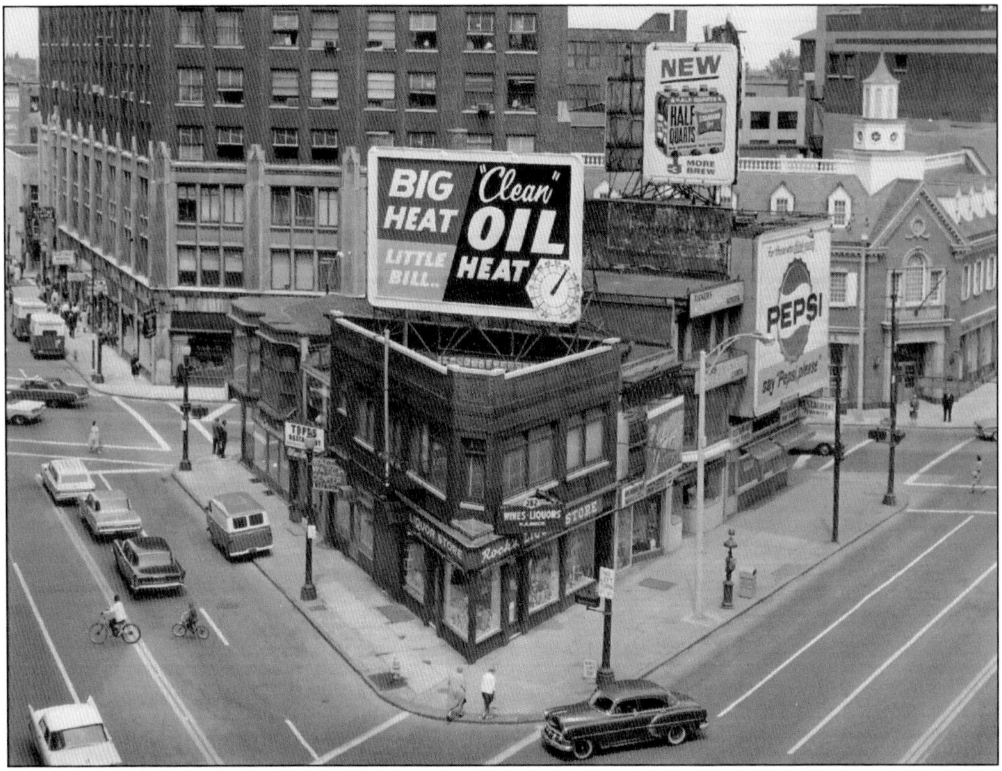

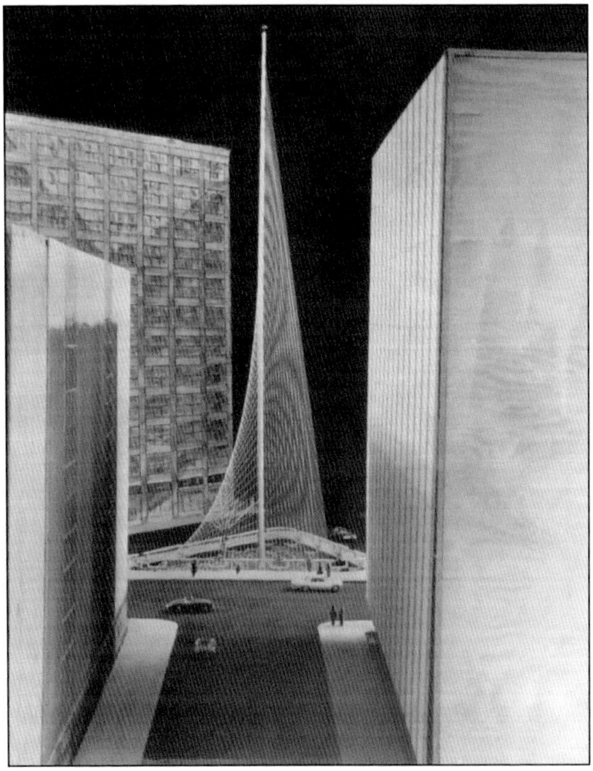

For decades after the second Liberty Pole collapsed, the land on which it stood was occupied by a triangle of two- and three-story buildings. In 1964, a competition was held to design a replacement for the Liberty Pole. Artists and architects from around the nation participated in the competition. (RMA.)

Local architect James Johnson's entry of a stainless-steel shaft supported by cables represented a modern homage to the original monument. An "eternal flame" memorial would grace the base of the 190-foot pole. It won first prize and was completed in 1965. (RMA.)

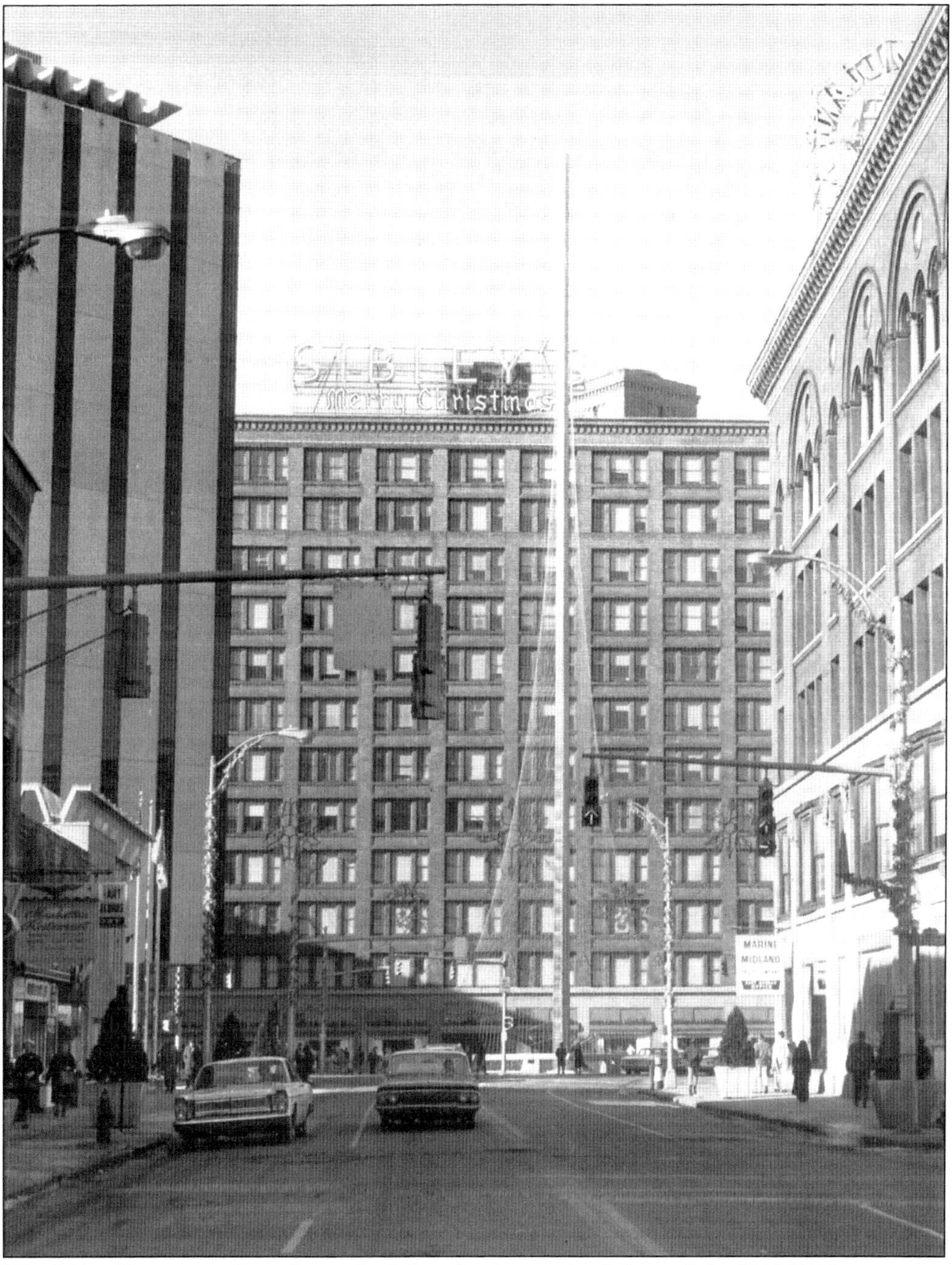

The Sibley Tower provides a fitting backdrop for the soaring Liberty Pole. (RLLHD.)

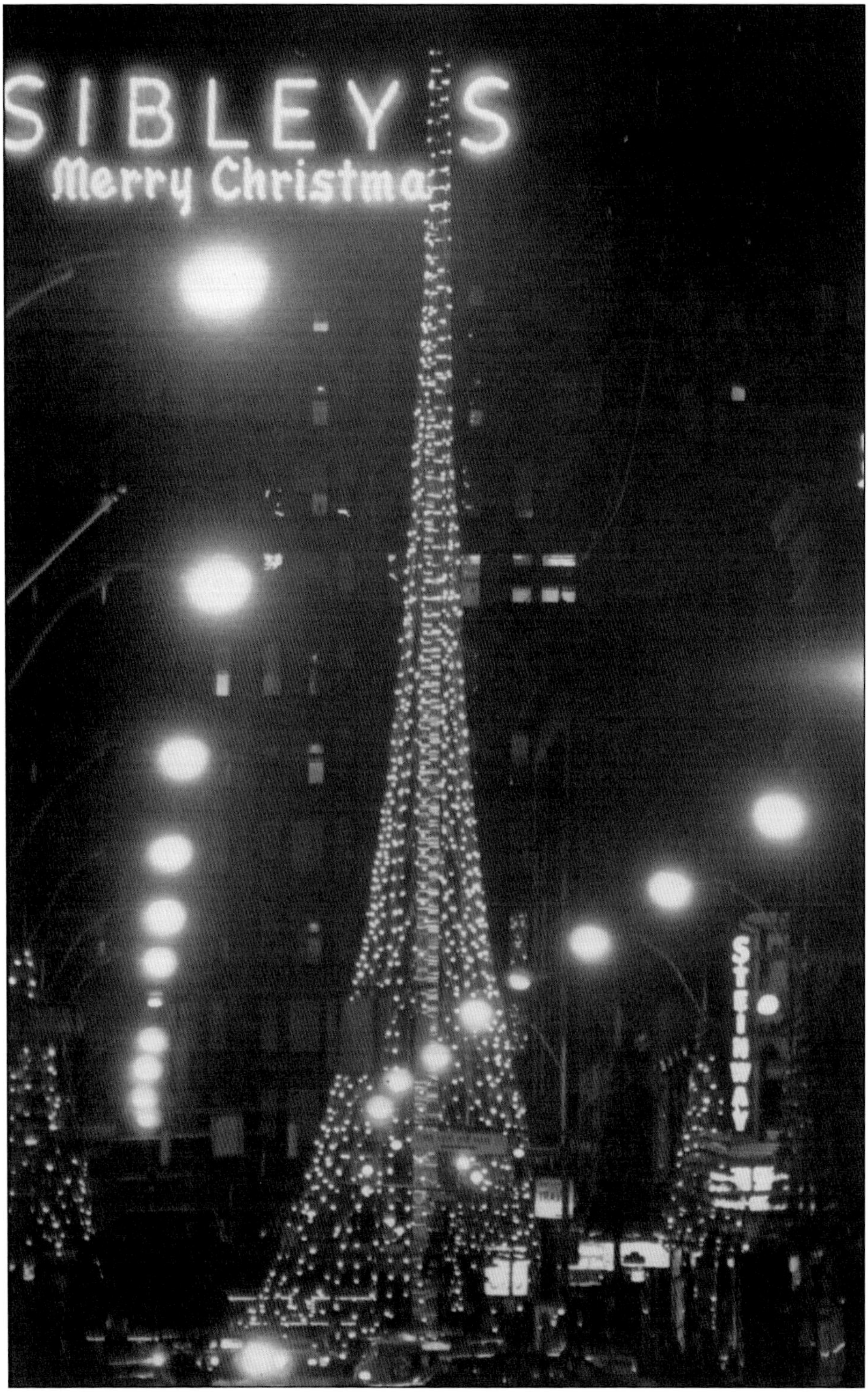

During the holidays, lights strung along the cables cause the monument to resemble a minimalist Christmas tree. (*Democrat and Chronicle*.)

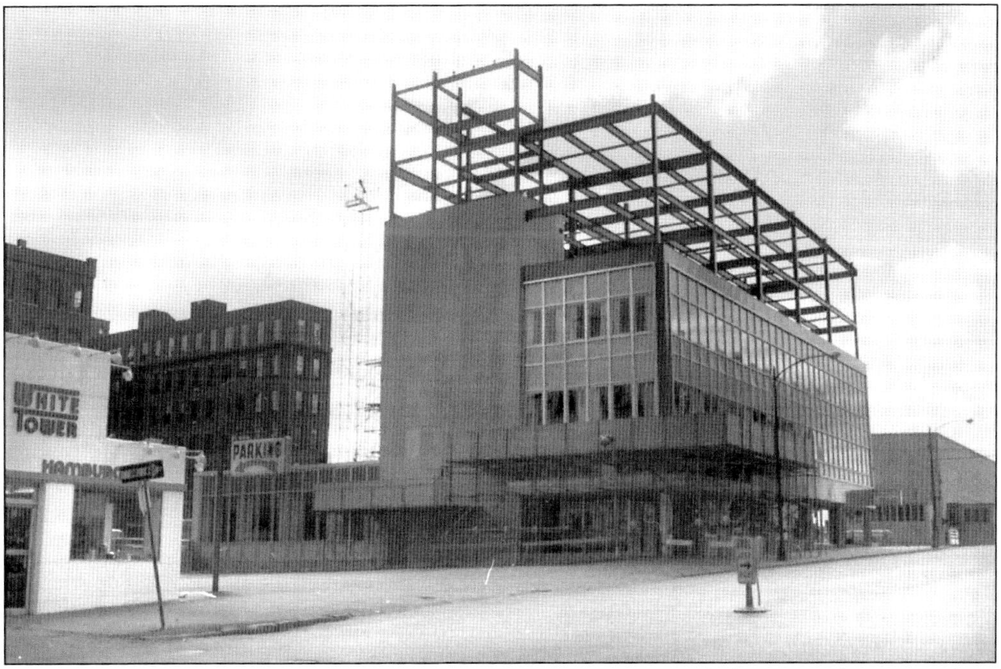

The top two floors of this building on Exchange Street are mere skeletons in this image from 1964. It was originally constructed from designs by architect Carl R. Traver as a three-story bank and office building for the Central Trust Company. The White Tower hamburger restaurant to the left of the bank is still in use. It now serves as an Asian takeout restaurant. (RLLHD.)

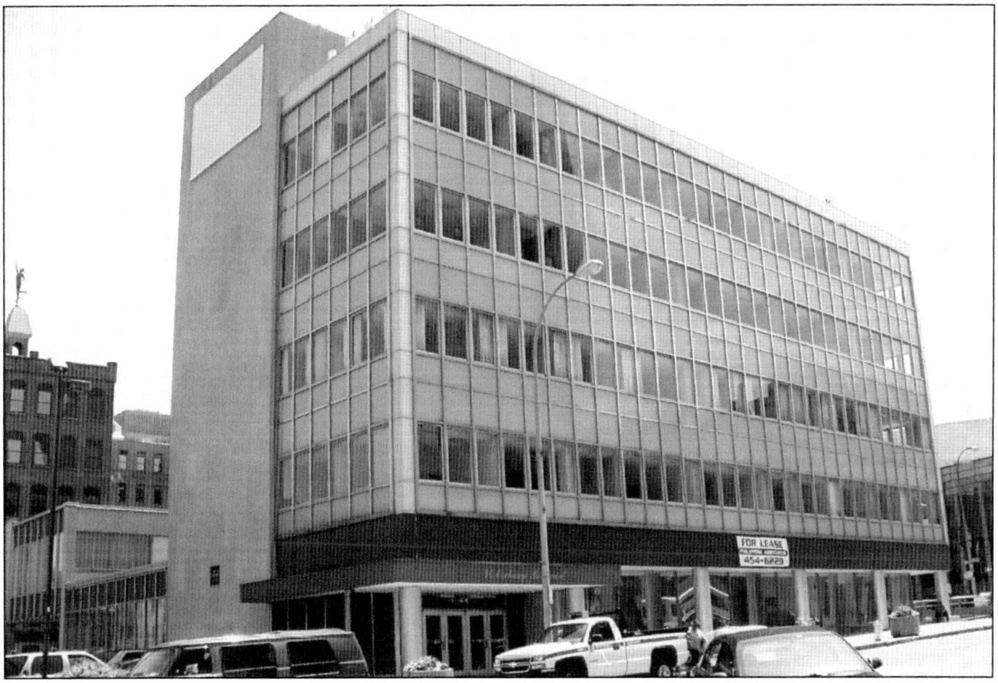

Forty years later, the former Central Trust Company Building stands vacant and awaits a conversion into apartments. (RMA.)

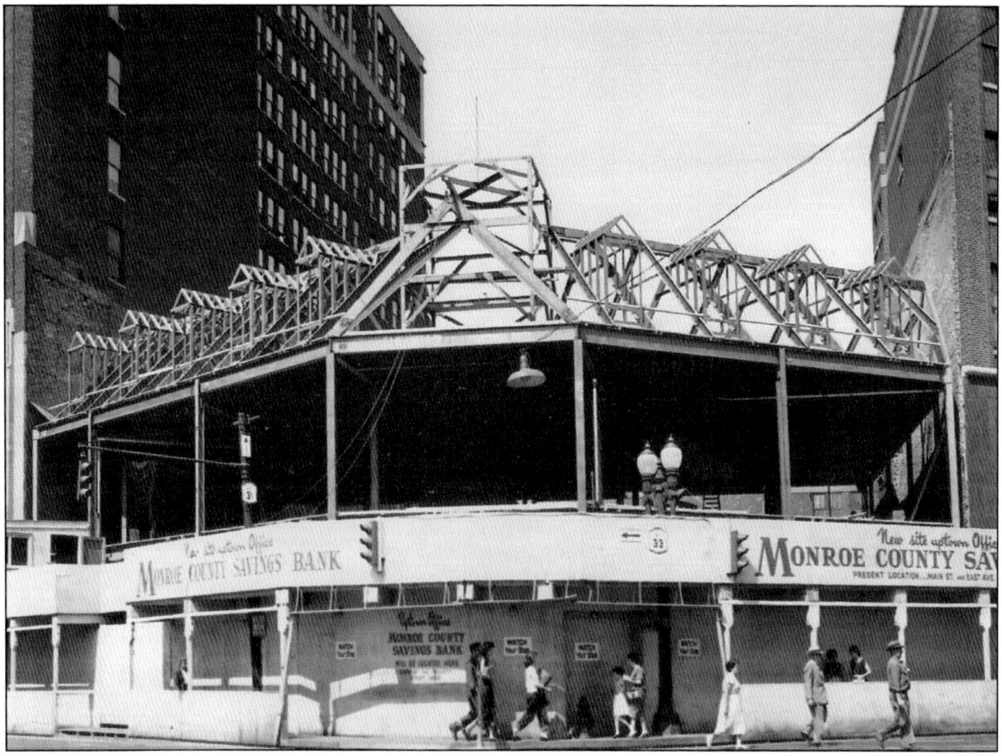

In the fall of 1954, the Monroe County Savings Bank, at the corner of Franklin and East Main Streets, reached the point where its shape was apparent, but confusing. It had what appeared to be dormers that looked out of place on a modern building. The tall structure on the left is the interesting, mixed-use church and office tower known as the Temple Building. (RMA.)

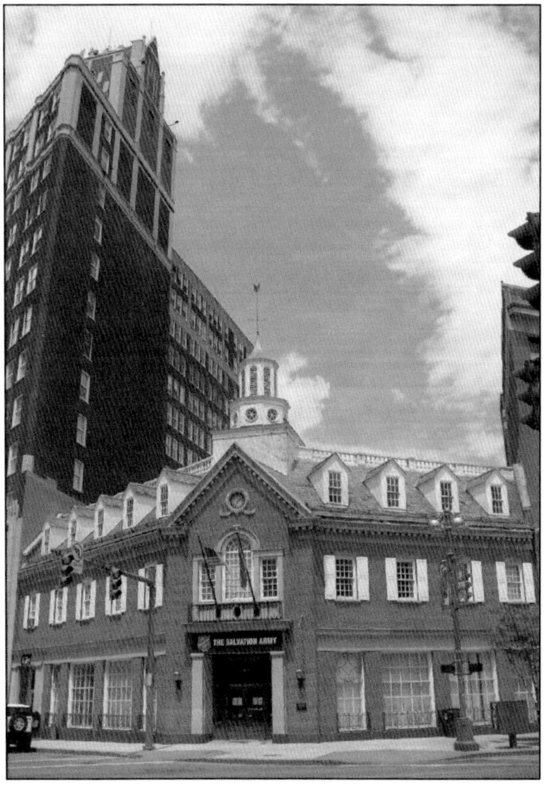

Looking like it would be at home in colonial Boston, this "modern" bank building exhibits one of the exceptions to the functionalist rule. Many banks and churches from the 1950s still referenced, if not outright copied, historical styles, such as neo-Gothic, for their structures. This example displays a Georgian Revival motif. (RMA.)

Since 1857, the Rochester Savings Bank had stood on the corner of West Main and Fitzhugh Streets. At one time, the bank had a copper dome flanked by lions, but the space was needed for additional rooms, and the dome and lions came down. One hundred years after it opened, the old landmark would be demolished to make way for a new bank branch that a local newspaper compared to the Tiffany Building in New York City. (RLLHD.)

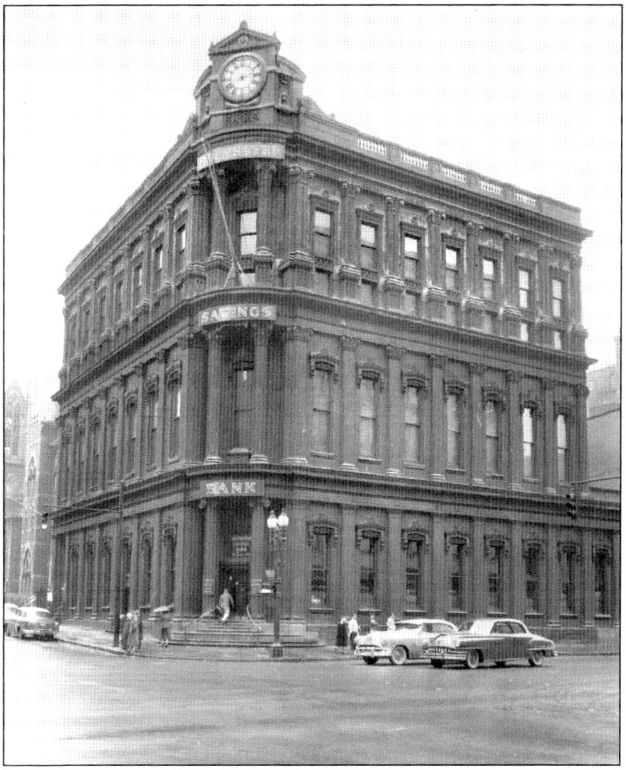

By early 1956, the old building is gone, and the site is ready for construction to begin. A few "sidewalk superintendents" can be seen on the corner peeking into the site. The Rochester Academy Building and St. Luke's church can be seen in the background. (RLLHD.)

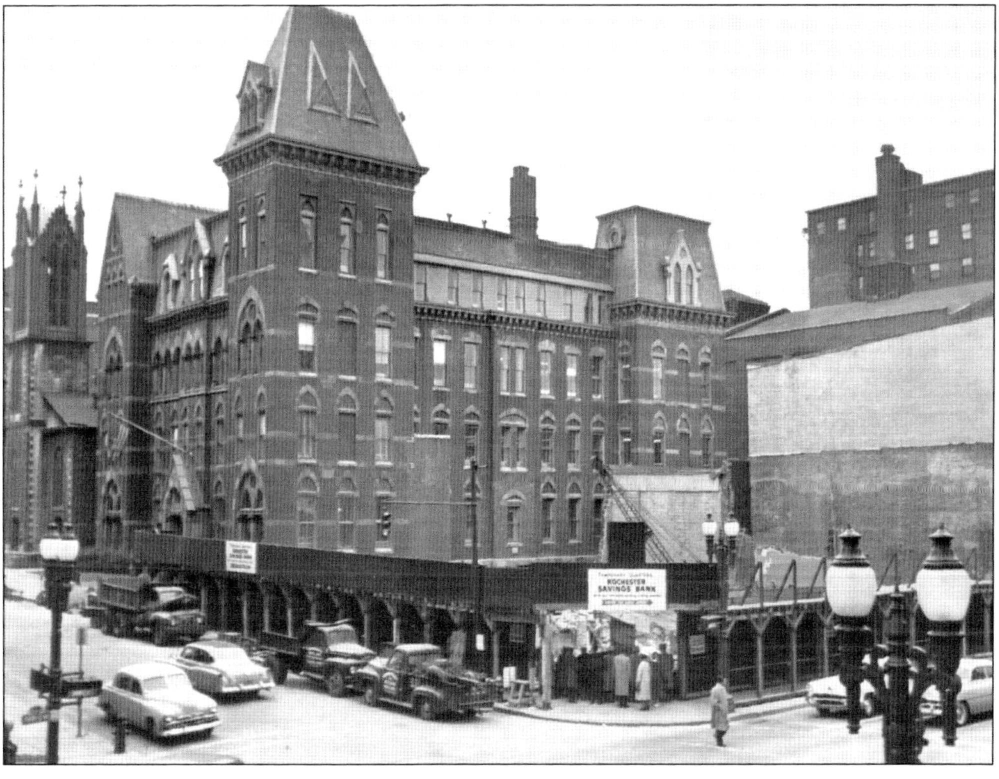

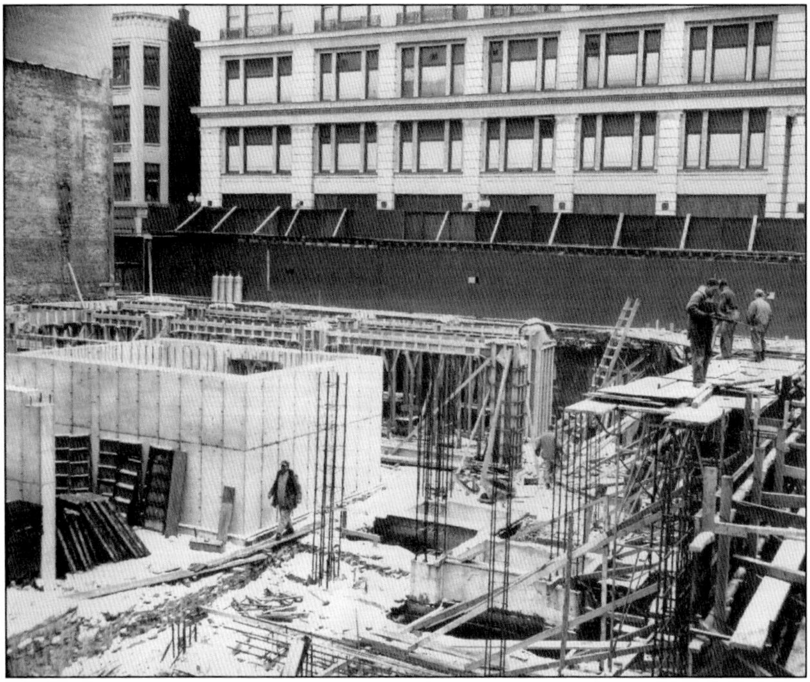

The concrete core has been poured and cured. Soon the new Rochester Savings Bank building would begin to rise above the wooden barrier. The Duffy-Powers building can be seen in the background. (RLLHD.)

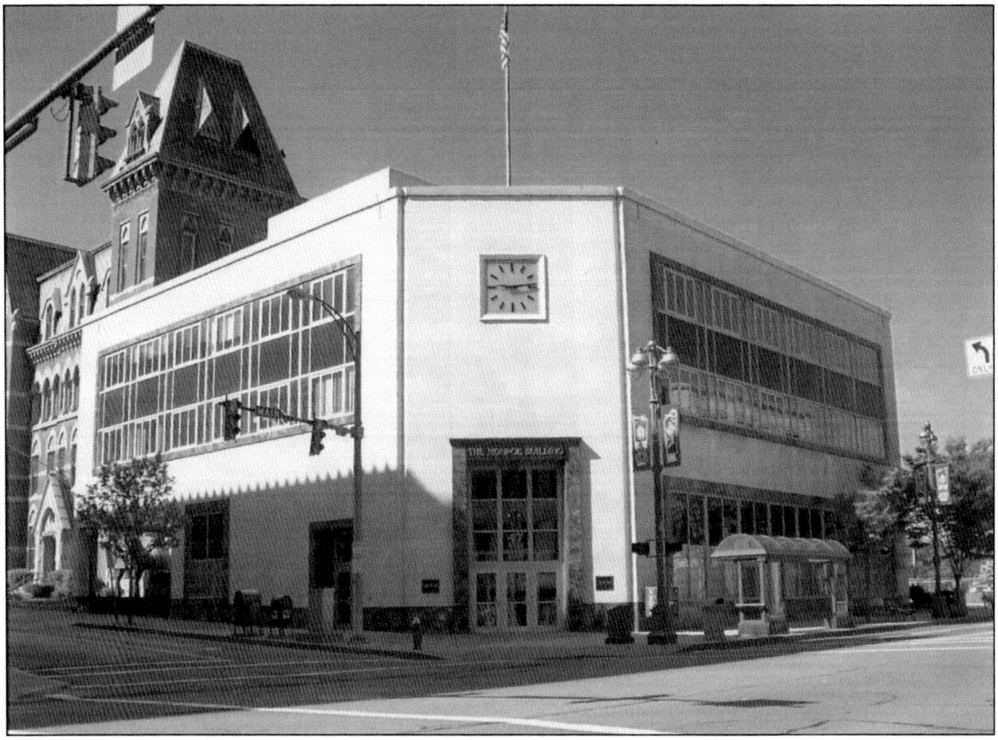

Opened on May 13, 1957, the new Rochester Savings Bank is a restrained design covered in fine materials. Clad in marble and granite, the bank relates well to the older buildings that surround it while offering the modern banking amenities, such as drive-through banking, that were becoming essential to its survival. (RMA.)

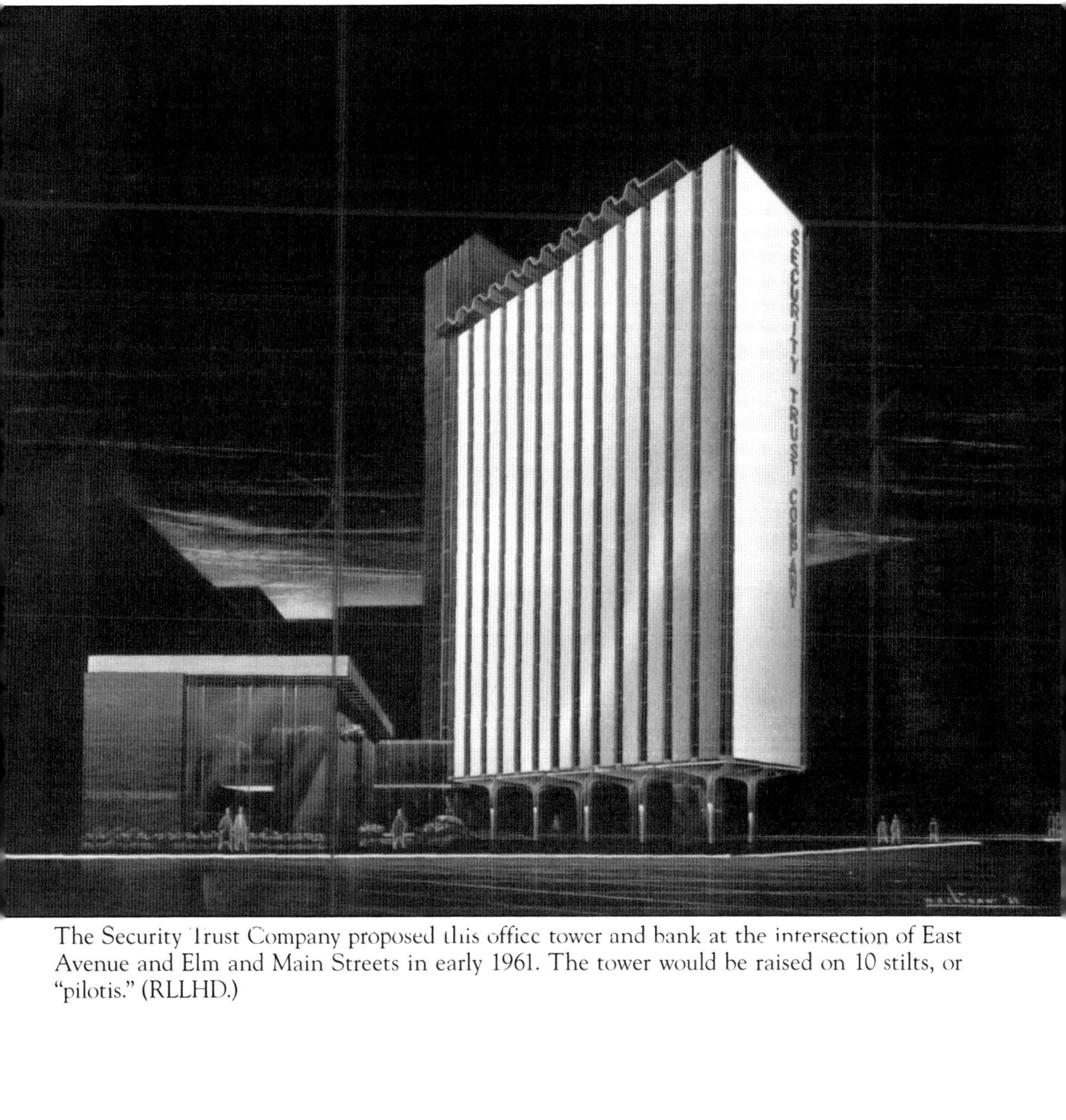

The Security Trust Company proposed this office tower and bank at the intersection of East Avenue and Elm and Main Streets in early 1961. The tower would be raised on 10 stilts, or "pilotis." (RLLHD.)

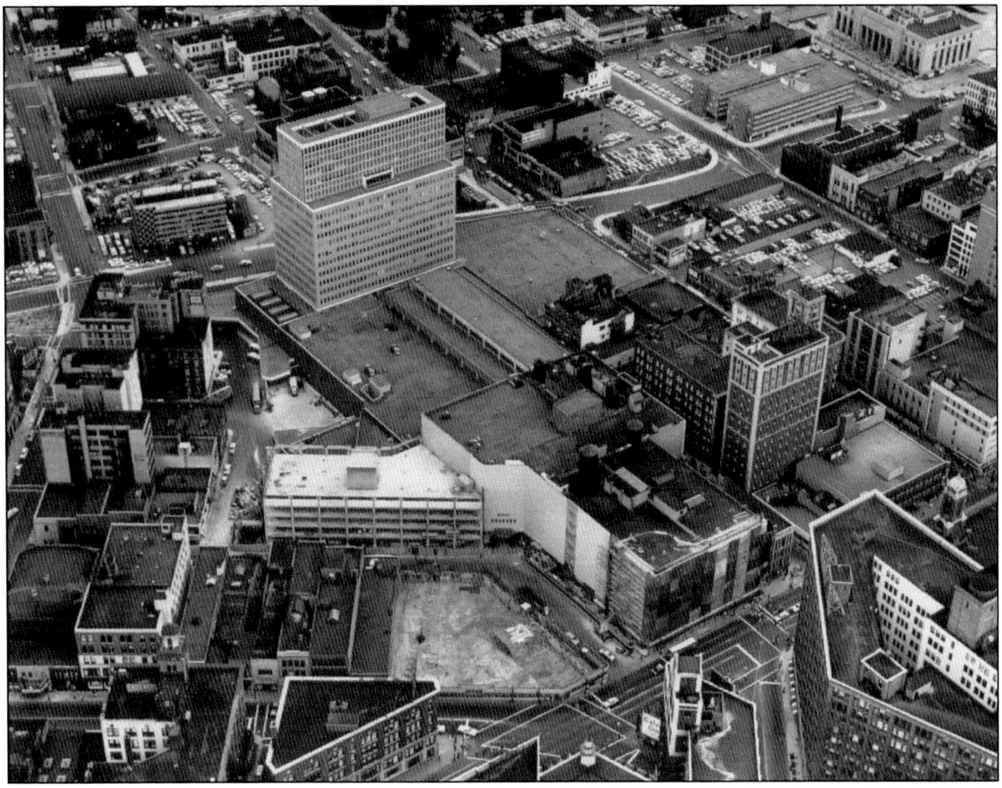

While the Midtown Plaza complex nears completion in the background, the Security Trust Company Building is only at the foundation stage. The structure under construction at Midtown Plaza would house the Rochester Telephone Company. The new extension of Broad Street can be seen just behind the Midtown Tower. (RLLHD.)

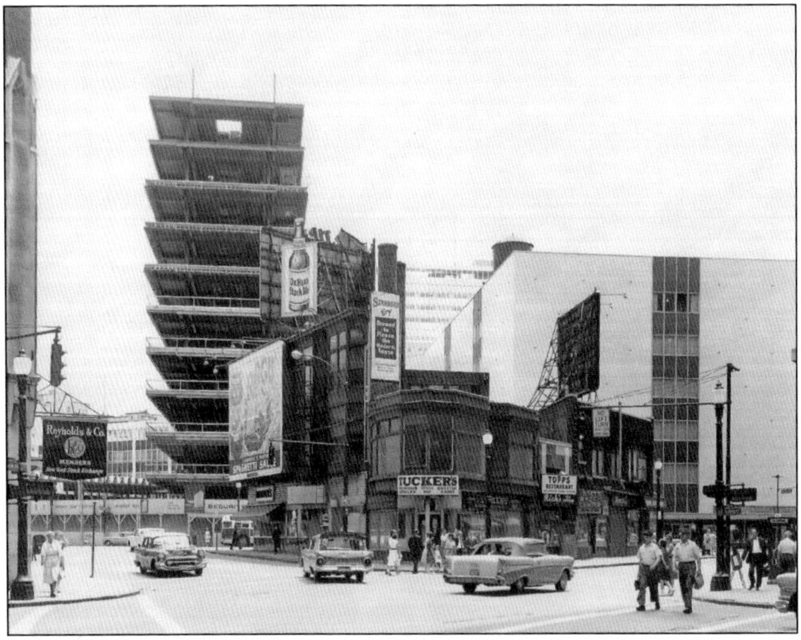

Seeming to float above Main Street, the innovative structure of the Security Trust Company Building is on full display in this image from its construction. The 10 main columns carry the weight of the tower's floors, thus providing easily reconfigured office space. (RLLHD.)

Nearing completion, the Security Trust Company Building is seen in this image from the fall of 1964. The tower's top floor is a glass-enclosed penthouse with a folded plate roof. To the rear of the tower, clad in brick, is the elevator and staircase service core. (RLLHD.)

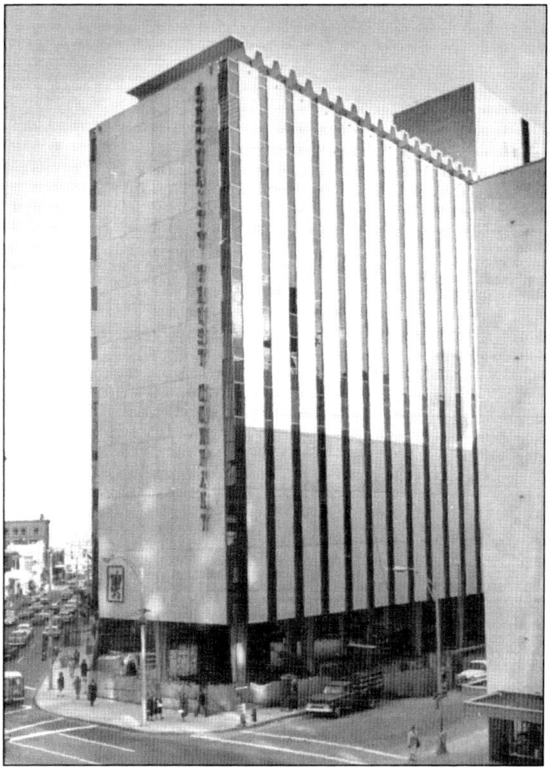

The use of a reinforced concrete, folded plate roof allowed the two-story-high banking room to have a clear span ceiling. The mural along the back wall of the bank is the work of John Menihan. (RMA.)

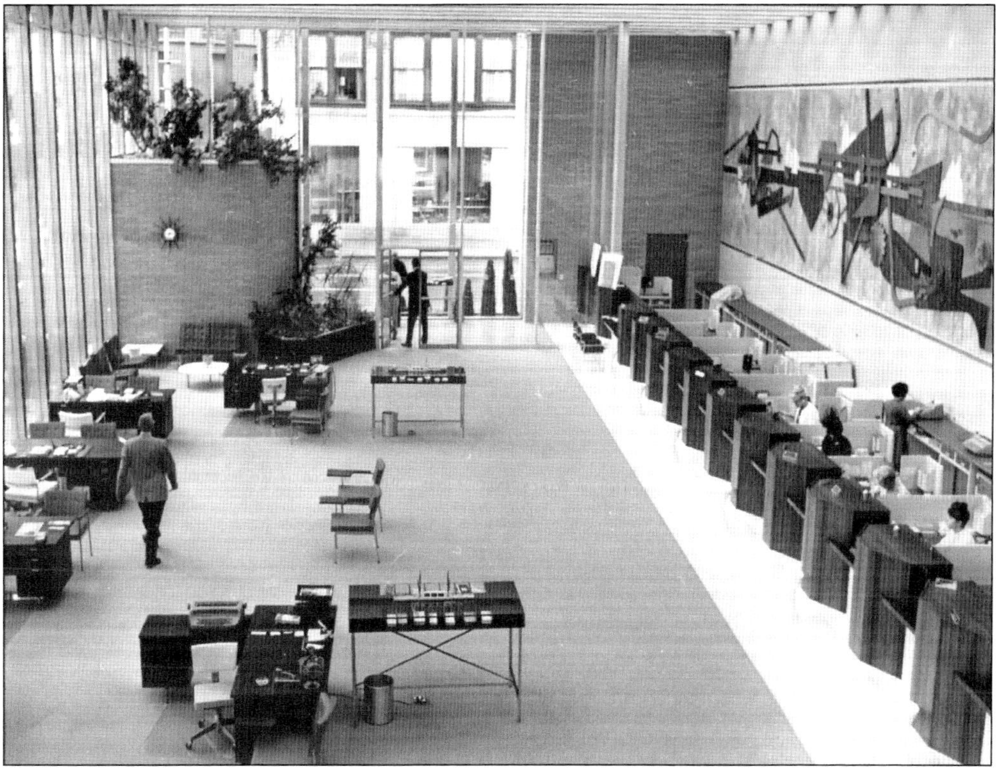

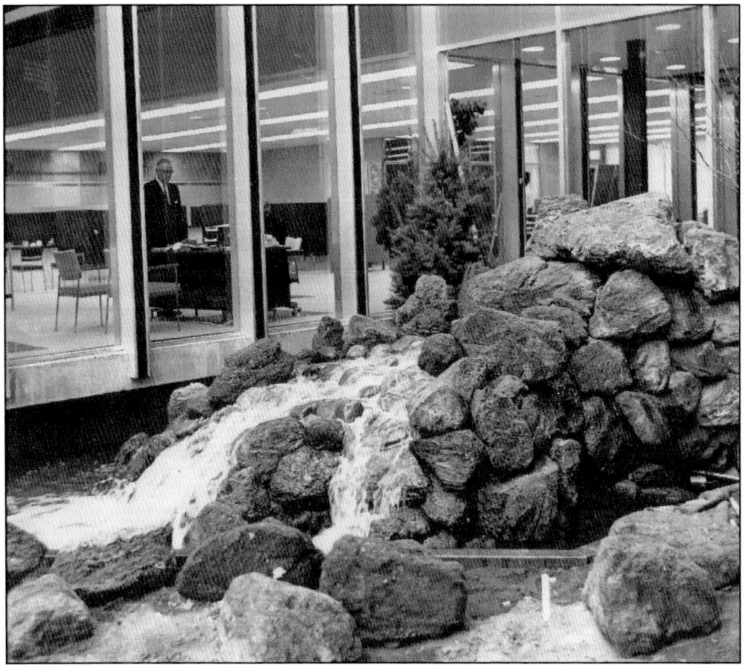

In the V-shaped plaza of the Security Trust Company Building, a rock garden and fountain gives bankers and pedestrians something tranquil to enjoy in the midst of a bustling city. Like all the other bank companies in this chapter, the Security Trust Company would be swallowed up by a larger, national bank. Today the building is the home of Bank of America's downtown office and banking branch. (RMA.)

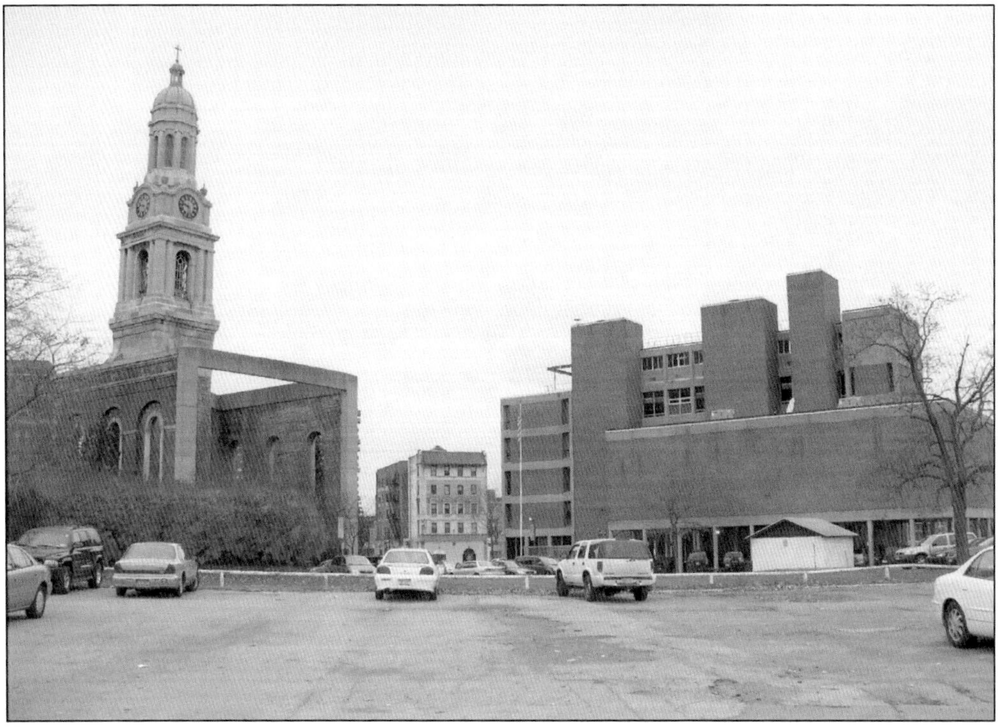

Designed by Edward Ribson in a style reminiscent of Louis I. Kahn's work at the University of Pennsylvania, the school for girls at St. Joseph's Church is a modern counterpoint to the adjacent 1840s-era church. Due to the large debt load from the construction and maintenance of the school, the church was forced to close it in 1972. The Landmark Society of Western New York later turned the church's empty shell into an interesting urban park. (RMA.)

In the early 1970s, prominent architecture firm Gruzen and Partners was hired to design the mixed-income high-rise housing at the Southeast Loop Urban Renewal Project, adjacent to the ultra-modern Manhattan Square Park. This architect's rendering is a view to the west from the Inner Loop. (RLLHD.)

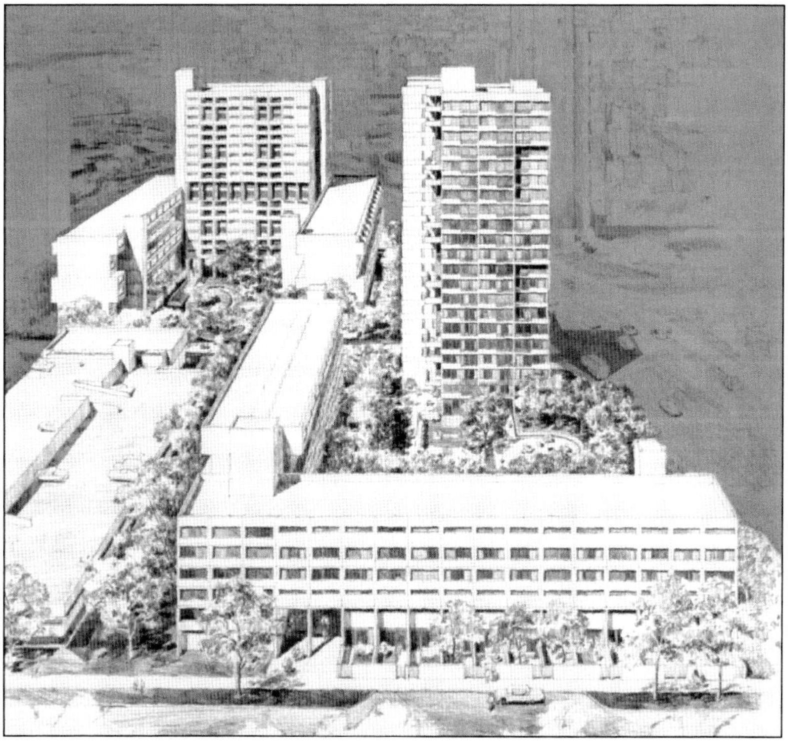

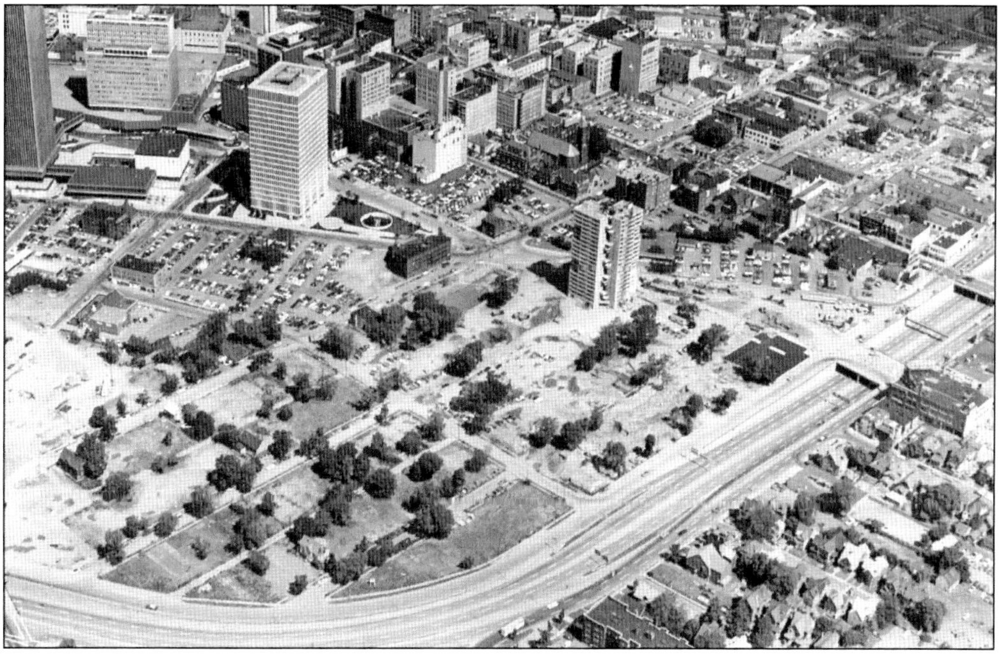

Like the other urban renewal projects, the Manhattan Square project required the clearing of a large swath of land, this time on the southeastern edge of the Inner Loop expressway. In addition to the complex in the previous image, parkland and other residential space was planned. The park would be built, but in the place of more housing would stand the Strong International Museum of Play. (RMA.)

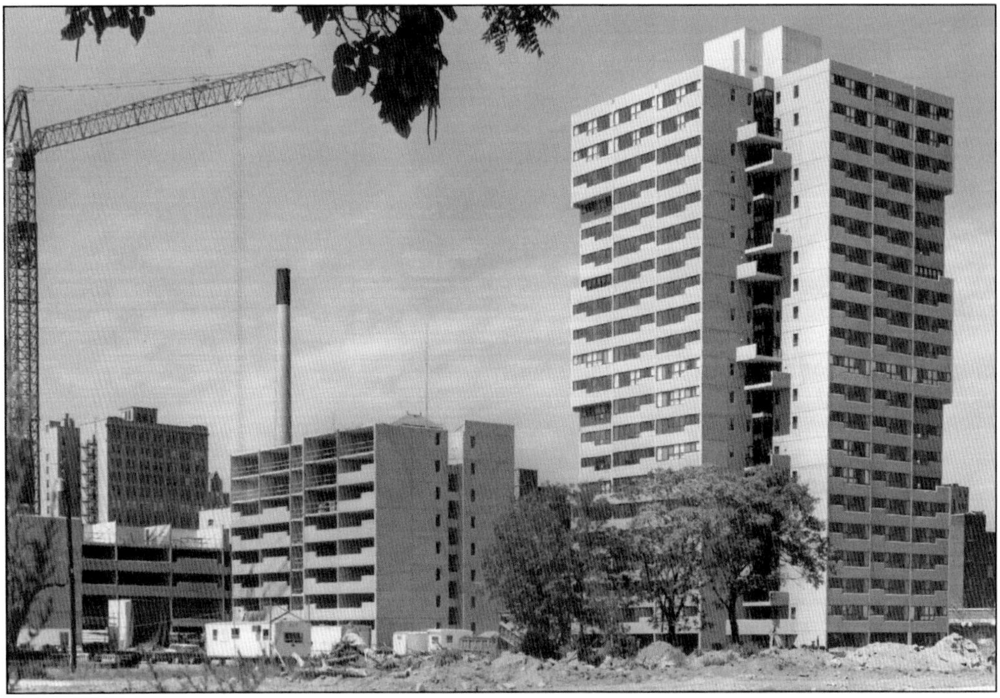

The precast concrete structure of the Savannah Apartments rises next to the finished senior citizen high-rise, Midtown Manor. Intimate and tree-lined parks with ample seating would be built between the towers to provide social opportunities in the summer months. (RMA.)

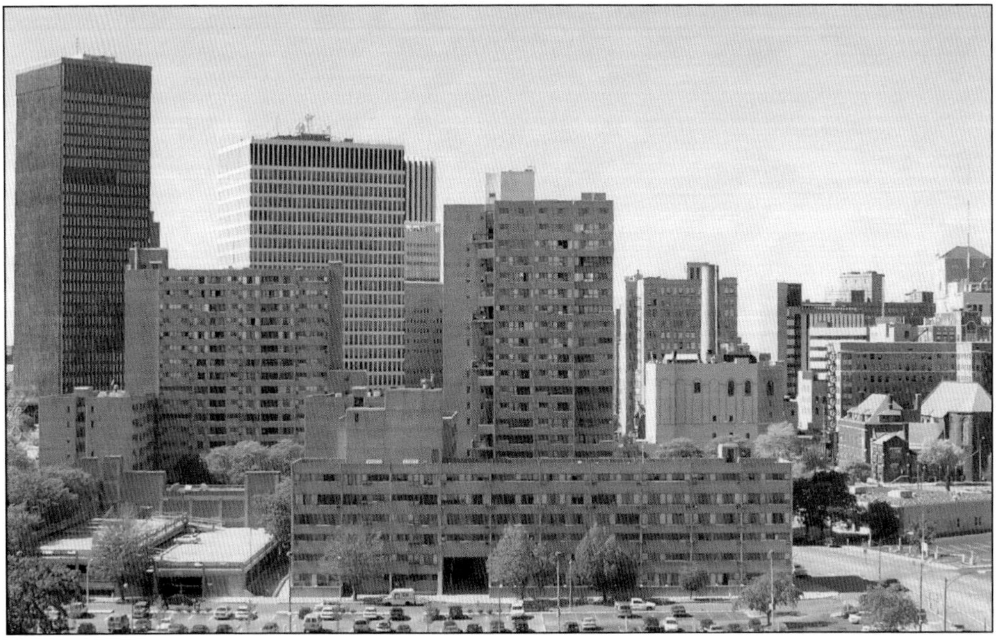

In its completed form, the apartment complex at Manhattan Square closely resembles the drawing a few pages back. Some criticized the Brutalist design of the buildings as being cold and unattractive. The complex would encounter vacancy issues early in its life but has proven to be popular with senior citizens and lower-income families. (RMA.)

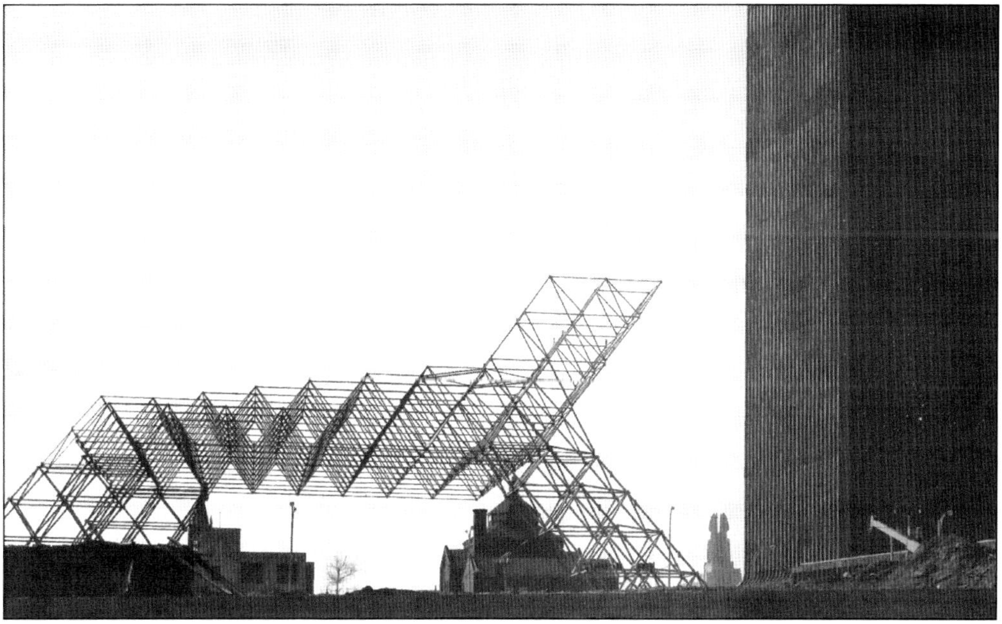

The Xerox Tower dwarfs the 100-foot space frame observation tower under construction at Manhattan Square Park. Below the space frame is a sculptural concrete fountain and amphitheater that would be used for civic events and concerts. Years later, the space frame was deemed unsafe to allow people to climb to the top, and it was closed to the public. (RLLHD.)

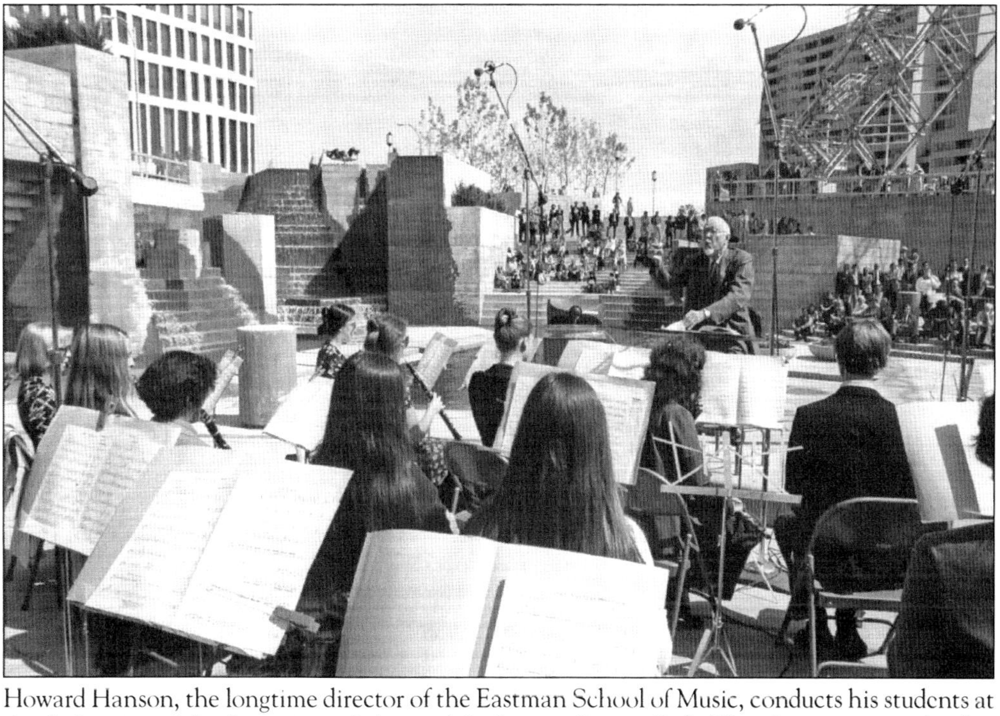

Howard Hanson, the longtime director of the Eastman School of Music, conducts his students at the dedication of the fountain and plaza at Manhattan Square Park. The plaza was named in his honor on that day. Hanson was a world-renowned composer and conductor prior to his 40-year tenure at the school. (RLLHD.)

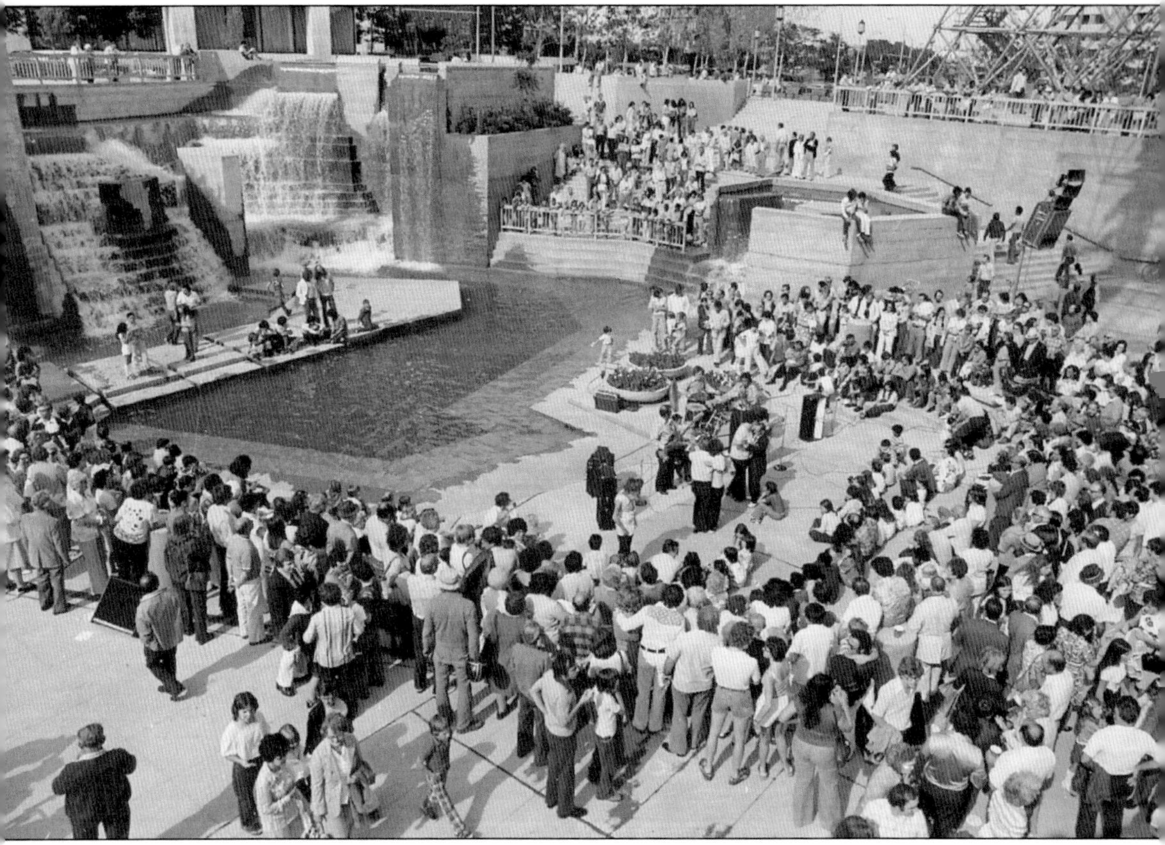

The tiered and cascading fountains provide an impressive backdrop for a concert on a sunny day in the 1970s. The fountain area would prove popular with office workers during lunchtime. Skateboard-riding youths found its concrete tiers and metal railings irresistible. Families enjoyed skating during the winter weather at the park's ice rink, a short walk away from the fountain. In the early 2000s, the ice rink was rebuilt and now serves as a reflecting pool in the warmer months. (RMA.)

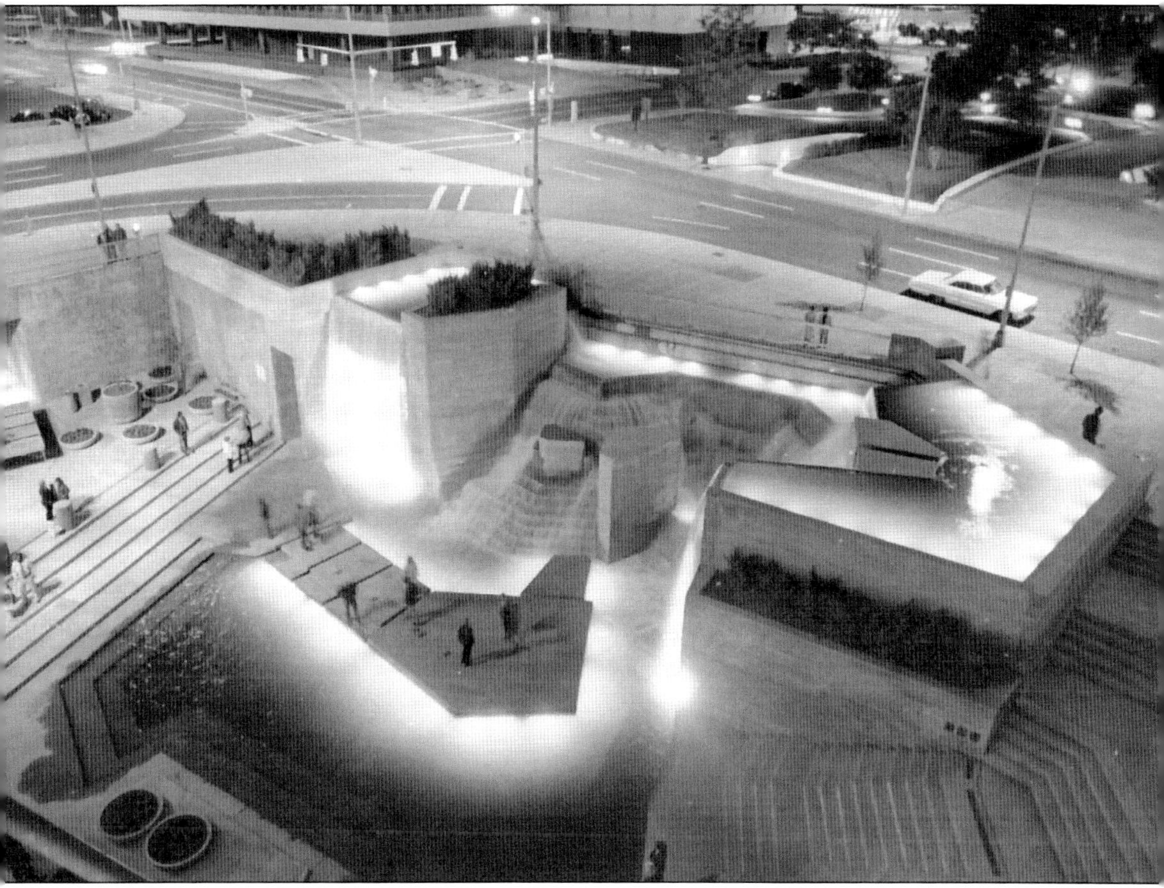

The architect of Manhattan Square Park was well aware that there would be high-rise apartments built near his park. Therefore, he designed the park to be enjoyed from the air as much as from the ground. This view of the fountain at night clearly illustrates his intentions. (RMA.)

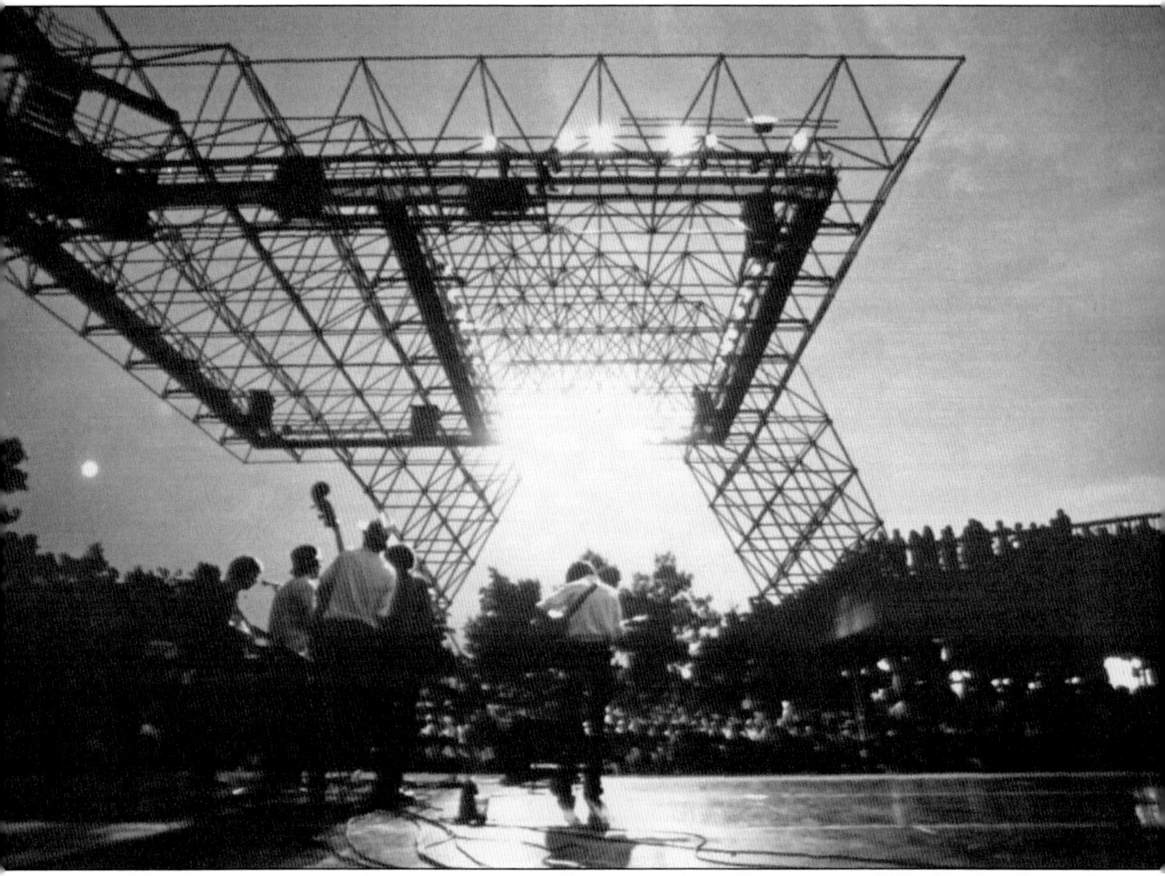

The sun sets on yet another concert under the space frame. Concerts would be held at the park regularly for decades to come. A renovation plan for the fountains and space frame necessitated the movement of the weekly summer concert series to another site downtown. Once the renovations are complete, the fountains will once again flow, and the community will be welcome to attend free events at the park. (RLLHD.)

Six

Garages and Highways

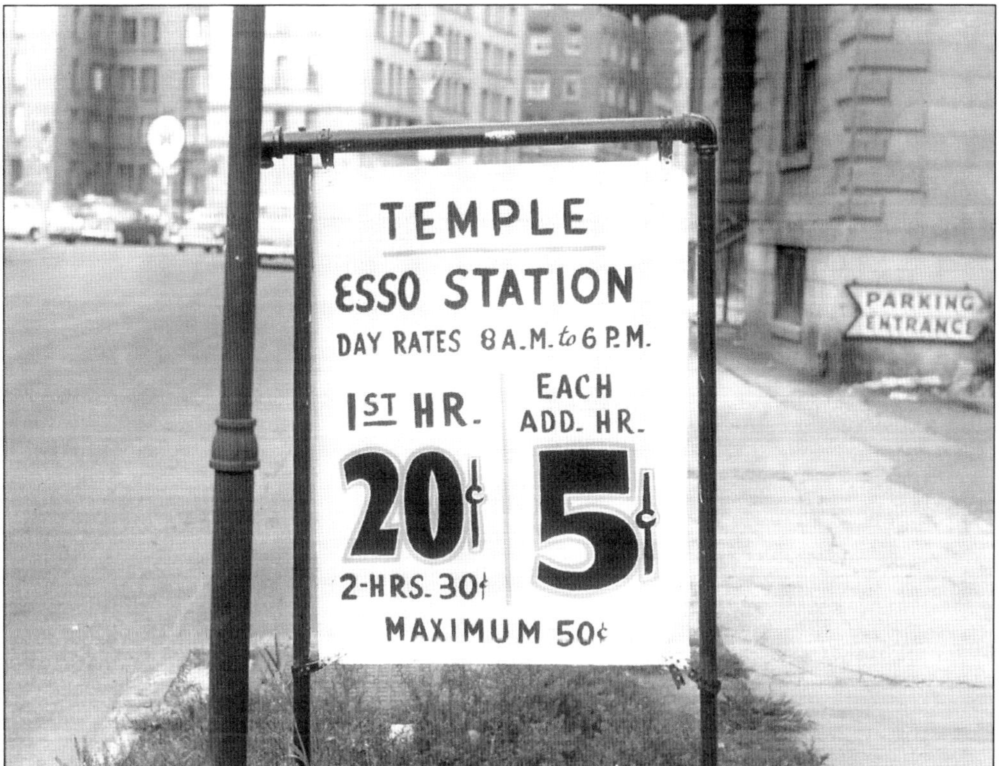

A 50¢ daily parking rate in the heart of downtown must have meant it was 1956. Sometimes the "good old days" really were that good. By this time, downtown was becoming riddled with surface parking lots that could not keep up with demand. Parking would have to go vertical to meet the needs of downtown residents and workers. (RMA.)

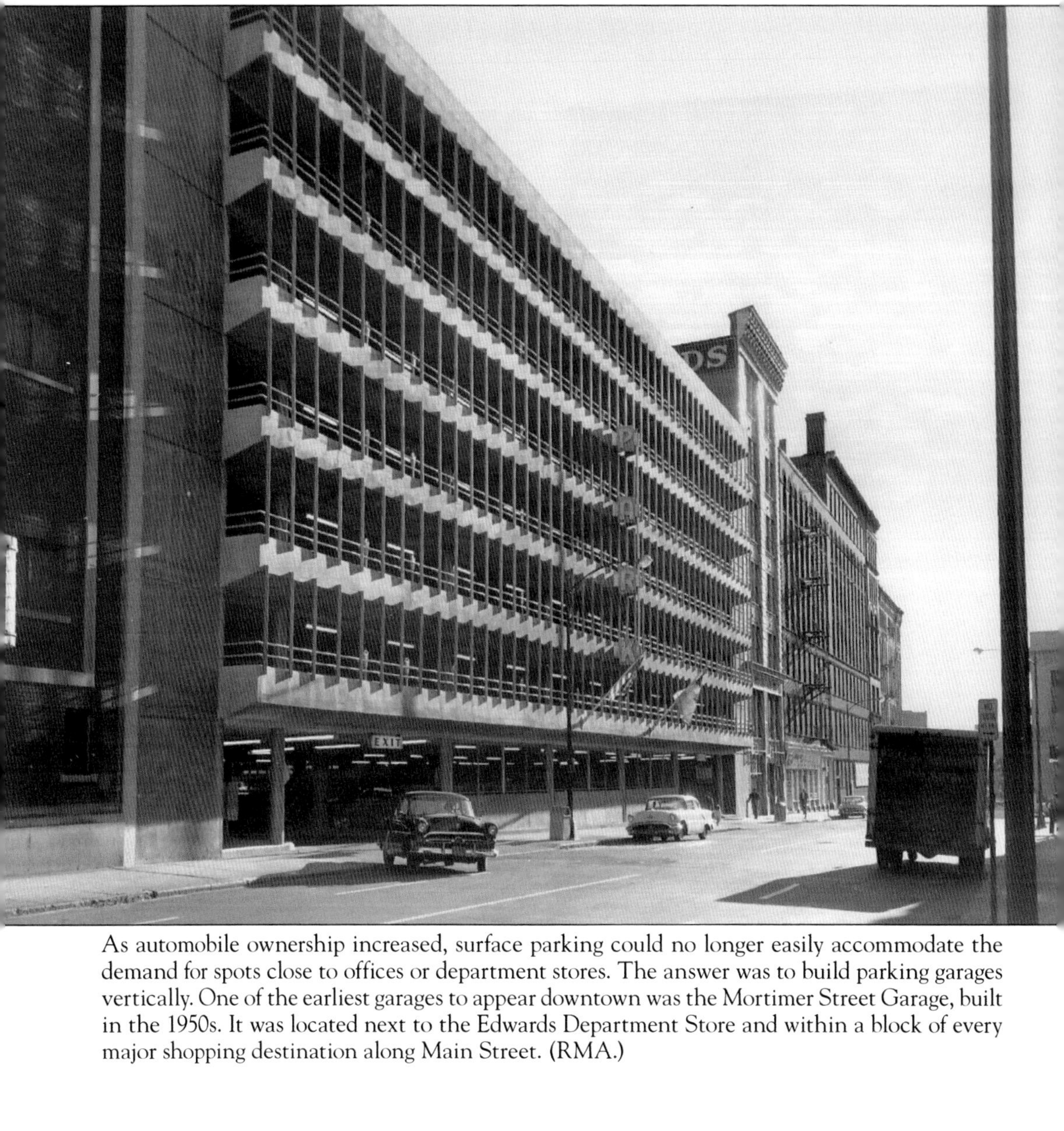

As automobile ownership increased, surface parking could no longer easily accommodate the demand for spots close to offices or department stores. The answer was to build parking garages vertically. One of the earliest garages to appear downtown was the Mortimer Street Garage, built in the 1950s. It was located next to the Edwards Department Store and within a block of every major shopping destination along Main Street. (RMA.)

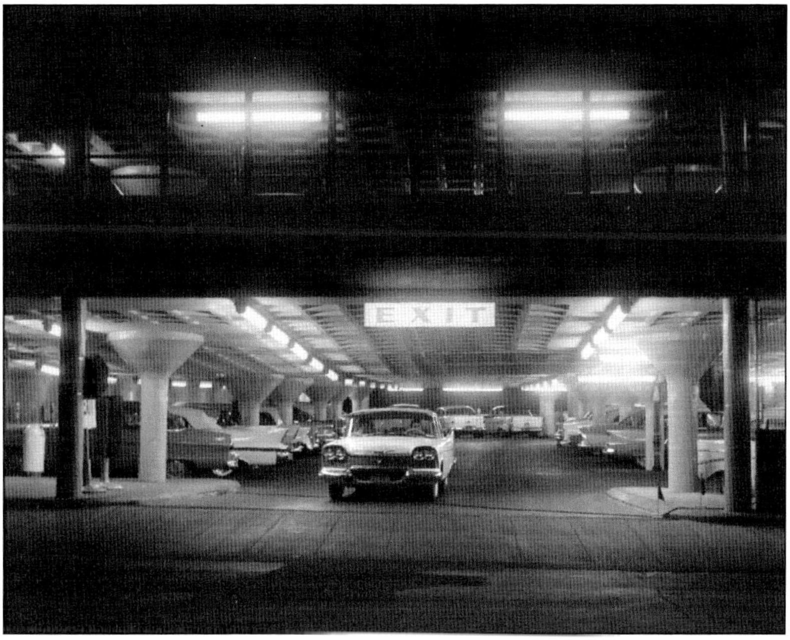

The mushroom columns and coffered concrete floors are the basic structures of the garage and are in full view in this nighttime image. The sculptural blankness of the structure and the futuristic swoops and curves of the chrome-finned machines seem to be made for each other. In many ways, they were. (RMA.)

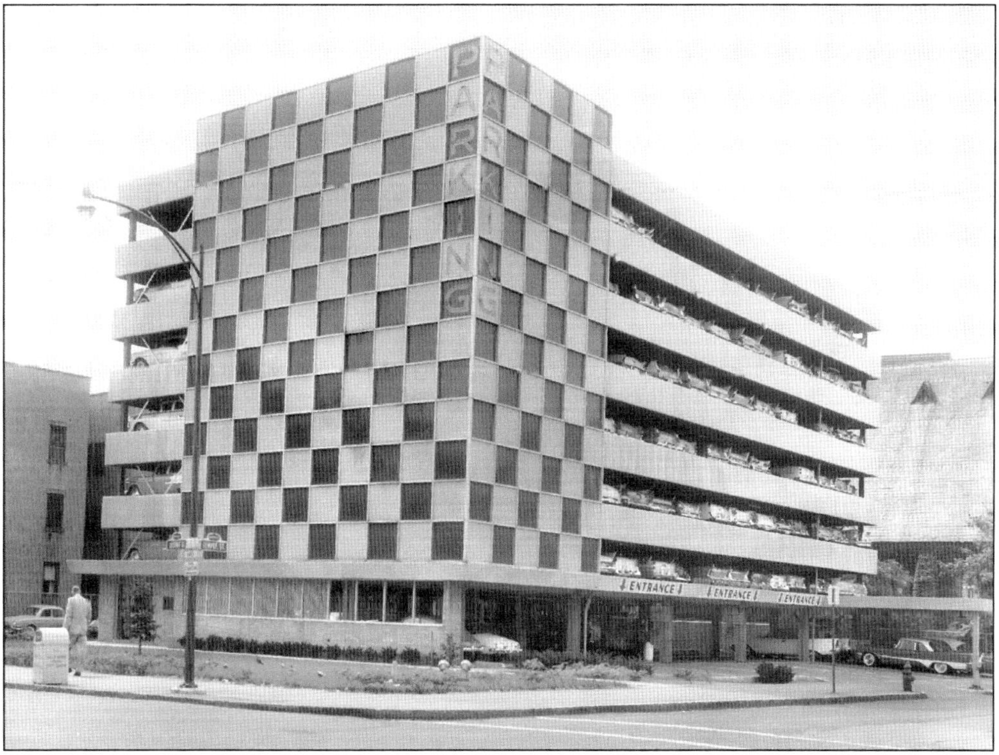

An oddity of the 1950s was the Pigeonhole self-parking garage. Fully automated and made for a narrow site, the owner would park the car at street level, after which a modified elevator would grab the car from underneath, lift it to the desired floor, and then place the car in its spot. When the owner returned, the process would occur in reverse. This example was demolished to make way for construction of Xerox Square in the 1960s. (RLLHD.)

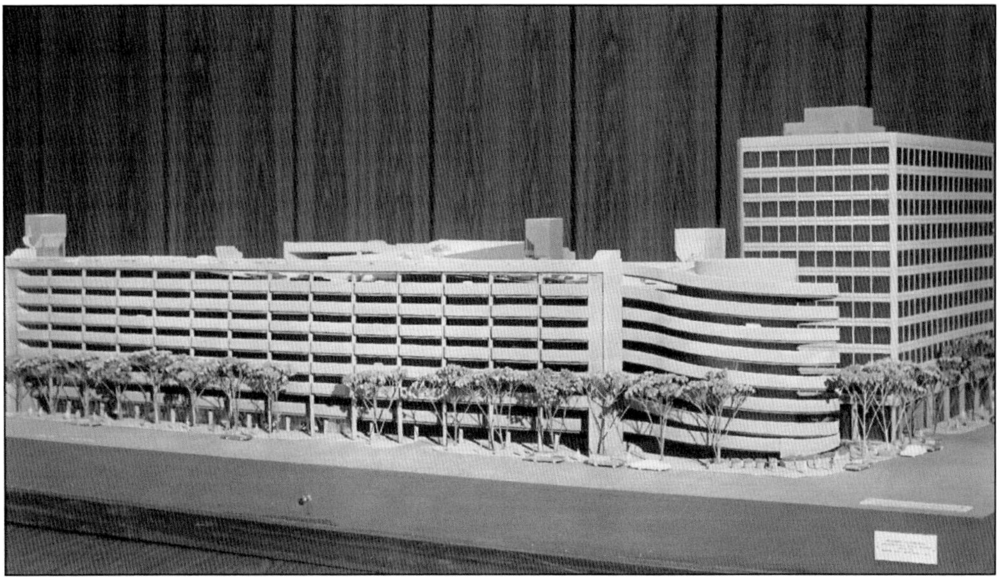

An 11-story office building and garage, with an 1,800-car capacity, was planned for the northeast corner of Broad Street and South Avenue. These two structures were part of the Genesee Crossroads Urban Renewal Project. Even though the office building was not constructed, the garage's plan moved forward. Vice mayor John R. Parrinello was in attendance for the ground-breaking ceremonies that took place on June 23, 1972. (RMA.)

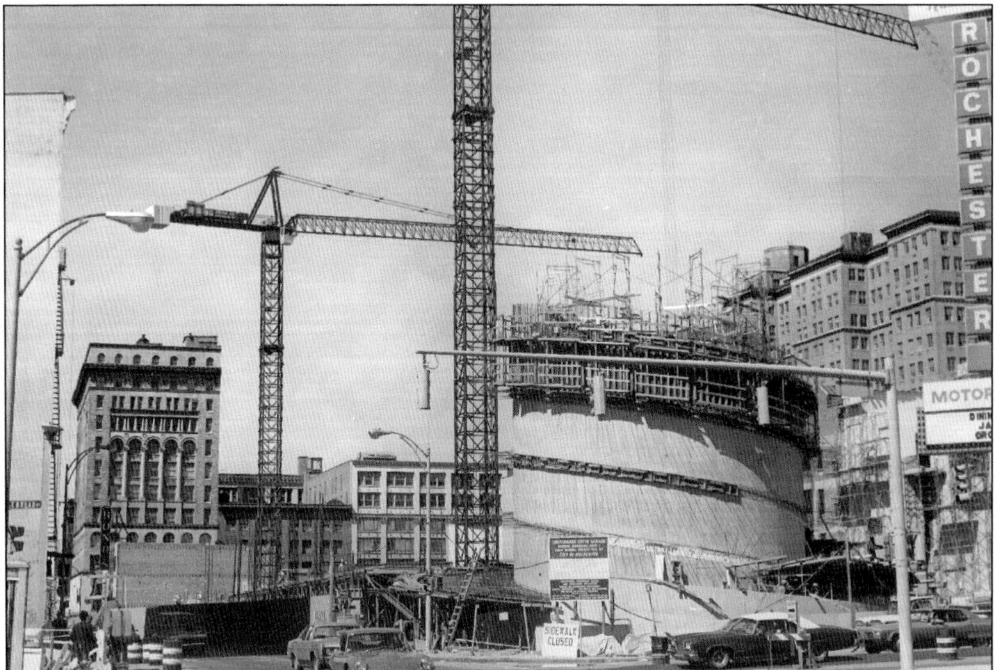

The core of the helix exit ramp begins to rise over the site as another crane works on the main structure of the parking garage. The Granite Building is seen in the background. (RMA.)

The helix continues to rise and is being ringed with the reinforced concrete structure of the exit ramp. In the background rises the main structure of the South Street Garage. The Lincoln First Tower looms behind the circular structure. (RLLHD.)

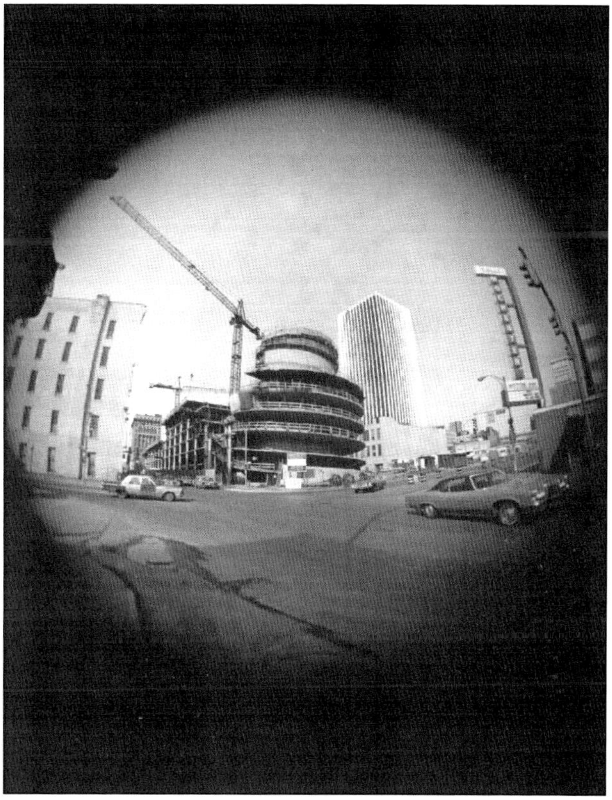

The South Avenue Garage, as it is known today, is a post-tensioned structure. Cables within the concrete are tensioned to provide added support and to allow longer spans of concrete floor, while reducing the number of vertical supports that occupy space intended for parked cars. (RMA.)

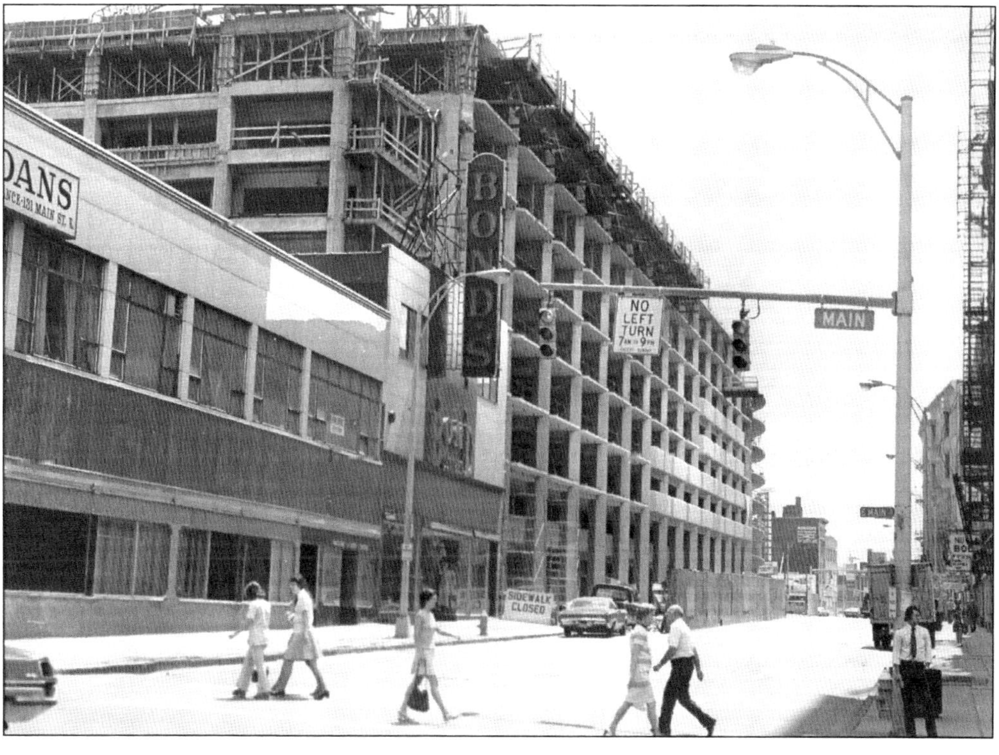

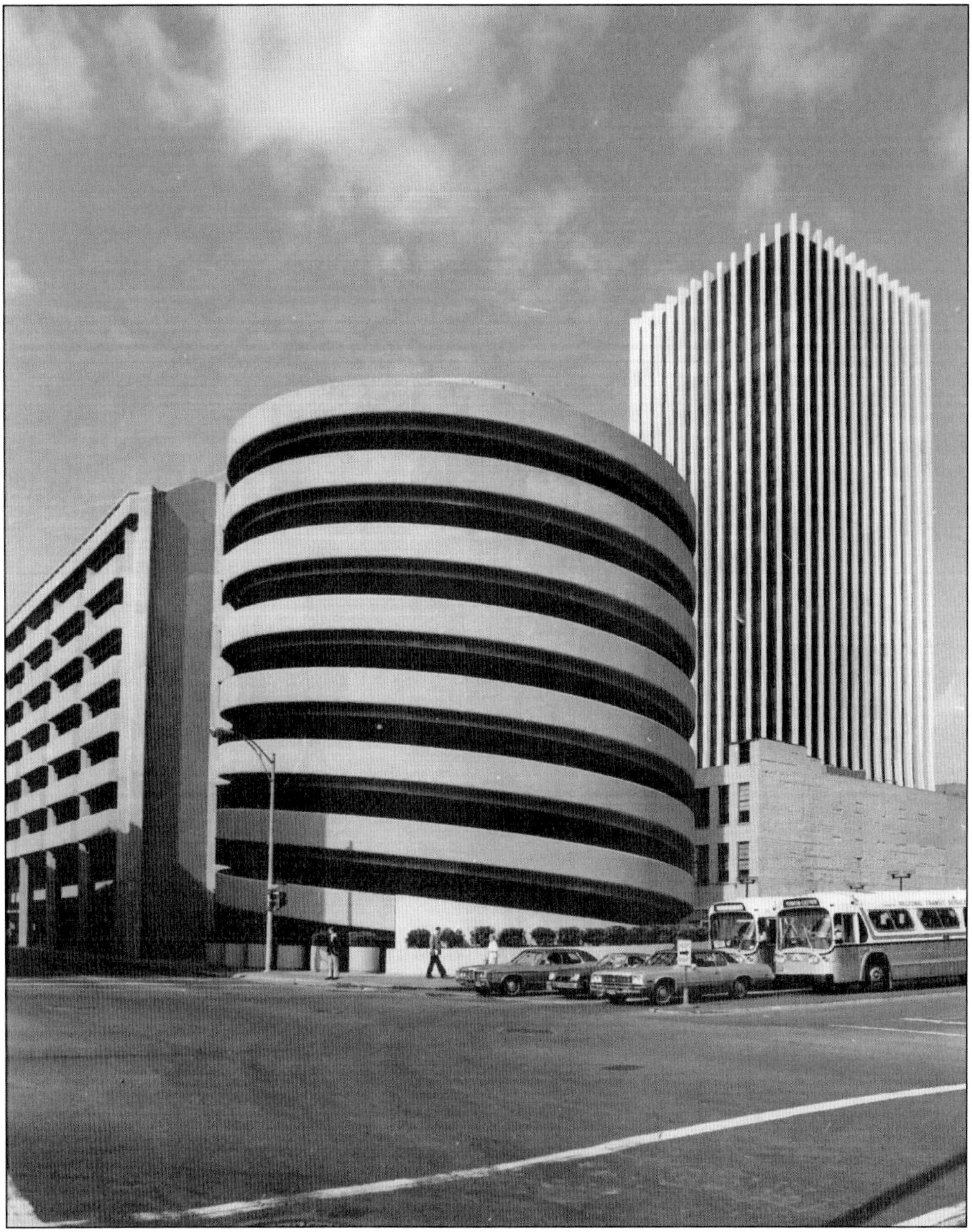

The circle and the rectangle play off each other in this image of the finished South Avenue Garage and the Lincoln First Tower. Some compared the look of the helix ramp to the famous Guggenheim Museum in New York City. Unfortunately, years of road salt took its toll on the steel cables embedded in the concrete of the helix, and it collapsed in the early 2000s. Fortunately only a few cars were on the ramp, and no one was seriously injured. (RMA.)

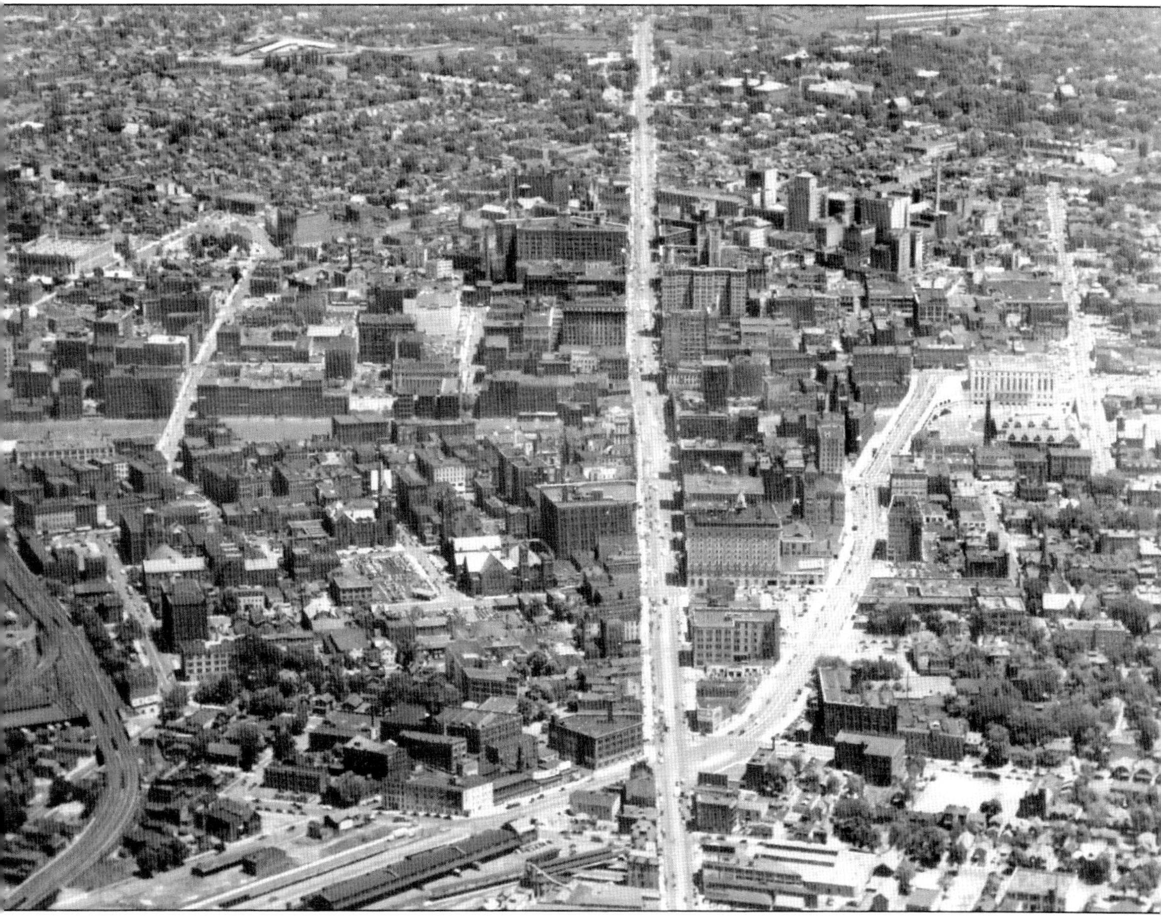

In this early-20th-century aerial view of Rochester, the only major road downtown is Main Street. Broad Street ends at the Osborn House on South Avenue. It would be decades before the expansion of downtown streets and expressway building would make traveling through the city much easier. It would not be without its costs to the social and physical fabric of downtown Rochester. (RMA.)

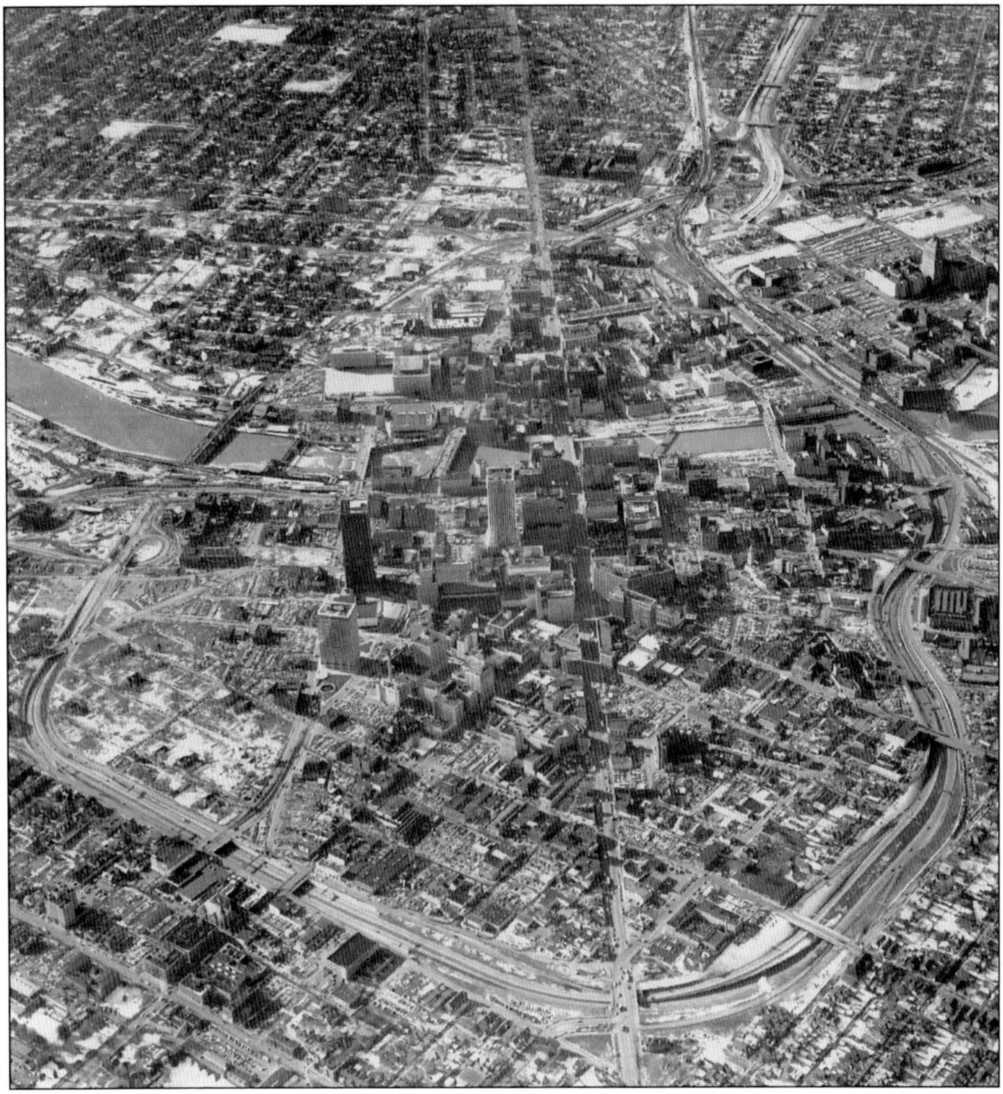

Main Street still cuts across the center of downtown but is now joined by an extended Broad Street and is surrounded by the sunken Inner Loop expressway. The connection of the Eastern and Western Expressways is under construction at the upper left of this aerial view from the 1970s. Most of the urban renewal projects have been finished, with the exception of the Manhattan Square Park and apartment complex to the left of Marine Midland Plaza. Save a few major buildings going up in the 1990s and 2000s, not much has changed in downtown Rochester in the past 35 years. (RLLHD.)

Seven

Rochester City Hall

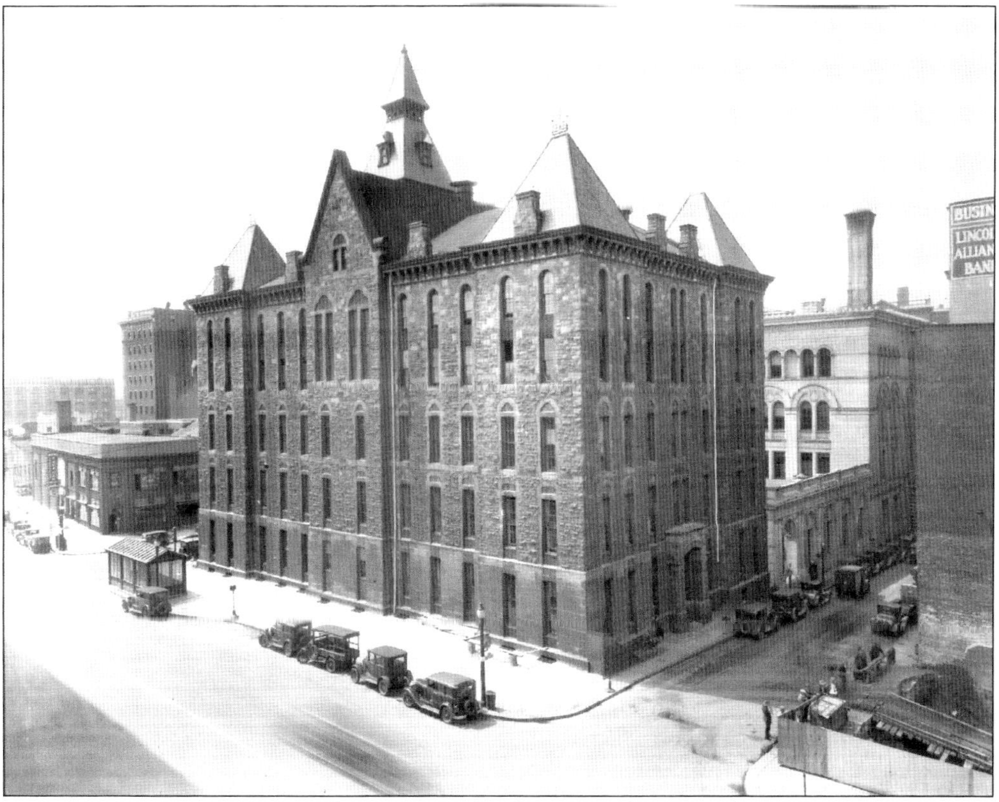

Completed in 1876 at a cost of $335,684.39, the first city hall was, and is, an important fixture of the west side of downtown, which was originally known as the "100 Acre Tract." It was not large enough to satisfy the needs of a growing city for long, and the search for additional space became necessary. (RMA.)

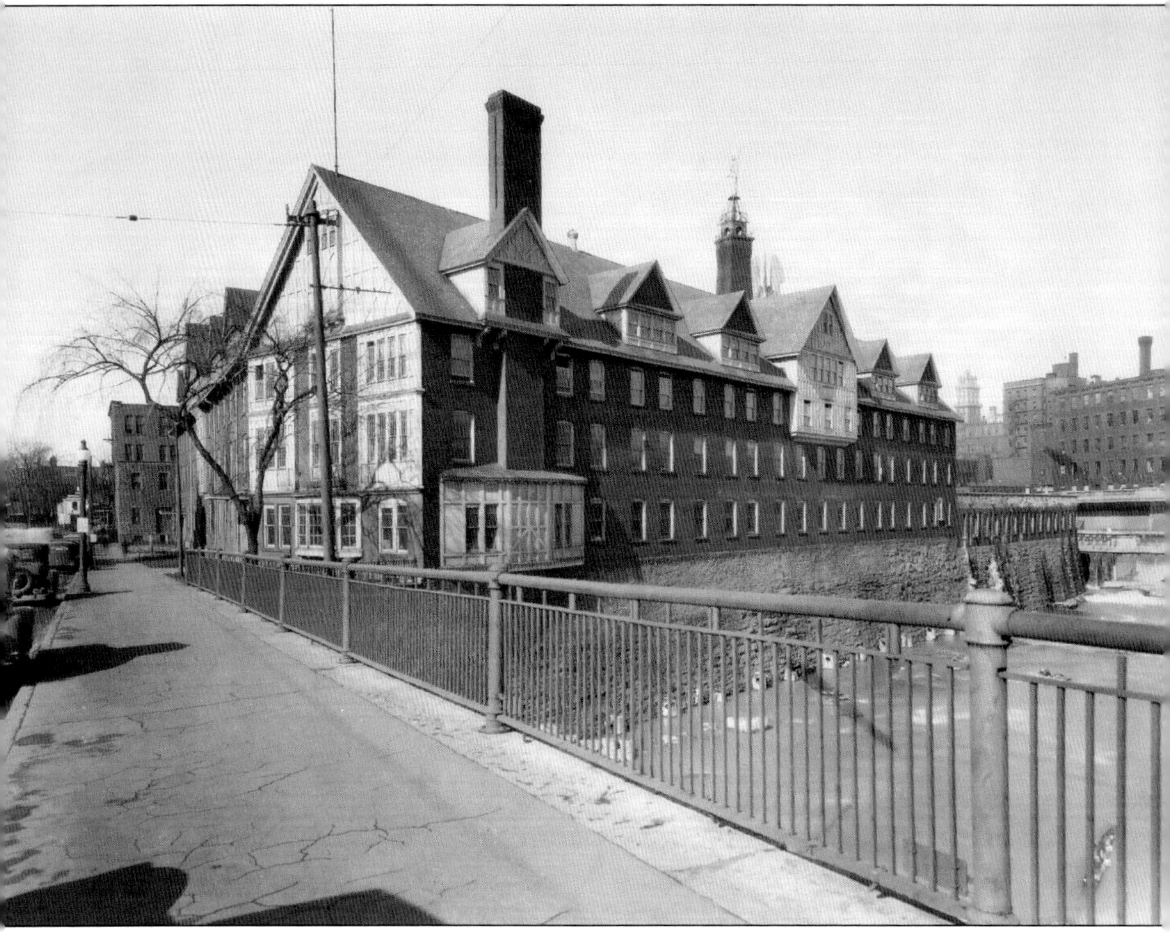

In 1924, George Eastman leased the former Kimball Tobacco Factory for a nominal fee to the city for use as the City Hall Annex. It would continue to serve in this capacity until the 1950s, when it would be demolished to make way for the Community War Memorial. (RLLHD.)

When plans for a city office building at the Monroe County Civic Center failed to be realized, the city government had to look elsewhere for a suitable home. They found it in an unlikely place. In 1973, the federal government moved its local offices to the new marble temple on State Street, thereby abandoning this magnificent Richardsonian Romanesque fortress of brown sandstone on Church Street. (RMA.)

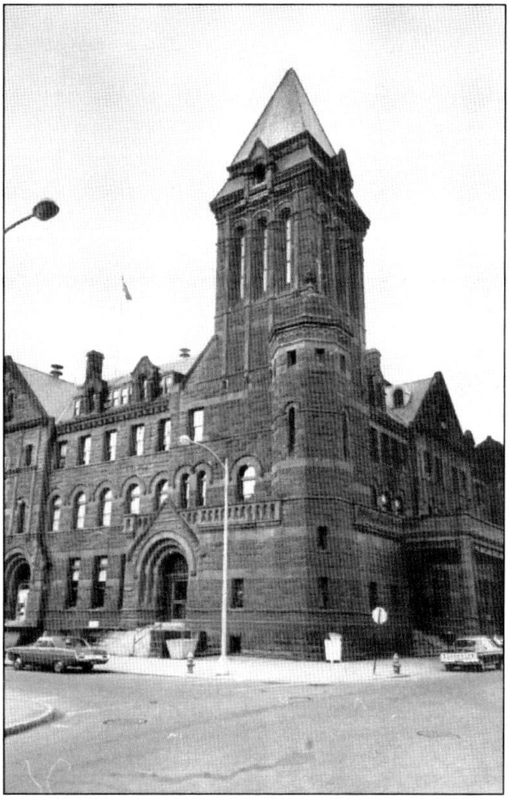

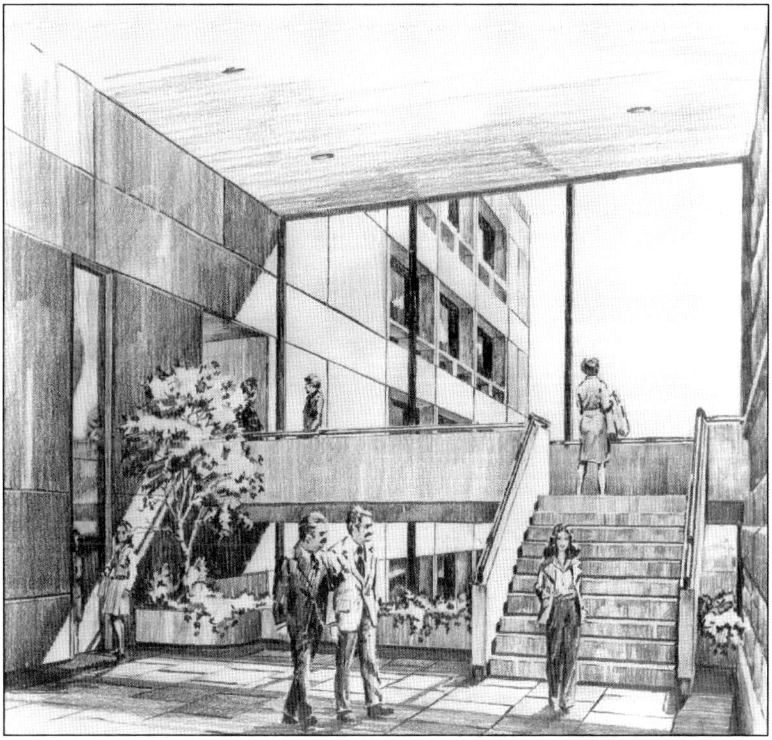

The city purchased the former Federal Building for $1 in 1975 and began the process of renovating and expanding the structure to meet the needs of an ever-changing modern city. This rendering shows the lobby between the original building and the new annex wing. (RMA.)

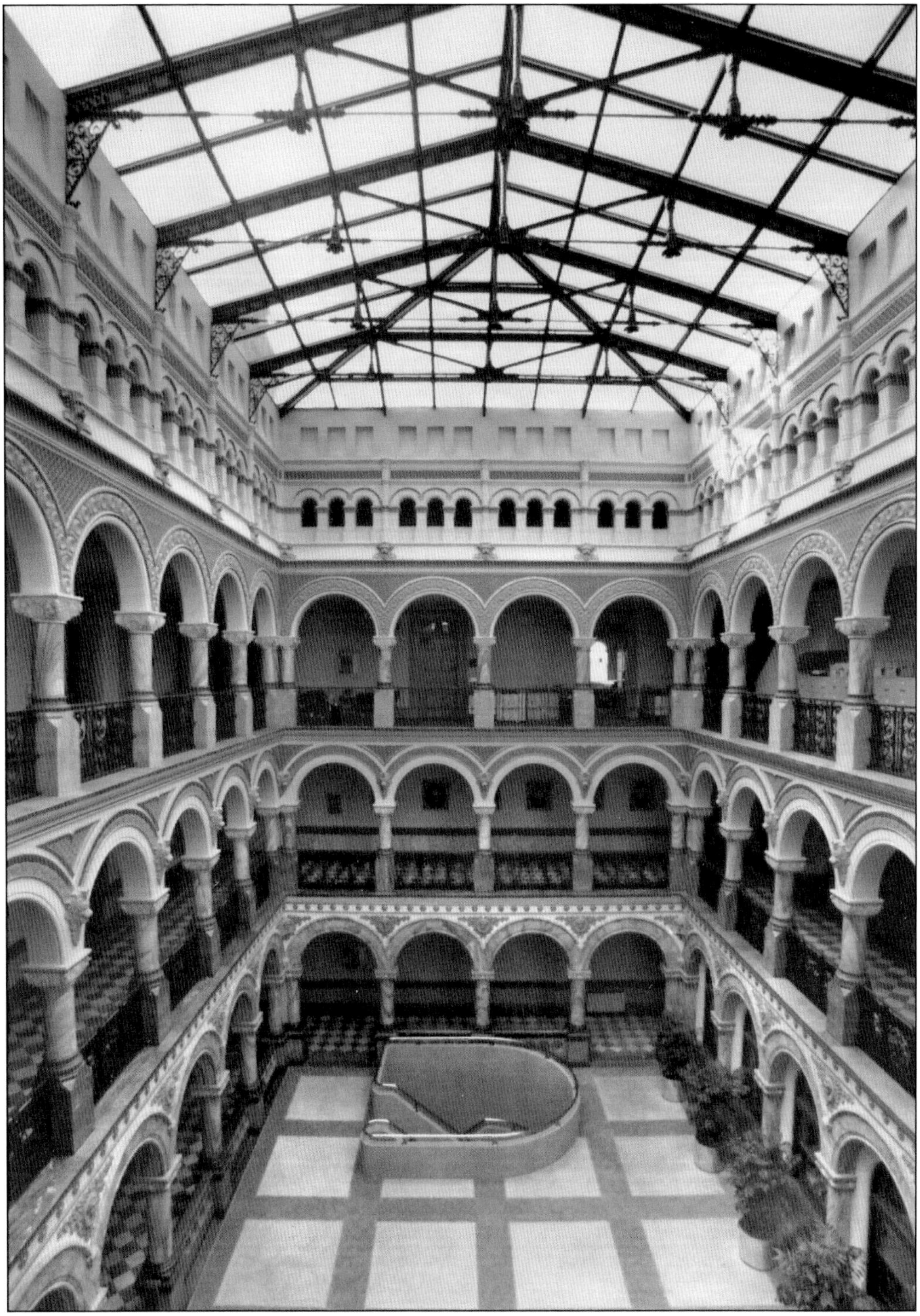

This magnificent three-story atrium was once a mere light well. The atrium's floor was installed in place of the glass panels that once fed light into the windowless lower floors. The atrium is a popular setting for weddings and public events. The staircase in the center of the image leads to the main entrance of the building. (RMA.)

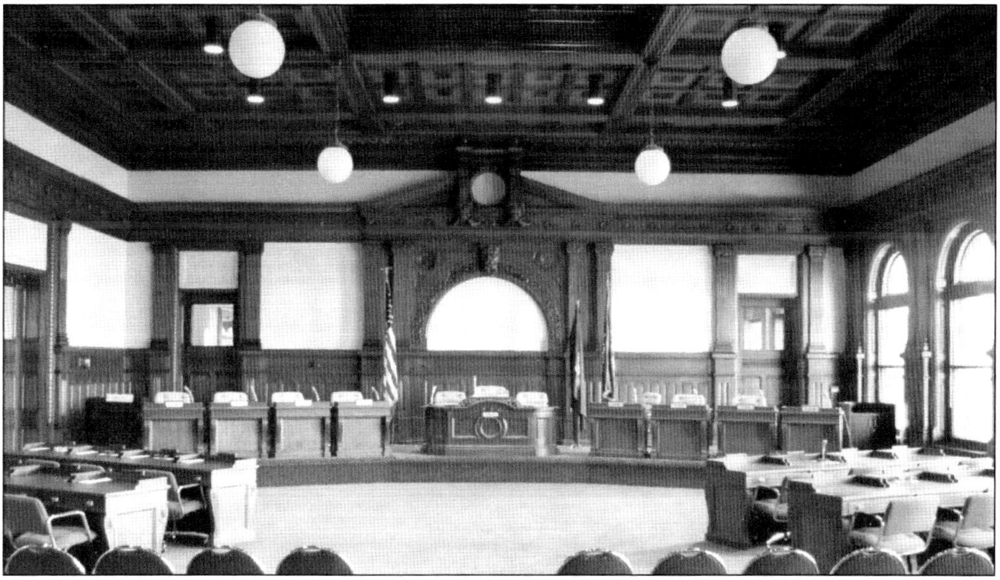

Gorgeous wood carvings, a coffered ceiling, and large arched windows lend an air of officiousness and dignity to the proceedings of Rochester's city council, when held in this chamber. The building was designed by local architect Harvey Ellis, in association with architects from the federal government. (RLLHD.)

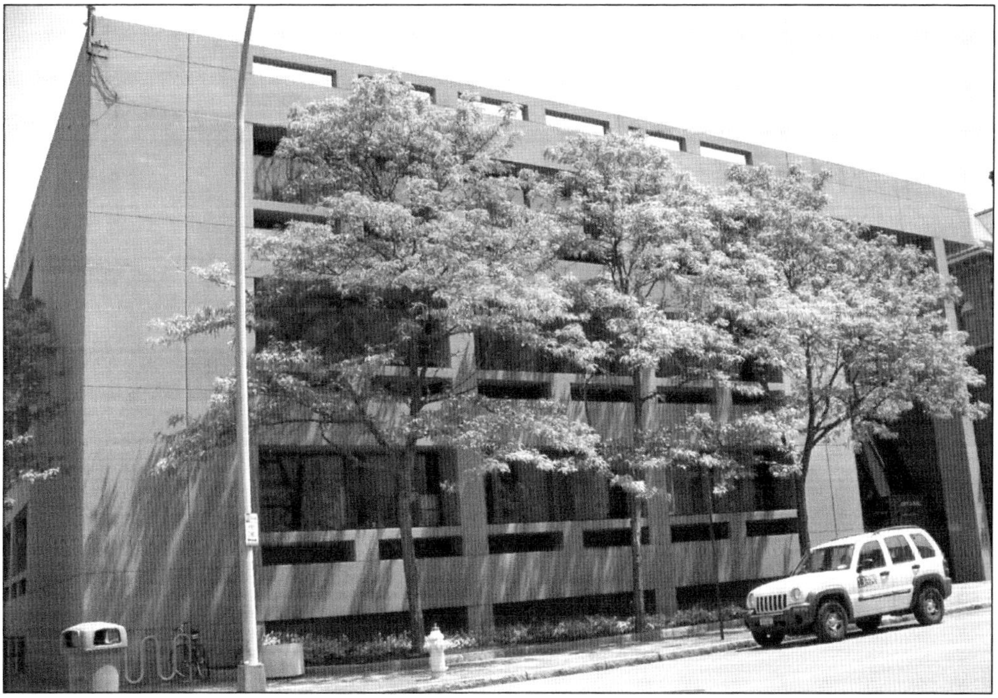

To avoid the capacity problems that plagued the former city hall building, an annex was built to add 45,000 square feet of office space. Clad in concrete panels tinted to compliment the brown sandstone of the older structure, the annex is a subdued building that does not attempt to outdo its neighbor. An attractive sculpture garden was built between the old and new buildings, and it provides a refuge from the hustle and bustle of the city's political world. (RMA.)